CELT AND ROMAN

Also by Peter Berresford Ellis

Celtic Inheritance
The Celtic Revolution
A Dictionary of Irish Mythology
The Celtic Empire
A Guide to Early Celtic Remains in Britain
A Dictionary of Celtic Mythology
Celt and Saxon
Celtic Dawn
The Druids
Celtic Women
Celt and Greek

Peter Berresford Ellis

CELT AND ROMAN

The Celts of Italy

St. Martin's Press

New York

CELT AND ROMAN

Copyright © 1998 by Peter Berresford Ellis

All rights reserved. No part of this book may be used or
reproduced in any manner whatsoever without written permission
except in the case of brief quotations embodied in critical articles or
reviews. For information, address:

St. Martin's Press, Scholarly and Reference Division, 175
Fifth Avenue, New York, N.Y. 10010

First published in the United States of America in 1998
Printed in Great Britain

ISBN 0-312-21419-7

Library of Congress Cataloging-in-Publication Data

Ellis, Peter Berresford.
    Celt and Roman: the Celts of Italy / Peter Berresford Ellis.
        p.   cm.
    Includes bibliographical references and index.
    ISBN 0-312-21419-7
        1. Celts—Rome—History.   2. Rome—History—Republic. 510-30 B.C.—
Historiography.   3. Civilization, Celtic.   I. Title.
DG225.C44E44   1998
937'.009416—dc21   98-4886
                                                                      CIP

In memory of C. Desmond Greaves (1913–1988), historian, biographer, poet and political philosopher, whose critical encouragement of my work was always deeply appreciated.

Contents

Note on Terminology   xi
1 'Alliensis': 18 July 390 BC   1
2 The Arrival of the Celts in Italy   17
3 Italians and the Celts   45
4 The Fall of Rome   62
5 Celtic Warriors   86
6 The Return of the Celts   104
7 'The Celtic Terror'   121
8 Celt, Etruscan and Samnite   131
9 Pyrrhos, Carthage and the Celts   142
10 Telamon!   150
11 Hannibal and the Celts   167
12 Litana: A Forgotten Celtic Victory   182
13 The Conquest of Cisalpine Gaul   201
14 The Colonisation of Cisalpine Gaul   219
15 The Last Kicks at Rome   231
16 The Cisalpine Celtic Legacy to Rome   246
Acknowledgements and Bibliography   264
Index   273

Illustrations

between pages 114 and 115

Carving depicting the Celtic god Cernunnos (*Seminario e Centro Camundo di Studi Preistorici, Brescia*)

Representation of Cernunnos from the third century BC (*Balzeaux-Zodiaque, France*)

Bronze head of a Celtic war goddess of the first century BC (*Musée de Bretagne, Rennes*)

Detail from a gold brooch showing Celtic warrior with helmet, shield and sword (*Private Collection*)

Horde of Celtic silver coins of the second century BC (*Civiche Raccolte Archeologiche del Castello Sfozesco, Milan*)

Selection of coins of the Taurini from the second/first century BC (*Nardoni Mzei, Ljubjana*)

One of the earliest known Celtic coins from the third century BC (*Bibliothèque Nationale, Paris*)

Gold leaf crown dated to late fourth century/early third century BC (*Museo Civico Archeologia, Bologna*)

Bronze figure of a second century BC Celtic warrior (*Musée Departmental de l'Oise, Beauvais*)

Figure of Epona, the horse goddess (*Musée Alesia, Alise-Sainte-Reine*)

Celtic statue from the first century (*Musée Calvet, Avignon*)

Figures of Celtic warriors from the second century BC (*Museo Nazionale della Marche, Ancona*)

One of the earliest known Celtic inscriptions dated to the fifth century BC (*Museo Archeologico del Liviano, Padova*)

Etruscan stone from the fifth century BC (*Museo Civico, Bologna*)

Stones inscribed in Celtic and Latin dated late third or early second centuries BC (*Museo Gregoriano, Rome*)

ix

Celtic helmet from the late fourth century/early third century BC (*Museo Civico Archeologico, Bologna*)

Two Celtic war helmets of the type worn by the Senones, fourth century BC (*Staatlichen Museen, Berlin*)

Celtic war helmet from the third century BC (*Muzuel de Istoire al RSR, Bucharest*)

Etruscan style flagon of the third century BC (*Museo Civico Archeologico, Bologna*)

Note on Terminology

To the Greeks the Celts were known as the *Keltoi* (Celts) and *Galatai* (Galatians) but to the Romans they were more popularly known as *Galli* (Gauls) although the terms *Celtae* and *Galatae* were also used. I have generally followed the modern usage of 'Celt' when transcribing the words of Classical writers, whatever term they use, for easier and consistent reading, and only left in the term 'Gaul' when directly quoting more recent writers who have opted for that term. Today, of course, the term 'Gaul' tends to mean specifically a Celt from the area of what is now modern France and Belgium.

Gallia or Gaul, the 'land of the Celts', was divided in early Roman perception into *Gallia Cisalpina* or Cisalpine Gaul, *Gallia* this side (*cis*) of the Alps, and *Gallia Transalpina* or Transalpine Gaul, *Gallia* beyond the Alps. Other Celtic lands would eventually become known to the Romans such as *Gallia Narbonensis* or *Gallia Provincia*, which is still known as Provence, and *Gallograecia* or Galatia, in modern central Turkey.

Cisalpine Gaul, the Po Valley in northern Italy, was, after the Roman conquest, often called *Gallia Togata*, the land of the Celts who wear the toga. Transalpine Gaul was referred to as *Gallia Comata*, 'hairy Gaul', to denote they were not Romanised. Cisalpine Gaul was additionally divided into *Cispadana*, the country south of the Po (Padus) and Transpadana, the country north of the Po, particularly north-west of the Po.

A word on Roman personal names: Romans usually had three names, the *praenomen*, the *nomen* and the *cognomen*. The first name was a personal name, the second name was their *gens* or family name and the last name was their nickname. Thus Marcus Manlius Capitolinus was of the Manlius *gens* or family who received the nickname Capitolinus because of his defence of the Capitol.

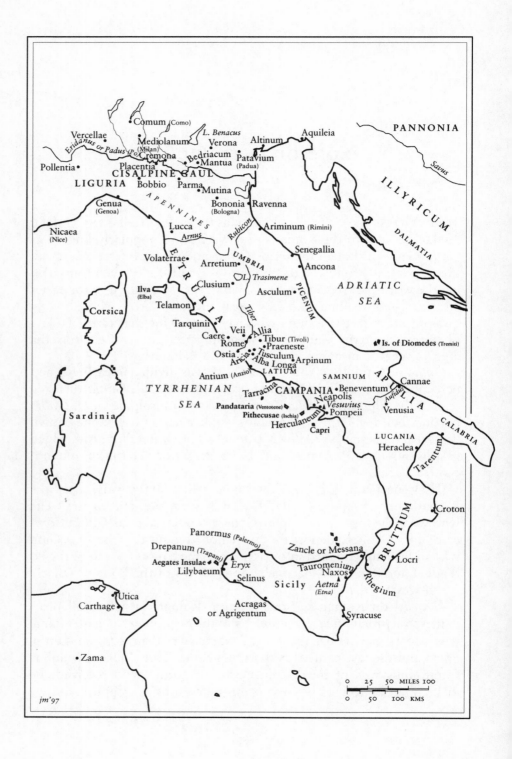

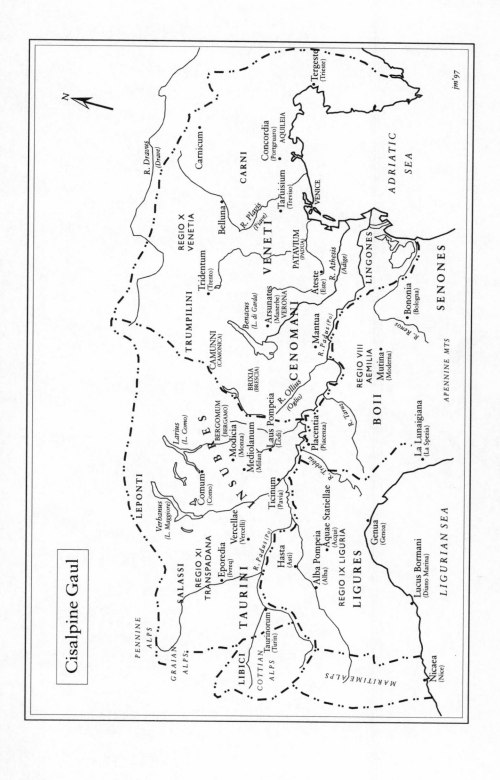

Cisalpine Gaul

'Alliensis': 18 July 390 BC*

DAWN had broken across the sharp-peaked Sabine mountains, to the east of the long meandering valley through which the River Tiber flowed on its south-westerly passage to the waters of the Mediterranean. Where the River Allia gushed into the Tiber, a spot just 11 miles north of the city of Rome, two large armies stood waiting to test each other's strength and resolve.

The powerful and so far undefeated legions of the Roman republic had drawn up near the waters of the Allia, on a broad front in the valley. The river, now the Fosso della Bettina north of Fidenae, was a small tributary of the Tiber, scarcely more than a stream, its swift-flowing waters rising in a deep gully in the foothills of the Sabine mountains near the city of Crustumeria. The Roman reserves had been placed on some high ground a little to the right of the main battle lines, overlooking the river. The command of the Roman legions had been assigned by the Senate into the hands of newly elected consuls and military tribunes. One of the consuls was Quintus Fabius, son of Marcus Fabius Ambustus. The Fabii *gens* were one of the oldest patrician families in Rome. Quintus Fabius had been appointed consul for the patricians for the first time that year. Two consuls were appointed each year as the supreme civil and military magistrates. From the fourth century BC, one consul had to be a patrician, an aristocrat, while the other had to be a plebeian, a representative of the people.

The Roman historian, Titus Livius, Livy (59 BC–AD 17), tells us that in overall command of the Roman legions was Quintus Sulpicius Lagus. He had been appointed consul for the plebeians. The Sulpicius family were, plebeians or not, one of the most powerful

---

* The date is given by Livy's reckoning, which is generally accepted, but Polybius gives references placing the day in 387/386 BC.

and influential in Rome and would continue to be so for centuries to come. Sulpicius Lagus was one of Rome's foremost generals.

The military tribunes were two brothers of the consul Fabius together with Quintus Servilius Fidenas and Publius Cornelius Maluginensis.

This was no amateur, untried army nor one which had inexperienced generals to lead it. Rome had been at war with her neighbours almost since the foundation of the city nearly four centuries before. War had become a way of life for Rome. After the expulsion of the Roman kings and the establishment of a republic, Rome had survived continuous warfare with the neighbouring Etruscan empire, with the Latin cities, with the Sabines and other peoples of the Italian peninsula. By the beginning of the fourth century BC, Rome's military star was well in the ascendant: she had forced an alliance with the Latin cities, defeated the Etruscans and the Aequi of Latium and, most importantly, captured the Etruscan city of Veii (modern Veio) which had for so long been her bitter rival. Veii had fallen only six years before, in 396 BC.

Two of the military tribunes of the army now gathered beside the Allia were veterans of countless previous campaigns. They were also trusted, victorious generals of Rome. Publius Cornelius Maluginensis had already been elected a military tribune twice before. Quintus Servilius Fidenas had been elected on no fewer than four previous occasions. Of the six commanders, only the brothers Fabius had not, as yet, distinguished themselves in senatorial command. But, while considered headstrong and arrogant, they too were veterans of several military campaigns as junior commanders.

Gathered in battle array before the Roman army was a Celtic army. Its commander was known to the Romans as Brennus, *princeps* of the Senones. But this name might well have been the native form of his title for one of the Celtic words for 'king' was *brennin*, which still survives in modern Welsh. The tribal name of Senones signifies 'the old ones', or perhaps a better interpretation would be 'the veterans'. The Celts were an unknown quantity to most of the Roman soldiers on the battlefield that day. While the Romans had heard stories of these people who had, for some centuries, lived north of the Apennine mountains, they had never encountered them before as military antagonists. Roman traders, trading with Etruscan, Greek and Carthaginian merchants, knew that the Celts dwelt in the lands to the north. Greek geographers and ethnographers had written accounts about them which, as Greek was the language of the learned classes in Rome, were known to the educated Romans. But to the ordinary Roman soldiers gathered at the Allia, they were a new and outlandish people. They viewed them, perhaps, with some awe, as they watched their opponents' light cavalry position itself; as the terrifying war chariots drew up in lines and the outwardly undisciplined infantry took up their positions. This was a great tribal army in which the ranks were divided into septs, sub-divisions and clans. For the Roman soldiers 'the air was loud with the dreadful din of the fierce war songs and discordant shouts of a people whose very life is wild adventure', observed Livy. They sung boastful war songs, roared battle cries and shouted taunts towards the serried ranks of Romans. They were brightly attired, wore patterned trousers, a sight few Romans had seen before, and colourful cloaks. Their leaders wore gold torques around their necks and other rich jewellery. They carried long shields and equally long slashing swords.

It was the Celtic leader, Brennus, who signalled his war trumpets to sound the commencement of battle.

It was early in the morning of a day in the month of Quintilis, the fifth month of the Roman year 363 *ab urbe condita* (from the foundation of Rome); a day which later calendars would record as 18 July 390 BC. A day which afterwards would be marked in the Roman calendars as *'dies Alliensis'*, a day of bad auspices; an unlucky day; a day on which future generations of Romans would refuse to undertake any public enterprise. The poet Publius Vergilius Maro, Virgil (70–19 BC) would speak of *'infaustum Alliae nomen'* – the unlucky name of Allia. It was to be the day of Rome's most disastrous defeat. The blow to her prestige would be terrible. It would take the city nearly fifty years to recover.

The battle of Allia could have been avoided had it not been for the arrogance of Rome's ambassadors.

The Etruscans had been at war not only with the Romans on their southern borders but with the Celts on their northern frontier. For centuries the Celts had pushed into the Po Valley, defeating Etruscan armies, occupying what had formerly been Etruscan cities and establishing themselves firmly north of the Apennine mountain range. The

Celtic tribes had settled in the Po Valley, pursuing their agricultural and pastoral life without encroaching into Etruria proper. The Senones had, according to Livy, been one of the most recent Celtic arrivals in the area. There was no room for new settlers in the Po Valley and so, led by their king, Brennus, they decided to cross through the inhospitable passes of the Apennines southward in search of land to settle. This was an entire nation on the march, not just isolated bands of warriors but women, children and the elderly, together with their baggage, wagons and pack animals, as well as chariots and columns of cavalry. The Senones arrived at the Etruscan town of Clusium (Chiusi) some 80 miles north of Rome. Livy repeats a tradition that a citizen of Clusium, one Arruns, had invited the Celts to come to Clusium and had even suggested that they attack the town. The story is repeated by Plutarch – Ploutarchos of Chaeronea in Boeotia (c.AD 46–c.120), the Greek historian and biographer. Arruns had invited the Celts, so it was explained, as vengeance for the seduction of his wife by a man named Lucumo, who was a powerful official of the city. According to Plutarch, Lucumo was an orphan, heir to the greatest wealth of the city, who had been raised by Arruns. In fact, *lucumo* was the title 'king' in Etruscan, one of the few Etruscan words that we can decipher. Lucumo was, Livy says, 'a man in too powerful a position to be punished except by the help of foreigners called in for the purpose'. Plutarch says that Lucumo and Arruns' wife had kept their affair a secret but 'at last the passions of both culprits increased upon them so that they could neither put away their desires nor longer hide them, wherefore the young man made open attempt to remove the woman and have her to wife. Her husband brought the case to trial but was defeated by Lucumo, owing to the multitude of his friends and his lavish outlays of money . . .'

The tradition has it that it was Arruns himself who guided the Celts through the mountain passes to Clusium. Even Livy, so fond of citing traditions as historical fact, points out that this was only a legend and not regarded as factual history. Plutarch, in his biography of Camillus, believes it to be true.

What is certain is that the Senones arrived outside Clusium in their thousands and asked the city fathers to grant them lands on which to settle. According to Livy:

The plight of Clusium was a most alarming one; strange men in thousands were at the gates, men the like of whom the townsfolk had never seen, outlandish warriors armed with strange weapons, who were rumoured already to have scattered the Etruscan legions on both sides of the Po; it was a terrible situation . . .

Rome had only recently exerted its military power through most of Etruria and agreed some treaties with Etruscan cities who promised to recognise Rome's overlordship. The city elders of Clusium decided to send to the Senate of Rome asking for military aid in case the newcomers became a threat.

Military aid was not granted [says Livy] but the three sons of Marcus Fabius Ambustus were sent to remonstrate with the Celts in the Senate's name and to ask them not to molest a people who had done them no wrong and were, moreover, friends and allies of Rome. Rome, they added, would be bound to protect them, even by force, should need arise, though it would be better, if possible, to avoid recourse to arms and to become acquainted with the new immigrants in a peaceful manner.

Of the three brothers, we learn the name of only one, Quintus Fabius, who appears to be the eldest. On arrival in Clusium, a council was held with the Celtic leaders and the city fathers. Plutarch mentions the Senones king, Brennus, as being at this meeting. When the ambassadors from Rome had supported the refusal of Clusium to allow any of their land to be used for settlement by the Senones, the Celtic leader made the following observation:

This is the first time we have heard of Rome, but we can believe none the less that you Romans are men of worth, for Clusium would never otherwise have sought your help in time of trouble. You say that you prefer to help your friends by negotiation rather than by force, and you offer us peace. We, for our part, need land, but we are prepared to accept your offer on condition that the people of Clusium cede to us a portion of their territory – for they have more than they can manage. You can have peace on no other terms. We wish to receive your answer in your presence; should it be a refusal then you will see us fight and thus be in a position

5

to tell your compatriots by how much the Celts exceed all other men in valour.

The young offspring of the Fabii clan were indignant and took offence at this candid reply. After all, they claimed to trace their ancestry back to Hercules himself and to Evander, son of Hermes, who established the first settlement on the Palatine hill of Rome. The family had held seven consulships in the last fifty years. The clan had, almost entirely on its own, pursued the war with the Etruscan town of Veii. The Fabii were arrogant and headstrong young men. Livy is moved to comment: 'The object of the mission was wholly conciliatory; unhappily, however, the ambassadors behaved more like savage Celts than civilised Romans.' In spite of the obvious prejudice revealed by his choice of words, Livy's account shows that the Celts were scrupulous in their diplomacy.

When the Roman ambassadors asked by what right and justice did the Celts demand land from its rightful owners under threat of violence, and what right had the Celts to be in Etruria anyway, Plutarch says that Brennus laughed at the posturing of the Romans. He argued that the people of Clusium had extensive territory but only worked a small area of it and could easily share it with the Senones. To refuse was wrong. But Brennus went further. He pointed out that Rome had marched against many of her neighbours, including the cities of Etruria.

> You marched against these peoples and if they would not share their goods with you, you enslaved them, you despoiled them and razed their cities to the ground; not that in so doing you claim in any wise to be cruel or unjust but that you are but obeying that most ancient of all laws which gives to the stronger the goods of his weaker neighbours . . . Cease, therefore, to pretend to pity the people of Clusium when we besiege them that you may not teach us Celts to be kind and full of pity towards those who have been conquered by the Romans.

Livy recounts the reply more simply, ignoring the subtle irony in which Plutarch phrases it. 'All things belonged to those who carried justice on the point of their swords.' In other words, might was the right. Whatever their arguments were, according to Livy, the Roman

6

ambassadors lost their diplomatic 'cool'. Angry passions were aroused. Negotiations were broken off.

The Etruscan army marched out of Clusium and lined up under the city walls to face the Senones. 'Then it was,' says Livy, 'that the Roman ambassadors took their fatal step. Urged by the evil star which even then had risen over Rome, they broke the law of nations and took up arms.' Instead of adhering to their neutral role as ambassadors and negotiators, the Fabii actually joined the ranks of the Etruscan army. Quintus Fabius saw a Celtic chieftain making for the Etruscan standards. He killed the warrior with a spearthrust through the side and, in spite of the heat of the battle, stopped to strip the Celt of his armour and weapons as token of his victory. According to Livy:

> It was then that the Celts realised who he was, and word was passed through their ranks that he was the envoy from Rome. At once the trumpets sounded the withdrawal; the quarrel with Clusium was forgotten and the anger of the barbarian army was turned upon Rome.

The Romans would eventually learn that the Celts were strict believers in law, both domestic and international. The role of ambassadors held a sacred trust for them. Indeed, the Romans would later incorporate into Latin the Celtic word *ambactus* which would give the word 'ambassador' to many languages. Naturally, the Celts were horrified at this 'crime' by Rome's envoys.

The council of the Senones met. Some of the younger chieftains urged that the Senones should march immediately upon Rome to take retribution for this appalling breach of international law. Other Celtic chieftains, perhaps older and wiser, decided that the Senones should send their own ambassadors to Rome. Livy says that

> ... envoys were sent to lodge a complaint against the breach of international law and to demand the surrender of the Fabii to justice.

The Senate, having listened to what the Celtic envoys had to say, by no means approved the conduct of their own envoys; but though they admitted to themselves that the Celtic demand was a fair one, they refused, where three men of such rank were

7

concerned, to take what they really knew to be the proper action; their own interests as the governing elders prevented them. Accordingly, to avoid the responsibility for any losses which might result from a clash with the Celts, they referred the ambassadors' demands to the people of Rome for decision, with the result that the three guilty men, whose punishment was supposed to be under discussion, were elected as military tribunes with consular powers for the following year; such was the influence on the mind of the populace of wealth and position. The Celtic envoys were naturally – and rightly – indignant, and before leaving the city openly threatened war.

Plutarch confirms this account and says that many members of the Senate denounced the Fabii brothers, especially the *fetiales*, a college of Roman priests, selected for life among the patrician class, who represented the people in their dealings with other nations. They were a group concerned particularly with the rituals of making a treaty or declaring war. They were said to have been instituted by the legendary king of Rome, Numa Pompilius (715–673 BC) but their office lapsed in the last century of the republic to be revived again under Augustus. In other words, the *fetiales* were international lawyers and they realised that the Celtic complaint was just.

The Senate referred the matter to the people, and although the priests with one accord denounced Fabius, the multitude so scorned and mocked at religion as to appoint him [Quintus Fabius] military tribune, along with his brothers.

These Celtic ambassadors returned to the Senones, who were still encamped near Clusium. They doubtless brought with them descriptions of Rome and its riches, its great temples and buildings. More importantly, they must have brought with them military knowledge, of the city's defences, its walls and gates and strategic places.

The Celts, for their part, wasted no time, the instant they knew of the insult to their embassy and the promotion to command of the men who had violated the unwritten law of all mankind, they flamed into uncontrollable anger which is characteristic of their race, and set forward, with terrible speed, on the path to Rome.

Terrified townships rushed to arms as the avengers went roaring by; men fled from the fields for their lives; and from all the immense host, covering miles of ground with its straggling masses of horse and foot, the cry went up 'To Rome!'

Some historians use this as the basis to present a picture of the Celtic army ravaging the countryside, looting, burning, raping and slaughtering people, as they surged towards Rome. However, Plutarch says: 'Contrary to all expectation the Celts did them [the people of the countryside] no harm, nor took aught from their fields, but even as they passed close by their cities, shouted out that they were marching on Rome and had declared war only on the Romans, but the rest of the people they regarded as friends.'

Livy is at pains to point out that the Roman generals had sought no portents from the gods, either from flights of birds or from searching the entrails of slaughtered animals. 'Because the military tribune Sulpicius had apparently not obtained favourable omens before offering sacrifice on 16 July and two days later had exposed the Roman army to the enemy without gaining the gods' favour, some think that it was also decreed that religious rites should not be held on the days following the Ides . . .' That is the 15th of the month. Livy says that the gods were forgotten. In this he is supported by Plutarch. 'They neglected all religious rites, having neither sacrificed with good omens, nor consulted the prophets as was meet before the perils of a battle.' To reinforce the symbolism, Plutarch says that the battle was fought on the same day as a former great disaster when 300 men of the Fabii clan had been cut to pieces by the Etruscans.

Indeed, Livy gives various other excuses for the forthcoming Roman defeat. The Roman commanders had taken no military precautions, he says. They had secured no regular defensive positions. Plutarch is quick to support him. He argued that the problem lay in the fact that there was no dictator and too many sub-commanders. Whenever the Roman armies were defeated, they were, according to Roman historians, always outnumbered and Livy claims the Roman legions were vastly outnumbered by the Celts on this occasion. Estimates of the Celtic army were put in the region of 30,000 men, which, as it is reported that only the Senones were involved, would have made them a pretty formidable tribe to field such a military host.

However, we may take all these figures with a pinch of salt. M. Cary and H. H. Scullard in their *History of Rome* are still inclined to accept the Roman view of a vast Celtic army. 'The Romans had perhaps 15,000 men; the Gauls are variously put at 30,000–70,000.' If a single tribal army could field such strength of fighting men then the size of the tribe would, indeed, have been colossal. But not all sources agree on the ratio. Plutarch actually gives the Roman legions as constituting 40,000 men and states: 'They [the Romans] were not inferior in numbers, being no fewer than 40,000 men but most of them were untrained, and had never handled weapons before.'

In this instance, I think we are safe in saying that the Roman defence force would have had the edge in numbers over the fighting men of the Senones who had also just completed an exhausting forced march of 80 miles to do battle. Assuming that the Romans had, as their minimum force, four legions – for each consul usually had two legions under his command – and given that each legion numbered at this time 6000 men not counting auxiliaries, the Roman army would have been about 24,000. The Senones' tribal army could scarcely have been more than 12,000 fighting men even by a conservative estimate based on a populous tribe.

As for Livy's reference to the inefficiency of Rome's generals, the arrival of a hostile army – only 11 miles from the city – would have caused Rome to have thrown all the fighting men who were available into battle with their best commanders at their head. There is no doubt that the Roman forces were veteran troops and their generals the most worthy that the Senate could appoint. The reason for the defeat of Rome was, simply, that Brennus of the Senones was a better general. Even Livy has to finally admit, when he has made all his excuses: 'Alas, not only good fortune but good generalship was on the Celtic side.'

Brennus observed the placement of the Roman legions and saw the reserves on the hillside to the Roman right. Livy thinks that he might have suspected that these reserves, placed in such an unusual position, were actually the main Roman force who would launch their attack on his flank if he went forward on the main lines. He decided to deliver a surprise attack on these reserves, rushing on them from the flank and from the rear. At the same time, he launched another wing of his army to engage the Roman front and centre. His fierce attack on the Roman reserves threw them into panic. They had been expecting to stand by and watch the opening of the battle, only being called in if things turned dangerous for the main force. Now they were attacked without warning and began streaming down on their own centre, causing alarm and eventually panic there.

Doubtless, one of the 'surprise weapons' that the Celts had at Allia was their war chariots and, while we have no detailed contemporary descriptions of them, we can assume that their tactics were much the same as those frequently mentioned in subsequent engagements. Diodorus Siculus (c.60–30 BC), quoting Posidonius (c.135–c.50 BC), is specific on the Celtic chariot in battle: 'When travelling and in war, they [the Celts] use chariots which seat a driver and a warrior. When they encounter horsemen in war they hurl javelins against the foe and then dismounting engage the enemy with the sword.' Over 300 years after Allia, Julius Caesar (100–44 BC), describes the Celtic chariot tactics which he encountered in Britain in a similar fashion: 'They first drive about in all directions and hurl missiles; by the terror of the horses and noise of the wheels they throw the ranks of the enemy into confusion.' Once the chariots had penetrated the ranks of the cavalry, the warriors jumped down and fought on foot while their charioteers withdrew but stood ready to rescue the warriors if things went badly, thus combining 'the mobility of cavalry and the stability of infantry'.

At Allia, according to Livy:

The main body of the [Roman] army, at the first sound of the Celtic war cry on their flank and in their rear, hardly waited even to see their strange enemy from the ends of the earth; they made no attempt at resistance; they had not courage even to answer his shouted challenge, but fled before they had lost a single man. None fell fighting; they were cut down from behind as they struggled to force a way to safety through the heaving mass of their fellow fugitives.

Livy is unfairly scathing about the courage of the Roman soldiers.

In the lines of the legionaries – officers and men alike – there was no trace of the old Roman manhood. They fled in panic, so blinded to everything but saving their skins that, in spite of the fact that the Tiber lay in their way, most of them tried to get to Veii, once an enemy town, instead of making for their own homes in Rome.

He goes on to say that there were heavy Roman casualties on the banks of the Tiber. The entire left wing of the Roman army had fled towards the Tiber, making for the Etruscan city of Veii which was situated on the opposite bank. The Romans, says Livy, tried to swim across but many were exhausted and were dragged under the water by the weight of their armour and equipment and drowned. Others drowned simply because they could not swim. He estimates that more than half of this left wing perished in the Tiber while the rest reached the depopulated city and fortified themselves inside. Those who reached safety failed to send news to Rome of their defeat nor did they make any attempt to send to the city units to help prepare a defence.

However, the survivors of the right wing of the Roman army certainly made for Rome and some reached it, rushing into the city and, surprisingly, not even bothering to close the city gates behind them. These took refuge on the northern summit of the Capitoline hill known as the *arx* or citadel. Both summits of the hill – the south-west summit was the official Capitol – constituted the religious centre, the site of the temple to Jupiter, Juno and Minerva. It was the most sacred part of Rome, where sacrifices were carried out and victorious generals were accorded their triumphs. It was also the most strategic area of the city, and the most defendable. Among the survivors who made it to the safety of the Capitoline hill was the commander-in-chief himself, the consul, Quintus Sulpicius Lagus. Accounts indicate that he was not the only military commander to escape from Allia but, alas, the names of the others are not given. We hear no more of the Fabii brothers. Perhaps they perished in the battle. We learn the names of the senior Roman officers who survived, including one Marcus Manlius, a former consul.

The Roman Senate believed that the few survivors who had reached Rome were all that were left of its legions. Rome became a place of lamentation and of panic. News came that the Celts were now marching triumphantly on the city. It was agreed that there was no hope of defending Rome with the handful of surviving troops. The perimeter walls of the city were too vast for them to defend properly. The decision was taken to withdraw all the men capable of bearing arms, with women and children, to the defensive position of the Capitol. According to Livy:

> It was felt that if the Citadel, home of the city's tutelary gods, could survive the impending ruin – if the few men still able to fight, if the Senate, fountain-head of true government, could escape the general disaster, it would be tolerable to leave, in the city below, the aged and useless, who had not, in any case, much longer to live. It was a stern decision, and to make it easier for the commons to bear, the old aristocrats who long before had served as consuls or celebrated their Triumphs said that they would die side by side with their humble compatriots, and never consent to burden the inadequate stores of the fighting few with bodies which could no longer bear arms in the country's defence. To tell each other of this noble resolve was the only consolation of the doomed men, who turned to address words of encouragement to the young and vigorous whom they were seeing on their way to the Capitol, and to commend to the valour of their youth whatever good fortune might yet remain for a city which for three hundred and fifty years had never been defeated.

In fact, the Capitol was just a small fortress within the city and it was intended to hold only combatants. The thousands of ordinary citizens of Rome, the poor, the women and the children, were ordered to leave the city and scatter into the countryside before the Celtic army arrived. Most of them streamed in an unbroken line westward across the Sublican Bridge over the Tiber towards the Janiculum hill. The bridge had been built by Ancus Martius and took its name from the *sublicae*, wooden piles, on which it was constructed. From early times the Janiculum hill had been a defensive outpost of Rome on which a flag always flew. Its removal signified the approach of danger. From the Janiculum, the refugees dispersed, making for shelter in neighbouring towns and villages.

The priests and priestess of Vesta, the ancient Roman goddess of the hearth, worshipped in every Roman house, were ordered to remove the sacred emblems of their cult and flee the city to a place of safety. This included the removal of the sacred eternal fire in the symbolic hearth of state, kept in a small round temple in the Forum which was looked after by the Vestal Virgins. These maidens, who served the order, were chosen from the families of ancient kings and warriors of Rome. Any Vestal found to be unchaste was entombed alive, a practice still in use in the first century BC. They were held in high repute and great weight was attached to their intervention on behalf of those in trouble.

The Vestal Virgins, and the priests of Quirinus, gathered to discuss what should be done. Quirinus was originally a local deity of the community settled on the Quirinal hill before the foundation of Rome and, with Mars and Jupiter, was incorporated as a state god and eventually identified with the deified Romulus by many Romans of the later republic. These priests realised that they could not transport all the sacred artifacts of their religions and so they decided to store them in boxes and jars and bury them in a shrine near the chief priest's house said to be in the Forum Boarium or cattle market. Livy says that in his day it was still forbidden to spit near that spot as it was considered sacrilegious. It was called the *doliola*, place of the casks. Other items they carried with them, along the road, over the pile-bridge across the Tiber towards the Janiculum.

According to Livy:

> On the slope of the hill they were noticed by a man of humble birth named Albinus, who was driving his wife and family in a cart, amongst the rabble of other non-combatants escaping from the city. Even at such a moment Albinus could remember the difference between what was due to the gods and what to man, and feeling it to be an impious thing that he and his family should be seen driving while priestesses of the state toiled along on foot carrying the nation's sacred emblems, he told his wife to get out of the cart with her little boys, took up the Vestals and their burdens instead, and drove them to their destination in Caere.

Caere was a very ancient city of Etruria, 15 miles east of Veii. One questions whether Lucius Albinus, in abandoning his wife and children in the face of an oncoming enemy army, in order to save the priests and priestesses and their treasures, was to be applauded. One can't help wondering what his wife and her children thought about Albinus and, indeed, what fate they suffered.

The story is also given by the polymath, Marcus Terentius Varro (116–27 BC), and by the compiler of anecdotes, Valerius Maximus (*c.* early first century AD), as well as being repeated by Plutarch who says: 'This pious act of Albinus, and the conspicuous honour which he showed the gods in a season of the greatest danger, could not well be passed over in silence.'

Livy tells us that the grey-haired senators, the elder statesmen and retired officials of the city, had gone to their homes to await the arrival of the Celts.

> It was the wish of those who had held the highest offices of the state to dress for death in the outward signs of such rank as they had enjoyed or service they had rendered in the days of their former fortunes; so putting on the ceremonial robes of the dignitaries who, at the Circensian Games, escort the chariots of the gods, or of generals who enter the City in triumph, they took their seats, each in the courtyard of his house, on the ivory inlaid chairs of the *curule* magistrates, having first – we are told – repeated after Marcus Folius, the Pontifex Maximus, a solemn vow to offer themselves as a sacrifice for their country and the Roman people.

The Pontifex Maximus was the head of the college of pontiffs, or priests, who exercised disciplinary functions over them and was responsible for the publishing of laws. During the subsequent empire it was an office held only by the emperors. The *curule* magistrates belonged to an office which originated in Etruria and were the highest rank of magistrates entitled to use the *stella curulis* or chair of state, a folding stool inlaid with ivory, from which justice was administered by them. However, if the ageing former senators, officials and generals were seated in their chairs of office in the *atria*, or courtyards, of their houses, awaiting the coming of the enemy, they had a long wait before them.

It was sunset before the forward scouting cavalry units of the Celtic army reached the outskirts of Rome. The Roman historians, such as Livy, made the Celts astonished at the magnitude and sumptuousness of Rome. This was merely to embellish Rome's greatness, of course, because the Celts had encountered other equally impressive cities. They had seen, and, indeed, captured, many Etruscan cities of the north. Livy claims that the Celts were too frightened to attack the city at night, which is a rather strange notion but probably put in to reinforce the idea that the Celts were backward savages. The

Celtic scouts made a careful reconnaissance of the walls and gates of the city, in case a new Roman army lay in wait to entrap them. From the Celtic ambassadors who had returned from Rome, they knew the extent and general layout of the city. The advance guard did not attempt to enter Rome but awaited the arrival of the main body of the army. It then being dusk they encamped somewhere between the River Anio, the modern Aniene, and the city walls.

Throughout the night, those Romans still within the city could hear the Celts singing songs around their camp fires or, as Livy would have it, 'cries like the howling of wolves and barbaric songs could be heard'.

> All the time, between then and the following dawn was filled with unbearable suspense. When would the assault come? Again and again they [the Romans] believed it to be imminent; they expected it on the first appearance of the Celts – for why had they marched on the city, and not stayed at the Allia, unless this had been their intention? They expected it at sunset – because there was little daylight left, and surely it would come before dark? Then, when darkness had fallen, they thought it had been deliberately postponed in order to multiply its terrors. But the night passed, and dawn, when it drew near, made them almost desperate; and then at last, hard upon this long drawn-out and insupportable anxiety, came the thing itself, and the enemy entered the gates.

Just after dawn, on the morning of the day which was later to be recorded as 19 July 390 BC, the advance guard of the Celtic army moved slowly through the wide open Porta Collina, or Colline Gate, on the north-east side of the city, near the Quirinal hill from which, just hours before, the priests of Quirinus had fled.

Rome, which its citizens had come to believe was an impregnable city, had fallen to the victorious Celtic army of Brennus of the Senones.

[2]

The Arrival of the Celts in Italy

WHO were these Celts who had achieved the unthinkable; who had brushed aside the armies of Rome and captured the city itself? Where had they come from?

According to archaeological evidence, the Celtic peoples descend from a mixture of the Bronze Age Tumulus culture (*c*.1550–1250 BC) and the Urnfield culture (*c*.1200 BC). Drs Jacquetta and Christopher Hawkes, in the 1940s, first identified these cultures as what they termed 'proto-Celtic'. The archaeologist, Dr John X. W. P. Corcoran, in his essay 'The Origin of the Celts', states:

> With the emergence of the Urnfield culture of Central Europe, there appeared a people whom some scholars regard as being 'proto-Celtic', in that they may have spoken, as is suggested by the evidence of place-names, an early form of Celtic, a sub-group of the Indo-European family of languages. Apart from the influence of some immigrants from the east during the early first millennium BC, there is little to distinguish the Urnfield people from their descendants of the Hallstatt culture, other than the latter's use of iron. Again it would seem that the thread of continuity is strong.

In other words, in the Bronze Age Tumulus and Urnfield cultures we see the early beginnings of what we now call Celtic civilisation. This civilisation, as we would recognise it, emerged in what is now eastern France, north Alpine Switzerland and south-west Germany, at the headwaters of the Danube, the Rhine and the Rhône. All three rivers still bear their Celtic names. The Danuvius (Danube) was named after the Celtic Mother Goddess, Danu, the 'divine waters'; the Renos (Rhine) takes its name from an ancient Celtic word for sea, still observed in the Old Irish *rian*; while Rhodanus (Rhône) also bears the name of the goddess Danu with the prefix *ro* meaning 'great', 'exceeding' or 'complete'. There is also a Rodanus which is an affluence of the Moselle.

Archaeologists have identified a fully developed Celtic society from the eighth century BC, in an iron-using economy known as the Hallstatt culture. Hallstatt is a village in the Salzkammergut in Austria at which was found an important cemetery. The Hallstatt culture is identified by a mainly geometric-based art which evolved from Urnfield antecedents; iron was in full use and spacious chamber graves beneath a mound or barrow were common, containing rich burials. A feature of these burials of 'chieftains' was that the bodies were laid out on four-wheeled wagons with splendidly decorative yokes and harnesses. The sophistication of the wagons and their means of construction indicate that the Celts had become highly advanced in methods of transport. The archaeological evidence also shows that the Celts of this period were developing a trade with the Mediterranean world: artifacts from Greece, Etruria and Carthage have been found in these tombs.

The Hallstatt culture eventually gave place to a new form known as La Tène, from the area based on the north-eastern end of Lake Neuchâtel in Switzerland. This culture saw the birth in Celtic society of remarkable decorative art forms whose patrons were the wealthy kings and chieftains of the tribal societies. It saw the emergence of fast two-wheeled war chariots and other transport innovations. Living standards were high. By the seventh century BC, the Celts were being identified by Greek and Phoenician explorers and traders who formed colonies in the western Mediterranean. Indeed, the Celts were the first Transalpine people to emerge into recorded history.

From their earliest appearance in written records, they are clearly identified by the fact that they spoke languages which can be distinguished from other European languages by the term 'Celtic'. The Celtic languages constitute a branch of the Indo-European family which covers most of Europe as well as Iran and northern India. An Indo-European family presupposes the existence at some time in remote antiquity of a unified, primitive parent language whose dialects developed into the ancestors of the present major language groups. Professor Myles Dillon argued for the start of the separation of Celtic from the hypothesised Indo-European parent around the start of the second millennium BC and Professor Stuart Piggott agrees with this dating. The Celtic languages spread rapidly during the first millennium BC as the Celtic tribes became advanced in the field of iron-working and were able to construct roads through the previously impenetrable forests of northern Europe. Dr Nora Chadwick believed that the Celts reached Ireland even before the start of the second millennium BC, earlier than most scholars accept, but certainly the Celts were in neighbouring Britain by the eighth century BC as well as having settled in the Iberian peninsula (Spain).

The answer to the question of when the Celts began to move across the Alps to settle in the Po Valley, between the Alps and Apennines, is still a matter of scholastic debate. According to Professor Otto-Herman Frey: 'All in all, the sequence of the Celtic immigration to Italy remains problematic because of the contradictory and, in part, very fragmentary nature of the documentary evidence.' The earliest date argued is at the start of the first millennium BC. Archaeologist Alexandre Bertrand (*Archéologie celtique et gauloise*, Paris, 1879) placed the descent of the Celts into the Po Valley at this time. However, Dr Bertrand saw no difference between the Celts and the Umbrians, arguing that Umbrian was an Indo-European dialect, which, at this stage, was the same dialect as Celtic Indo-European. Dr Marco Tizzoni points to the settlements of the plain of Lombardy and Emilia Romagna and argues that the few La Tène 'A' class archaeological finds should be thought of as merely 'imports'. He would argue for a date no earlier than 388 BC for the Celtic settlements. On the other hand, Dr G. Dobesch has argued for a date of the sixth century BC and presents evidence to substantiate his claims. The written records from most ancient historians, with the notable exception of Livy, place them as entering the valley at the end of the fifth century BC.

Henri Hubert argued for an early date in a paper in the *Revue Celtique* (vol. xxxiv) and made the suggestion that the Celts arrived, from the evidence of archaeological finds along the Ticino, about the end of the eighth century BC. Sir John Rhŷs, who spent some time in the Po Valley deciphering Celtic inscriptions, and delivered a series of papers on them to the British Academy between 1906 and 1914, appeared to approve of this contention. In 'Gleanings in the Italian Field of Celtic Epigraphy', read to the Academy on 27 May 1914, Sir John, first holder of the chair of Celtic Studies at Oxford, argued that these early Celts were of the 'Q' Celtic linguistic group. It is accepted that 'Q' Celtic, from which the Goidelic family of Irish,

Manx and Scottish descends, was the more archaic form of Celtic. About the seventh century B C, some Celtic dialects began to modify away from this into the 'P' Celtic form, from which Welsh, Cornish and Breton derive and to which it is believed most forms of Continental Celtic belonged. The 'Q' sound, that is the sound in Indo-European which gave *qu* (*kw*) represented by 'c' in the modern 'Q' dialects, was substituted by 'P'. That is best demonstrated in the following examples: the Irish ma*c* (son) becomes, in Welsh, ma*p*; or the Irish *c*enn (head) becomes *p*en in Welsh; or the Irish *cách* (everyone) becomes *paup* in Welsh.

Sir John argued:

> . . . I venture to regard his [Hubert's] earliest Celts – I mean earliest in Italy in the archaeological sense – as having a claim to be racially identified with the earlier Celts in the philological sense. Who the latter were is open to no doubt; they were the Celts whose language had *qu* and with whom the Gaelic-speaking peoples of Erin, Man and Scotland have to be ranked, while the Brythons were Gauls and spoke a Celtic which was modified, among other things in that it had substituted *p* for *qu*, as for instance in *epos* 'a horse' for the older *equos* or in *magos* 'a boy, a son', Modern Irish *mac*, O. Welsh *map*, Modern Welsh *mab*, of the same meaning. The differentiation had taken place on the Continent, that is to say before the ancestors of the Goidels had reached Ireland and before the Gauls settled in Britain.

So Sir John is arguing for a linguistic change from 'Q' Celtic-speaking to 'P' Celtic-speaking also among the Celts of the Po Valley.

Bertrand, in trying to argue an earlier descent for all the Celts, pointed out that, according to Plutarch, a Greek poet named Simylos blamed the death of Tarpeia on the Celts and not the Sabines. Most sources say that during a war between Rome and the Sabines, at the time of the city's foundation in 753 B C, resulting from the Roman 'Rape of the Sabine Women', the Sabines exacted revenge, besieging the Capitol. Tarpeia, the daughter of the Roman commander, offered to betray the Capitol if the Sabines gave her 'what they wore on their left arm', meaning their gold bracelets. They agreed to the bargain. After she had betrayed the Roman garrison, the Sabines crushed her to death with their shields, which were also worn on the left arm. They, therefore, did not betray their word. Another version has it that Tarpeia was a heroine who had tried to gain possession of the Sabine shields. The name Tarpeia is, of course, Etruscan, and her role as a traitoress to Rome was underlined by the naming of the south-west rocky corner of the Capitoline hill as the Tarpeian Rock, from which those sentenced to death were hurled on the rocks below. Simylos, in shifting the blame for her death on to the Celts, puts this legendary story out of its time sequence and it does not really help Bertrand's argument.

Livy, who certainly used at least two Celtic historians as his sources – Cornelius Nepos, an Insubrean (c.100–c.25 BC) and Trogus Pompeius, of the Vocontii from Narbonensis Gaul (27 BC–AD 14) – places the historical arrival of the Celts around the late seventh century or early sixth century BC. Another main source would be the Alexandrian, Timagenes, captured by the Romans in 55 BC and brought to Rome, where he collected many traditions relating to the Celts; he is cited by other writers as an authority on the Celtic Druids. He might well have had access to now lost Greek sources, especially as Livy brings the foundation of the Greek city of Massilia (Marseilles) into his account. However, Livy, living in the Augustinian period, was born in Patavium (Padua) in Cisalpine Gaul and did not go to Rome until his adulthood. It has been argued that he could well have heard, in his youth, the oral historical traditions of the Celts. It has even been suggested that he might have been a Celt himself, for all his Roman name. This would account for his appearance of trying to be more Roman than the Romans.

Livy is the exception among historians for all the rest tie in the coming of the Celts into Italy with the battle of Allia and capture of Rome, that is between the years 396 and 386 BC. Even Cornelius Nepos places the date of their arrival at the time of the capture of Veii in 396 BC. Polybius (c.200–after 118 BC) says it happened during the time of the Archonship of Theodotos, the Peace of Antalcidas, the siege of Rhegion and the second year of the 98th Olympiad – that is 387–386 BC – while Dionysius of Halicarnassus (c.30 BC) places it in the Archonship of Pyrgion in Athens, which was 388–387 BC. According to Diodorus Siculus: 'At the time that Dionysius was besieging Rhegium [391 BC] the Celts, who had their homes in the regions beyond the Alps, streamed through the passes in great strength and seized the territory that lay between the Apennine

mountains and the Alps, expelling the Tyrrhenians who lived there.'
However, just for once, I believe that we can place more trust in
Livy, not only when he gives 390 BC as the date of the capture of
Rome but also when he suggests an early date for the Celtic
migrations into Italy.

Judging from what evidence we have, it is feasible that the first
Celts were settling south of the Alps in the eighth/seventh century
BC. Certainly they were well established in the Alpine valleys by this
date. We can argue that the Celts, entering Italy by the western passes
through the Alps, through Valais or Savoy, the Val d'Aosta, where
early archaeological traces of their passage have been discovered, had
crossed into Italy to join their Osco-Umbrian cousins some centuries
before the attack on Rome. The Senones, who captured Rome, were,
as I have pointed out, late-comers who did not initially settle among
their fellow Celts of the Po Valley but moved directly south over the
Apennines.

According to Livy:

The following account has come down to us of the Celtic
migrations. During the reign of Tarquinius Priscus in Rome, the
Celts, one of three Gallic peoples, were dominated by the Bituriges,
and their king was consequently a member of that tribe. At the
time we are concerned with, the king was one Ambicatus, who,
by his personal qualities, had attained to very considerable power;
indeed, under his rule Gaul [the Celtic homeland] became so rich
and populous that the effective control of such large numbers was
a matter of serious difficulty. The king therefore, being now an
old man and wishing to relieve his kingdom of the burdensome
excess of the population, announced his intention of sending his
two nephews, Bellovesus and Segovesus, both of them adventurous
young men, out into the world to find such new homes as the
gods, by signs from heaven, might point the way to; he was willing
to give them as many followers as they thought would ensure their
ability to overcome any opposition as they might encounter. The
gods were duly consulted, with the result that to Segovesus were
assigned the Hercynian uplands in South Germany while Bellovesus was granted the much more pleasant road into Italy; whereupon collecting the surplus population – Bituriges, Arverni,
Senones, Aedui, Ambarri, Carnutes, Aulerci – he set out with a

vast host, some mounted, some on foot, and reached the territory of the Tricastini at the foot of the Alps.

Livy's statements need some commentary.

To place this event in the reign of Tarquinius Priscus dates it precisely for Tarquin, or Tarquinius the Elder, was the fifth king of Rome ruling from 616 to 579 BC. Interestingly, in connection with the tradition about Arruns of Clusium having invited the Celts there to punish Lucumo for seducing his wife, later Roman writers claimed Tarquinius' original name was Lucumo but, of course, these historians did not realise that *lucumo* was an Etruscan word meaning 'king'. However, the Celtic personal names given by Livy seem authentic enough: Ambicatus, 'He who gives battle all round', Bellovesus, 'He who can kill', and Segovesus, 'He who can conquer'.

The names of the Celtic tribes are also genuine except that not all these tribes settled in the Po Valley.

Trogus Pompeius likened the Celtic movement into Italy to the *ver sacrum* or 'sacred spring' which was practised among the ancient Latins and also among some Greek communities. At a time of great emergency, when the population grew too large, those of twenty years of age were expelled from the country to go where they pleased and found a new community. The tradition was revived by the Romans after the Second Punic War in 217 BC.

Apart from slight differences, most of the main pro-Roman historians of the period set forth the facts of the coming of the Celts in a fairly similar manner: Plutarch, Dionysius of Halicarnassus, Polybius, Pliny the Elder (AD 23/4–79) Marcus Porcius Cato (234–149 BC), Appian of Alexandria (c.AD 160), Aulus Gellius (AD 130 –c.180), Diodorus Siculus and Flavius Petrus Sabbatius Justinianus or Justinian (c.AD 482–565). In every case they ascribe the agricultural riches of Italy as the reason why the Celts descended into the peninsula from what were considered to be the inhospitable Celtic regions. Pliny argued that the Celts were enticed by the lure of grapes and figs. In his *Natural History* he says:

The Celts, imprisoned as they were by the Alps . . . first found a motive for overflowing into Italy from the circumstance of a Celt from the Helvetii, named Helico, who had lived in Rome because of his skill as a craftsman, and brought back with him some dried figs and grapes and some samples of oil and wine; consequently we may excuse them for having sought to obtain these things even by means of war!

Plutarch paints a jaundiced picture:

At last they got a taste of wine, which was then for the first time brought to them from Italy. They admired the drink so much, and were all so beside themselves with the novel pleasure which it gave, that they seized their arms, took along their families, and made off to the Alps in quest of the land which produced such fruit, considering the rest of the world barren and wild.

The truth was, of course, that the Celts of the north were certainly importing wine from Greece and Etruria by the sixth century BC. An enormous bronze wine *krater* from Sparta (5 ft 4 ins high) was found in the grave of a sixth-century BC Celtic princess at Vix, near Mont Lassois in France. Also in the same grave were Etruscan wine flagons and cups. By 500 BC the Celts were trading with Massilia and Greek colonies at Spina and Adria and the new Etruscan settlements in the Po Valley. Even Ireland, on the western edge of the Celtic world, was trading with Greeks and Phoenicians and importing wine. Soon the vine was being cultivated over southern Gaul. Romans saw the Celts as over-indulging in wine, and frequently they are painted as drunken and unable to handle alcohol. The Roman views are rather like the general view held by white Americans of the native peoples of North America. We shall discuss the Roman prejudices later but certainly the view is an unfair one. We find that one Celtic tribe, the Nervii, a Belgae tribe living in the area of modern Schedlt in central Belgium, actually forbade the import or use of wine because they believed that it would make their young men too soft and effeminate. Ironically, the Celts did provide Latin with a word for a type of beer – *cervisia* which has survived in modern Spanish as *cerveza*.

Livy continues his narrative by recounting how, having reached the mountain barrier of the Alps, Bellovesus and his people halted awhile. The Alps, of course, bear a Celtic name – *alpes* meant 'a height' or 'high mountain'. It has been argued that they could have been named by the Romans because Latin has the word *albus* meaning 'white'. However, by the time Romans saw the Alps the Celts were well settled in and around them and had passed on their name for the mountains to the Greeks who first record it. While *alpes* was a Celtic word it would appear the Latin *albus* might have been a cognate, a word descended from a common ancestor word in Indo-European. Pliny goes to some trouble to point out that when he spoke of Albion, the earlier Celtic name for Britain, he was referring to the Celtic word for 'high country'.

So when Livy speaks of Bellovesus halting before the Alps, he is using the Celtic name for the mountains and what he doesn't say is that Celts were already domiciled in the Alpine valleys.

There in front of him [Bellovesus] stood the mountains. I am not surprised that they seemed an insuperable barrier, for as yet no track had led a traveller over them – at any rate within recorded time, unless one likes to believe the fabled exploits of Hercules. There, then, stood the Celtic host, brought to a halt by the towering wall, and looking for a way over those skyward rising peaks into another world. Another consideration also delayed them, for they had heard that a strange people – actually the Massiliots, who had sailed from Phocaea – were seeking for somewhere to settle and were in conflict with the Salui. The superstitious Celts took this as an omen of their own success and helped the strangers to such effect that they were enabled to establish themselves without serious opposition, at the spot where they had disembarked . . .

Again there are some interesting points raised in this passage. Greeks from Phocaea did, indeed, establish their city colony called Massilia (Marseilles) around 600 BC just east of the mouth of the Rhône. The Salui are, doubtless, the Saluvii who dwelt in this area. D'Arbois de Jubainville believes that they were a Celtic tribe, identifiable as the Salassi. This seems a dubious proposition and most writers clearly differentiate between the Saluvii of Provence and the Salassi of Savoy. Others have argued that they were Ligurians while a consensus makes them Celto-Ligurians, a mixed race of people. It is not beyond the bounds of possibility that the Celts of Bellovesus helped the Greek colonists establish their colony on the southern shores of what was eventually to become known as France just to the east of the great river called the Rhodanus (Rhône).

We will follow Livy's account for the moment.

> They then . . . crossed the Alps by the Taurine passes and the pass of Duria, defeated the Etruscans near the river Ticinus, and, having learnt that they were in what was known as the territory of the Insubres, the same name as one of the cantons of the Aedui, took it as another favourable omen and founded the town of Mediolanum.

Again, we need to look at this passage carefully. Bellovesus and his Celts crossed the Alps into the country of the Taurini, through the valley of Duria and into northern Italy. If Livy is claiming Bellovesus and his people were the first Celts to cross the Alps, we are at once confronted by a contradiction. The Taurini were a Celtic tribe who had established their capital at Taurinorum, modern Turin. This tribe was apparently eventually forced to move during the Roman conquest of the area and appears to have resettled in Noricum (Austria) by the first century BC. So we already find Celts domiciled south of the Alps when Bellovesus arrives.

And if this one tribe was not enough, Livy says that the Celts of Bellovesus learnt that the area around Mediolanum, modern Milan, 'was called the Plain of the Insubres'; this lay between the Rivers Ticinus (Ticina) and Ollius (Oglio). The Insubres were a major Celtic tribe whose name might indicate 'very wise ones' from the root *subro*, 'wise'. So yet again we have evidence that the Celts had already passed this way long before Bellovesus and settled.

Among the isolated valleys in the Alps is the Camonica Valley, which lies in the Italian Alps. It is a natural corridor 30 miles (50 kilometres) long in a difficult terrain through which the River Oglio flows. It had been inhabited since the Bronze Age because it was good hunting country where food was plentiful. The entrance to the valley from the south lies beyond Lake d'Iseo some 25 miles (40 kilometres) north of Brescia. By the Hallstatt period and into the La Tène period its population was identifiably Celtic. A record of the population had been carved on rocks from even the neolithic period, and this custom had become a religious ritual by the time we can identify the people as Celts. The dominant images on the rocks are weapons, the sun and stags. At Naquane, a piece of rock art identified to the seventh century BC shows a four-wheeled Celtic wagon pulled by two horses. A fourth-century BC carving at Pasparido shows a large male figure, standing upright in a long garment. He has a torque on his right arm and what seems to be another on his left while below this, near the left arm, hangs a horned snake. The male figure has antlers on his head. A smaller figure in similar posture stands by the side, or in front, of this 'deity' and is obviously a phallic symbol. Dr Miranda Green has pointed out that this is probably the earliest known representation of the antlered Celtic god Cernunnos. He is equated with the Irish The Dagda, the father of the gods, and the deity the Romans described as the Celtic *Dis Pater*. Dr Green says:

> Besides the sun and hunting cults, the Celtic Camunians also portrayed their funereal ritual on the rocks; death scenes are drawn, with four-wheeled wagons bearing urns (perhaps containing the ashes of the deceased) and accompanied by processions of worshippers or mourners. Indeed, a whole way of life and death, traditions, customs and religious perceptions are described at Camonica in a series of ritual acts which span a period of perhaps 3000 years.

There is also evidence of Celtic gods being worshipped in the passes of the Italian Alps. Poeninus had a sanctuary around the Great St Bernard Pass, where votive offerings were made during the La Tène period and later plaques were left during the Roman period when Poeninus had been converted to a persona of Jupiter. Indeed, Jupiter became connected with the mountains because this is how the Romans saw the Celtic sky gods. In the Austrian peaks the Celtic god Uxellinus (*uxellos*, high) was also named Jupiter as was Beissirissa in the Hautes-Pyrénées, Ladicus in north-west Spain and Parthinus in Dalmatia and Upper Moesia. The Celtic god Poeninus is not to be confused with the word Poeni, which was applied to the Carthaginians and from which the word Punic derives.

From archaeological evidence, and even his own contradictory account, it becomes clear that Livy is describing the passage of one tribe or group into the Italian peninsula after other Celtic tribes had already settled there. Bellovesus and his followers were simply one among several tribes who crossed the Alps at various periods. Before we go on to identify these various tribes, one other matter, neglected by Livy, needs some reflection. Whether we are speaking of the passage of one tribe at a time or groups of tribes, the movement through the Alps required the transportation of thousands of people, men, women and children and their baggage; the movement of chariots, wagons and carts, horses, pack animals, herds of cows and oxen, flocks of sheep, goats and other domestic animals. We know how difficult this movement was because of the details we have of the later crossing by Hannibal of Carthage and his army. If an army found it difficult, how much more so would an entire nation on the march! The movement of tens of thousands of Celts through the Alpine passes must have been a considerable undertaking. Today, Hannibal is acknowledged as the hero of the passage through the Alps while the crossing by Bellovesus and other unknown Celtic leaders centuries before him is not even considered.

The Celts had arrived in a great valley land where the River Padus (the Po) rose on the slopes of Monte Viso, in the Cotian Alps, and flowed across the broad North Italian Plain some 405 miles (670 kilometres) before dispersing through a delta into the Adriatic Sea. The area north of the Po became known to the Romans as Transpadana and that to the south was Cispadana. It was a rich and fertile country due to the fact that the plain was well watered not only by the Po itself but by smaller rivers which fed the Po or meandered through the valley on their own account. There were also a chain of *fontanili* to the north and south of the flood plain in which the Alpine and Apennine waters rose to the surface through impervious soil.

According to Livy, soon after the arrival of Bellovesus and his Celts into this rich but wild countryside:

Another wave, this time of the Cenomani, followed in their footsteps and crossing, under the leadership of Elitovius, by the same pass and without opposition from Bellovesus, settled near where the towns of Brixia [Brescia] and Verona are today. After them came the Libui, then the Salassi who settled on the Ticinus, near the ancient tribe of the Laevi Ligures. Then the Boii and Lingones came over by the Poenine Pass [Great St Bernard Pass], and finding all the country between the Alps and the Po already occupied, crossed the river on rafts and expelled not the Etruscans only but the Umbrians as well; they did not, however, pass south of the Apennines.

The Apennines, the mountain range running diagonally south-east through Italy, were called *Apennini*. Greek merchants and travellers again picked up the name from the Celts and it was adopted by the early Latin writers. The name was Celtic, derived from the root *pennos*, head or top. The word survives in modern Welsh, Breton and Cornish and in countless place-names throughout the Celtic world. There are also, of course, the Pennine Alps (Alpes Pennini), through which the Great St Bernard Pass thrusts its way. Livy is at pains to point out that the Alpes Pennini take their name from the Celtic deity Poeninus. So does Marius Servius Honoratus (early fifth century AD). Poeninus would be the 'god of the tops or heights'. Similarly, the mountain range and hill system now called 'the back-bone of England' still retains the original Celtic name, the Pennines. It has also been argued that the same root gives the name of the range in the basin of the Saale, north of Saxe-Weimar, south of Harz, in Germany, which has come down to us as The Finne. We do not know what the Etruscans called this mountain barrier.

Polybius describes the settlements of the Celts in northern Italy in these terms:

The Celts, who were much associated with the Etruscans because they were their neighbours, cast envious eyes upon the beauty of their country, and suddenly seized upon some trivial pretext to attack them with a large army, drove them out of the valley of the Po and occupied the area themselves. Those who first settled in the district near the source of the Po were the Laevi and Lebeccii; after them came the Insubres, the largest tribe of all, and finally the Cenomani, who lived along the banks of the river to the east of the Oglio. The part of the plain which borders the Adriatic had always belonged to another very ancient tribe, that is the Veneti; in their customs and their dress they scarcely differed from the Celts, but they spoke a different language and the tragic poets have many fabulous tales to tell about them.

On the southern bank of the Po, that is the side nearer the Apennines, the first settlers beginning from the west were the Anares and later the Boii. Eastwards of them in the direction of the Adriatic lived the Lingones, and beyond these and near the sea the Senones.

These are the names of the principal tribes which took possesion of this region. They lived in unwalled villages and had no knowledge of the refinements of civilisation. As they slept on straw and leaves, ate meat and practised no other pursuits but war and agriculture, their lives were very simple and they were completely unacquainted with any art or science. Their possessions consisted of cattle and gold, since these were the only objects which they could easily take with them whatever their circumstances and transport wherever they chose. It was of the greatest importance to them to have a following, and the man who was believed to have the greatest number of dependants and companions about him was the most feared and the most powerful of the tribe.

When they first arrived in Italy the Celts not only took possession of this northern region, but subjugated many of the neighbouring peoples and terrified them by their audacity. Not long afterwards they defeated the Romans and their allies in a pitched battle . . .

In these paragraphs, Polybius is letting his prejudices dictate his picture of Celtic society. Professor Arnold Toynbee echoes Polybius' prejudice by making the surprising statement: 'It is unquestionable that the advent of the Gauls was a set-back for civilisation in the Po basin, and that the subsequent advent of the Romans set civilisation moving there again on the upgrade.' One is almost stung to ask 'which civilisation'? However, having made this judgemental comment Professor Toynbee, because he is essentially fair, seems to realise the prejudice. He goes on: 'At the same time it is probable that the tale of this episode of Cisalpine history, as it has come down to us, does more than justice to the Romans, and less than justice to the Gauls. The telling of the tale was monopolised by the Romans; this Roman record therefore presents the picture as it appeared to Roman, not to Gallic eyes; and the Romans are no unprejudiced witnesses when they are testifying about the Gauls.'

Unfortunately we do not have any written accounts to help us other than the prejudiced reports of the Romans. Archaeology certainly paints a different picture of these tribes who had settled in Cisalpine Gaul, demonstrating that the Celts were in fact technologically advanced. With the exception of the Senones, who eventually settled along the mountain foothills and eastern seaboard, the Po Valley settlements were made on the plains suited for agricultural development. Unlike their Transalpine Hallstatt ancestors, Cisalpine Celts did not fortify themselves in hillforts to any extent. They remained mainly settled on the soil in small farms and villages, although walled towns are spoken of by the Romans. They were primarily agriculturists, crop growers, not the nomads and simple stock raisers which Polybius would have us believe. In fact, they developed a rich agricultural country, with settled industry and high artistic achievement.

The Celts were already an advanced agricultural and pastoral people when they settled in the Po Valley. Dr L. Homo, in *L'Italie primitive et les débuts de l'impérialisme romain*, argued that those Celts who settled south of the Po became Etruscanised while those who settled to the north of the river did not. Certainly there are grounds for arguing that the Celts did not totally efface Etruscan culture in the Po Valley, but, to some extent, assimilated it. They certainly assimilated some Etruscan ideas, such as writing using the Etruscan alphabet. Perhaps they also adopted some of the Etruscan technology, although the Celts were so advanced in metalwork that they would not have needed to borrow new methods. They took over the cultivation of vines and produced their own wine. It is interesting that Pliny the Elder lists wine first among the products of Gallia Cisalpina.

Our evidence of Celtic farming comes from archaeology. Livestock was an important part of Celtic farming with varieties of sheep, cattle and pigs. Sheep were reared for wool. Strabo points out that the wool trade from the area 'clothed the greater part of Italy' in his day: soft wool from the Boii country, coarser fabric from the east of Cisalpine Gaul and costly carpets and woollen covers from around Patavium (Padua). Goats were kept for milk and cheese. Oxen were used mainly for pulling ploughs and heavy wagons. Horses were particularly bred for transport and warfare. The Celts were great horse dealers. Chickens and cats were kept on the farms and dogs were bred mainly for hunting. These animals produced a range of raw materials which were important to the Celtic economy.

The Celtic farmers grew a number of cereals, particularly wheat and barley. However, Pliny the Elder pointed out that north of the Po, turnips ranked as the third crop of the area after wine and cereals. Beans, peas and lentils were among other cultivated crops. Polybius mentions that ordinary millet and panic (*pannicum*, or wild Italian millet) were used for bread. A porridge of millet was also made mixed with milk. The Taurini specialised in growing rye.

Celtic agriculture was highly praised by Pliny who observed that the Celtic plough, fitted with a mobile coulter, was greatly superior to the Roman swing plough of the same period. The Celts had also developed the practice of manuring as well as inventing a harvesting machine (*messor*, later called a *vallus*). According to Pliny, this was a 'big box, the edges armed with teeth and supported by two wheels, moved through the cornfield pushed by an ox; the ears of corn were uprooted by the teeth and fell into the box.' A stone relief from Brussels actually shows one of these Celtic harvesting machines.

Hunting was a popular pastime. The boar was a particular prey and an important Celtic symbol of power.

At the time the Celts settled in the Po Valley this alluvial river basin was a mixture of swampland and great forests. For centuries the various inhabitants had constructed and maintained an elaborate system of dykes, canals and dams. Sometimes the protection of the cultivated land from destructive flooding, brought on by heavy rains or the melting of mountain snows, was a problem. In 108 BC, according to Osequens, a great flood caused the loss of many thousands of lives; another flood occurred in 41 BC which inspired Virgil to write about it in the *Georgics*, his long poem about husbandry, in which he observes that the Po is the most violent of rivers. Lucan was also inspired by its turbulence. The waterways often changed their course and we hear, after the Roman conquest of the area, that controversies arose because the changing course of the waters would deprive an owner of land while endowing another with new alluvial soil. Sextus Julius Frontinus (c.AD 30–c.104) says, in his work *De aquis urbis Romae* (On the waters of Rome): 'These controversies are most common in Gallia Togata [Cisalpine Gaul]; the land is woven of many streams and conveys the enormous snows of the Alps to the sea, besides suffering damage from unforeseen floods due to sudden rainstorms.'

A Celtic appreciation of river flooding is seen in the name of the town of Trent, modern Trento, situated below the confluence of three rivers which gush south of the Po Valley. The Romans misinterpreted the Celtic word, thinking it referred to the three rivers, and named it Tridentum. But the Celtic name appears to lie in the roots *tri*, through, and *santon*, which is related to the Old Irish *sét*, a journey and the Welsh *hynt*, road. The concept would be that of a 'trespasser', implying a place by a river liable to flood. The name is also used for the English rivers Trent, Tarrant and *Trisantónos*, the early name for the River Arun in Sussex.

The efforts of the inhabitants of the Po Valley gradually wrested fertile fields from the great river, and water control systems were introduced. Strabo the Greek geographer (64 BC–after AD 24), in his *Geographica*, compared the Cisalpine system to that in operation in Egypt along the Nile. Swamps were drained and the river and its tributaries and affluences embanked so that the waters were subjugated to a network of intricate irrigation channels which made the swampland into productive estates. The Celts either originated some of the system of dykes and canals or took it over and maintained it.

The Celts came to know the land well for it is significant that few of their settlements and towns were placed by the River Po. As well as the fertile agricultural lands, the Po Valley was thick with great forests, particularly large oak forests. Tacitus mentions their fecundity as does Sidonius Apollinaris in a later age. Only in medieval and modern times have the tremendous forests of the Po Valley been destroyed. Timber was eventually exported from the Po Valley, floated down the rivers to the Adriatic ports. The Emperor Tiberius (AD 14–37) had larch wood sent to Rome because it was held to be more impervious to fire. Larches grew on both banks of the Po but while an emperor could afford to bring larch wood to Rome, Vitruvius Pollio (*c.*50–26 BC), the Roman architect and engineer, in his work *De architectura*, indicates that it was too expensive for ordinary people to do so. Importing this 'foreign' wood meant, of necessity, importing the foreign word to describe it. Pliny is one of the first to record *larix* and *laricis*. The Celtic name survives in modern Irish as *learóg* and in modern Welsh as *llarwydden*. The word seems to have the old Celtic root *lar*, 'ground', in it.

Polybius says that in his time the great oak forests were still extensive enough to provide acorns for fodder for vast herds of pigs. Cato was much impressed by the enormous flitches of bacon from pigs bred by the Insubreans. Strabo says that 'the forests bear such an abundance of acorns that Rome is largely fed on the herds of Cisalpine swine.' He points out the importance of this economy to the area, and also that of the pinewoods which produced pitch. Botanical evidence shows that the ratio of oaks to poplars and elms was at that time four to one. Later, of course, with a deteriorating climate, beech and chestnut displaced many areas of oak forest. But during the final conquest of Cisalpine Gaul there were still vast stretches of forest interspersed with cultivated tracts.

The Celts also developed small industries such as mining. Strabo points out that, as a result of the Roman invasion and conquest, the mines had fallen into disuse. Metalwork, the cutting and working of timber and even ship building, pottery and tile making as well as glass and jewellery production were carried on. P. A. Brunt comments:

> Polybius depicts the Gaels as a relatively savage people, who lived in open villages with no permanent buildings, who followed no pursuits but war and agriculture and whose property consisted in cattle and gold. This picture is evidently exaggerated. Details of the wars show that they had fortified towns and stocks of grain. Livy refers to the '*vasa aenea Gallica*' and to other rich booty which Roman generals secured, and archaeological evidence too shows that Polybius is wrong in thinking that they had no arts or crafts.

When the Romans finally secured a foothold in Cisalpine Gaul in the second century B C they found a flourishing economy in which coins were already being struck, especially in silver. Cisalpine Gaul had a local source of silver, and the Cisalpine Celts struck some of the earliest native coinage. The first coins were struck by the Insubres and Cenomani during the third century B C, at a time of mounting conflict with Rome. Let us put the date of Celtic coinage in context. By 289 B C, Rome had only just established its *triumviri monetales* to supervise the production of *aes signatum*, rectangular pieces of cast bronze bearing distinctive devices. Not until 269 B C did a Roman mint produce silver coinage which, like the Celtic silver coins, owed its origins to the Greeks. Rome was very slow to make use of coins as a means of exchange. The Celts appear to have adopted the model of the *drachma* of Massilia, struck in the fourth century B C. Fascinatingly, a hoard of Cisalpine coins ended up in Penzance, Cornwall. Bronze Celtic coins were struck as well as silver among the Insubres and Cenomani.

The last of the major Cisalpine Celtic silver coins was struck around 220 BC on the eve of the outbreak of the Second Punic War. The production of more coins at this time suggests that the Celts were preparing for the military cost of the war. Celtic coinage of Cisalpine Gaul came to an end with the Roman conquest and occupation. Coins struck in the second century BC were mainly for payment of native auxiliary troops under Roman leadership. The last native coinage seems to have been struck under the name *RIKOI* at the end of the second century.

The native *drachma*-based coinage of the Celts was structured on standards adjusted to local prices and conditions. The Romans used their *victoriatus*, comparable in weight, for standard payments during the second century. It seems likely that during this time some *victoriati* were actually struck in Cisalpine Gaul utilising the native silver. Later Roman *denarii* were struck in Transalpine Gaul.

We can see from this example alone, and it is not isolated, just how jaundiced the Roman view of the Celts was.

Celtic houses tended to be rectangular. At Monte Bibele, above Monterenzio and the valley of the Idige, in the Apennines, archaeologists have been able to excavate a Celtic village. The site was settled between 400 and 200 BC and it consisted of forty to fifty houses with a population of 200 to 300. There were two religious shrines here and a cemetery, where at least one noteworthy Celtic sword has been excavated, from 'Grave XIV'. The cemetery actually consisted of both Celtic and some Etruscan graves, mostly dating from between 350 and 330 BC. By this means archaeologists argued that the site was a mixed one, with the Etruscans and Celts merging their cultures.

The houses were built of stone and timber and probably thatched. Indications are that they had an upper floor. The houses were formed into a systematic pattern with clay hearths and water supplied from a nearby spring which fed into a well-constructed cistern. Weaving obviously took place for traces of looms were found. Pottery for storage and traces of a storehouse revealed remains of foodstuffs: wheat, oats, broad beans, lentils, peas, flax, acorns, olives, garlic, hazelnuts, apples and grape seeds. Significantly, the village was destroyed by fire about 200 BC which would point to its being destroyed during the Roman conquest of the area.

The Celts had developed herbal remedies for a wide variety of diseases and healing springs were popularly used. How advanced the Celtic general medical practices were has been demonstrated by one grave discovered at München-Obermenzing in Germany, dated to the third or second century BC, containing a collection of Celtic surgical implements, such as probes, retractors and a trephining saw. Trephining, making holes in the skull, was a skill that appears to have been widely used in the Celtic world. In 1935, at Ovingdean, near Brighton, Sussex, a human skull was found dated to about 100 BC. Two large round holes had been deliberately cut in the skull, one on either side of the brain. There had been a healing of the bone showing that the patient had survived the brain surgery, and not merely one operation but two. Another skull found at Katzeldorf, Austria, shows the surgeon attempting to cut a third hole, which is not complete. The fact that there is no sign of any bone healing on this skull demonstrates that this patient died. Many trephined skulls have been found throughout the Celtic world, especially in Austria.

As Dr Simon James observes: 'In medicine, as in so many other areas, the Celts stand favourable comparison with the Classical world . . .'

We can be certain that, at the time when the Senones won their victory at Allia, the northern region of Italy had already become largely Celtic-speaking and an integral part of the La Tène cultural world of the Celts. The Insubres had their capital in Mediolanum. The literal meaning is 'middle sanctuary' or, as D'Arbois de Jubainville describes it, the 'central sanctuary' of their tribe, implying that Mediolanum was a place of assembly and religious worship. Dr A. Holder, in *Alt-celtische Sprachschatz*, lists forty-two examples of the use of this place-name in the Celtic world such as the Mediolanum which is now Wolkersdorf, north of Venice, one on the borders of Bohemia and another at Gourney Moenneville, where there was, indeed, a famous Celtic sanctuary.

The Cenomani, whose name implies 'men of strength', had founded Brixia, modern Brescia, as their main town. Catullus, in pointing out that Brixia was a Cenomani foundation, calls it the mother of his own town of Verona with the implied meaning that the Cenomani also founded that city. Livy confirms this. Brixia held a sanctuary to the tribal god Brixianus who, after the Roman conquest, was linked with Jupiter. The Cenomani also founded towns at Tridentum, Trento, and nearby Cavereno. This name comes from *cauaros*, a hero, as in the Old Irish *caur* meaning a giant, and *renos* meaning sea or waters – perhaps applied to nearby Lake Garda.

Near here is a Celtic cemetery at Mechel in Nonsberg. The Cenomani were claimed to have originally been a sub-division of the Volcae tribe in Gaul proper.

The old Etruscan city of Felsina had been taken over by the Boii and renamed Bononia (modern Bologna). There were two other places we know of in the Celtic world which took the name Bononia: one, interestingly, in the Belgae area of Gaul which is now Boulogne, and the other on the Danube, where a remnant of the Boii were acknowledged to have moved, which is now known as Banostar. The Celts were certainly well established in Bologna by the fourth century BC and a Celtic cemetery has been found there dated to that period. Cato claimed they were the largest tribe in the Po Valley and that they were divided into 112 sub-tribes, a fact also quoted by Pliny.

The Lingones were settled in the Valli de Commachio in the Po delta where the great river divided into the Adriatic Sea. Livy mentions tribes such as the Libui and Salassi to which Polybius adds the Libici and Laevi north of the Po, and the Ananes, Anares or Anamari, south of it but west of the Boii. Perhaps Livy's Libui and Polybius' Libici were the same peoples. According to Pliny, taking information from Cato's *Origines*, they were a sub-division of the Salassi. The Salassi had as their tribal capital Eporedia, a distinctive Celtic name, which is the modern Ivrea on the Duria in Piedmont. The Libui had Vercellae, modern Vercelli, as their main settlement. In the territory was another settlement called Rigomagus, now Trino, 'plain of the kings'. One also wonders about the ending L*ibui* for it has an echo of Boii and it might be equally argued they were a sub-division of that tribe although other evidence indicates that they were part of the Insubrean hegemony.

Between the Libui/Libici and the Insubres was a tribe called the Vertamocori of Novara, identified by Pliny as being a sub-tribe of the Vocontii of Transalpine Gaul. North of the Vertamocori were, according to Pliny, the Leoponti established in the Val d'Ossola and the Val Leventina.

As well as the main tribes – the Insubres, Cenomani, Boii, Lingones, Taurini and the latecomers, the Senones, whose settlement we shall deal with later – Livy mentioned the Bituriges, Arverni, Aedui, Ambarri, Carnutes and Auleci. However, these later tribes do not appear to feature in what we know of the Italian settlement.

In the east of this large valley was a people called the Veneti. Some scholars have attempted to link the Veneti of Venetia, or modern Venice, with the Venetii of Vannes in Morbihan, Brittany. According to Dr Chilvers: 'In the eastern Transpadana we may suppose that the Veneti were more numerous than the Celts. But the customs and language of the two peoples were very similar and Strabo could put forward the theory that they were of the same origin.' However, it has also been argued that the tribal name survived in the different branches of Indo-European and, rather than the Veneti of Venice being a Celtic tribe, they were simply a related Indo-European-speaking people. It has already been mentioned that Livy thought they differed little from the Celts except in the all-important aspect of language, and he should know coming, as he did, from Patavium. Polybius echoes him. Support for this argument comes in the cognate word in Sanskrit, indicating an Indo-European ancestor, *vanóti*, those who win or conquer. This is related to *fian* in Old Irish, hence *fianna*. Archaeology has demonstrated that a 'Celticisation' of the Veneti was being carried out; they had adopted Celtic customs and dress. The one difference between the Veneti graves and Celtic graves is the absence of swords. Before the Celtic settlement in the Po Valley it was not the custom to place swords in the graves of males. The Celtic custom of doing so was soon reflected in all Po Valley burials of males with the exception of those of the Veneti, though it is noticeable that Celtic warriors' sword belt hooks and rings occur in the area of the Veneti.

Eastwards of the Veneti we find another Celtic tribe called the Carni, who give their name to the Alpi Carniche and who were settled over the plains of what is Udine, although Henri Hubert argues that they did not arrive in the area until 186 BC. This is disputed by other scholars who believe they had crossed south in the Alpine foothills and Udine plains long before this and had already given their name to the mountain range.

The Celtic settlements south of the Alps were obviously not just one single movement of people, as Roman historians paint it, but several movements spread over several centuries. Their settlements were well established by the time of Allia. We can disagree with the early writers' perception that the migration of the Celts into Italy, and the capture of Rome, happened within a short space of time as one continuous movement.

P. A. Brunt estimates that the population of the actual Po Valley, not counting the surrounding foothills, at the start of the Roman conquest in 225 BC, was around 1,400,000. He makes this estimate on the basis of computing numbers of the tribal armies as enumerated by the Roman accounts.

The settlement of the Po Valley by the Celtic tribes was not, of course, without conflict. Around the seventh century BC the Etruscans had crossed north over the Apennines into the Po Valley and had begun to subjugate the Umbrian tribes there and so extend their empire. Plutarch speaks of the eighteen fine cities which the Etruscans established north of the Apennines and Strabo expressed his belief that it was the riches of these Etruscan cities that led to their downfall, attracting the attention of the Celts. It can be argued, on dating, that the Etruscans, moving north, and the Celts, moving south, clashed over who should occupy the area.

Etruscan pillar stones (stelae) found at Bologna show Etruscan horsemen fighting against Celtic foot soldiers, naked and with traditional long Celtic shields. Polybius points out that the Celts had been in contact with the Etruscans long before their descent on Clusium, which conflict led to Allia. This continuing contact between the Etruscans and Celts, not merely confined to warring clashes, must have left some mark on both peoples. From Monte Bibele we see them intermarrying. We know that the Celts enjoyed a trade with Etruscan merchants but, most significantly, it was Etruscan literacy that had an impact on the Celts.

The Etruscan language was represented in an alphabet of twenty-six characters and used mainly on funereal inscriptions. The Etruscans had learnt to write by the mid-seventh century BC and about ten thousand examples of Etruscan writing survive, a few of which are quite extensive such as one from Perugia. Livy believed in ancient times that Roman boys were 'schooled in Etruscan literature, as nowadays they are trained in Greek'. The frustrating thing is that Etruscan is not an identified Indo-European language nor does it bear any relationship to any other known tongue, alive or dead. So far, there has been no successful reading of the Etruscan texts.

Even Celtic has been conjured as a possible means of interpretation and translations attempted which are totally spurious, as I have discussed in my article 'Etruria-Celtica: A Rebuttal of the Etruscan-Celtic Theory' and in my book The Celtic Empire (1990). Etruscan literature vanished in the wake of the Roman conquest in the third century BC.

The oldest inscriptive monuments fashioned by the Celts were erected with Etruscan lettering. The earliest inscriptions accepted as being mainly in a Celtic language occur in the Lepontic area dating back to around 500 BC. There are some thirty-three inscriptions found between the Rivers Ticino and Adda, tributaries of the Po. However, after Sir John Rhŷs' work on these inscriptions, some Celtic scholars became dubious because it was realised that there were differences between these forms and other written Celtic remains. Dr Joshua Whatmough, in *Dialects of Ancient Gaul*, argued that the Celtic had been influenced by the Ligurians who had been pre-Indo-European but spoke an Indo-European dialect in historical times, presumably Celtic. For a while the Lepontic inscriptions were described as a form of Celto-Ligurian. Professor Michel Lejeune in 1971 argued that the inscriptions merely demonstrated two neighbouring dialects which were both variant but Celtic.

Of the 200 or more Celtic inscriptions we have dating from the fourth and third centuries BC, there are some seventy or more texts and inscriptions using the Etruscan alphabet. These are found mainly around the lakes of Como, Lugano, Maggiore and Orta. As Latin influences began to penetrate the Po Valley there was a change from Etruscan lettering to Latin characters. Graffiti on pottery, manufacturers' names and marks, and funereal inscriptions show that the Celts were far from illiterate as popular tradition would have it. Indeed, this idea that the Celts were illiterate arises from a misreading of Caesar who says that they 'believe that their religion forbids them to commit their teachings to writing, although for most other purposes, such as public and private accounts, the Celts use the Greek alphabet.' Certainly Caesar is accurate in this observation and we find many inscriptions in Celtic but using Greek characters.

Professor Schmidt has pointed out that the Celtic of the Continent was not a homogeneous single language but a series of dialects, developing over a wide territory, leaving aside the development around the seventh century BC of the Brythonic parent language evolving away from the more archaic Goidelic form. The interpretation of Continental Celtic sources has been found difficult because they are of a fragmentary nature and because they are the product of a mixture of peoples and dialects.

In the valley of the Tiber at Todi, south of Perugia, a funereal inscription was found in Celtic and Latin to honour one Ategnatos son of Druteos. It is the southernmost of the Celtic inscriptions in Italy, well inside Umbria but north of Latin territory. The Celtic domains did not reach so far. Was this a relic of a Celtic expedition like the tombs of Canossa, or a record that an individual Celt and his family settled here, among the Umbrians, at an early date before Rome began to encroach in the area? Why is Latin used instead of Umbrian as the second language in the bilingual inscription?

At the same time as Celtic tribes were crossing the western end of the Alps, there were Celts crossing the eastern end. Around the sixth century BC, the Celts entered into Styria and thence into Lombardy. In 1912, at Negau, Lower Styria, not far from Marburg on the Drave, some twenty bronze helmets were discovered. On two of them were graffiti written in an alphabet of Etruscan type. As Henri Hubert pointed out: 'All the words are proper names, and they are all Celtic. In each case a man's name is followed by that of his father . . .' These helmets are from both the seventh and sixth centuries BC and, says Dr Hubert, 'the date of these inscriptions is clearly that of the time of [the manufacture of] the helmets'.

Therefore, not only had Celtic tribes crossed south of the Alps by the sixth and fifth centuries BC, they had established enough social contact with the Etruscans to learn their alphabet and begin to write in it. At Zignano, in the Vara Valley, in 1827 a series of *cippi* were found; a *cippus* is a small, low column, usually inscribed. These stones depict armed warriors, and by the peculiarity of their armaments we may identify them as Celts. One depicts a woman. Some inscriptions are unreadable while another bears the name, in Etruscan letters, 'Mezunemusus'. By taking into account the values of the Etruscan 'z' one can read the name as Mediunemusus and translate it from the Celtic as 'he who measures [takes care of] holy places'. While Henri Hubert argued that this *cippus* was Celtic, Raffaello Battaglia, in *Studi etruschi* 7 (1933), believed it to be a merging of Celtic and Ligurian elements. However, Paul Kretschmer, in *Glotta* 30 (1943), considered the inscription to be Rhaetic. We can be assured, however, that this is a Celtic inscription. The date of these stones can be attested by the fact that the swords on them are of the Celtic type used during the Hallstatt period placing them well before the sixth century BC. For example, a stone found at Bocconi, classified as 'stone D', shows a typical Hallstatt period knife or sword.

To those who argue that the Celts may simply have been using antique weapons, it must be pointed out that Celts moving through Liguria in search of new lands to conquer and settle would hardly be using old-fashioned arms. Designs of the same period have also been found on buckets and bronze plaques and materials taken from Celtic cemeteries south of Lake Maggiore, from which Dr Hubert argued that one must conclude that the Celts descended into Italy far earlier than was usually supposed.

The cemeteries of Golasecca and Castelletto Ticino on the plateau of Somma Ticinese, south of Lake Maggiore, according to Dr Hubert, were the site of the first extensive Celtic settlements in Italy. He argues that the tombs and the pottery found there are similar to those found in clearly identified Celtic sites north of the Alps and even in Britain. Dr Hubert is of the opinion that the earliest Celts in Italy therefore lived in this area and that they were the Insubres. However, recent scholarship, as represented by Professor Otto-Herman Frey, claims that the Golasecca culture of the seventh and fifth centuries BC was developed from local older roots. 'There is,' he argues, 'no sign of a break, by which one could conclude the massive immigration of a foreign ("Celtic") ethnic group.' While placing the Golasecca culture within the 'Fazies Canegrate group' of 1200 BC, Professor Frey has to admit that it is clearly related to the Urnfield cultural developments beyond the Alps from which the Celts developed. 'This circumstance,' he adds, 'might explain the origins of the population, which is not "italic" in linguistic terms.'

One thing most Roman historians agree on is that early in the fourth century BC the Celts destroyed a large Etruscan army and captured an Etruscan city named Melpum, perhaps Melzo, west of Milan. Most Etruscan colonies north of the Apennines are thought to have been in Celtic hands by the beginning of that century. Pliny, thought to be quoting Cornelius Nepos, implies that the Etruscans were overrun by a confederation of the Boii, Insubres and Senones, on the same day that the Roman general Marcus Furius Camillus captured and occupied the southern Etruscan town of Veii – that is, in 396 BC.

If the Celts had been domiciled in the Po Valley for so long, it is logical to ask if Celtic place-names survive in the area to any large extent. We have already mentioned a few, which have evolved into Turin, Bologna and Milan. There are many others. The original name of Lake Garda, Benacus, was Celtic, meaning 'lake of points' (*benn* still appears in Old Irish as the word for 'point'.) River names in the Po Valley took Celtic form. The Reno, rising in the Apennines in Boii territory, takes the same name as the Rhine – Rhenos from *renos*, a sea. The Tanaro, then given as Tanaros, a tributary of the Po, was named for the Celtic god of thunder. Dr W. J. Watson points out that the name is usually given as Taranos but in Cisalpine Gaul it appears with a metathesis of the 'n' and 'r'. Another Tanaros is a tributary of the Garonne. There is a Tanar in Glen Tanar in Aberdeen, Scotland, a Tanner in Selkirk and a Tarenig, a tributary of the Wye, in Wales.

The Romans learnt that the great river north of the Apennines was named Padus (Po), but who had named it? Metrodorus of Scepsis, in the second century BC, thought that the Padus was a Ligurian word meaning 'unfathomable'. Yet if other rivers that were tributaries to the Po had Celtic names, could it be logically expected that the great river itself had received this name from the Celts?

Clearly, the type of Celtic spoken in the Po Valley in the fourth century BC was the 'P' Celtic form. Whatever the arguments about the language of the earliest Celtic settlers made by Sir John Rhŷs, when they emerged into recorded history they had already made the famous 'P' for 'Q' substitution. It has been suggested, therefore, that the Padus takes its name from a word denoting respect or esteem, to imply, perhaps, that it was a river to be respected. This would have been Old Celtic *padis*. This seems to have evolved in modern Welsh as *parch*. In Old Irish it appears in the 'Q' form as *cádus*, a word that seems to have fallen out of use in modern Irish although still noted by Dineen's *Irish Dictionary* in 1927. It appeared as the root *cáid* in the tenth-century *Cormac's Glossary (Sanas Chormaic)* in which it is glossed *sanctum* in Latin, and in the mid-sixteenth-century *Davoreen's Glossary* where it is glossed by the Irish word *uasal* for noble or one respected. When Dr Whitley Stokes edited this for Halle in 1904 he wrote: 'I do not understand this article, *cáidh* is glossed . . . by *uasal*.' He had obviously forgotten the root word. While this is still open to debate, the description of the Po, a river inclined to flooding and therefore dangerous, as being deserving of respect, is appropriate.

There is, however, an earlier name for the Po. Greek travellers called the river Eridanus. Herodotus (*c.*490–*c.*425 BC), the Greek historian, mentions it as lying to the north-west of Greece and as being a source of amber, but he was dubious of its existence. The Greeks introduced the Eridanus into their mythology as the river in which Phaethon, son of Helios the sungod and Clymene the nymph, drowned after Zeus had hurled a thunderbolt at him as he rode in his father's chariot through the sky, causing it to burn up and his blazing body to fall to earth. His sisters stood on the river bank and wept for him, turning into the poplars that grow along the banks of the Po, and their tears still oozing from the trees turned into amber. The local king, Cycnus, who was Phaethon's cousin, came and delivered a funeral dirge and was turned into a swan. Cycnus was a word of Greek origin meaning a swan. Hence 'swan song' entered the languages of the world. Cicero says that the former name of the river, Eridanus, was also used among Cisalpines as the name of the constellation Auriga, the charioteer. Auriga is named after the son of the Roman god Vulcan who was the first to devise a chariot. Could there be a link to Phaethon and his chariot or is there some other meaning overlooked in the transition from one culture to another?

But does the name Eridanus mean anything in Celtic? Well, we can easily spot the same element which occurs in the Celtic names for both the Danube (Danuvius) and the Rhône (Rhodanus) – Danu, the Celtic Mother Goddess. The first element, *eri*, has been argued to mean 'rising up', 'growing', 'leaping forth', and occurs as *eirge* in Old and Middle Irish (modern Irish *éirí*). In Irish myth, Danu had a daughter Eri who made love to a Fomorii and gave birth to Bres who became king of the Tuatha Dé Danaan.

Given the emerging picture of a continuing Celtic settlement north of the Apennines, it was inevitable that one day Celtic tribes, in search of new land on which to settle, would move across the mountain range into Etruria proper and threaten Rome itself.

[3]

Italians and the Celts

I N A S K I N G who the Celts were, it behoves us to ask who were the peoples populating the Italian peninsula at the time of the Celtic arrival. The Italian peninsula had begun to be peopled by Indo-European-speaking peoples, distant cousins of the Celts, at the start of the Italian Bronze Age, about 1800–1300 BC. But among the various cultures on the peninsula several non Indo-European ones had survived. The early Ligurians are claimed to have originally been outside the Indo-European linguistic family but their original language was submerged and when they emerged into recorded history they were speaking an early Celtic dialect. Then there were the Etruscans of whom we have already spoken. At the height of their power, from the seventh to the fourth centuries BC, the Etruscans controlled an empire from the River Po in the north to Campania in the south. Their empire for many years included Rome itself, then a small Latin trading town on their southern borders. Etruscan kings held sway there until 509 BC when the last of them was expelled from the city. Their southern territories had been mainly lost to Rome with the defeat at Aricia in c.504 BC and their naval supremacy had been destroyed by fleets from the ancient city of Cumae, in Campania, the home of the oracle, the Sibyl, and Syracuse, modern Siracusa, in a sea battle fought off Cumae in 474 BC. The Romans feared and therefore hated the Etruscans and thus began their conquest which finally eliminated them. As the Celts were also to find, the Romans were unrelenting and unforgiving enemies. Yet Rome was deeply indebted to the Etruscans for their art, architecture and engineering, and also for some of their religious practices such as augury based on the scrutiny of entrails, especially the livers of sacrificial animals (*haruspices*). It is curious that the Romans were later to criticise the Celts for following this method of augury.

The central southern Apennines were occupied by tribes known as the Umbro-Sabellians, of which the major tribes were the Umbri, Sabines or Sabelli and Osci. The area to the south of the Tiber, Latium, was populated by Latin tribes, such as the Aequi, Marsi and Volsci. The Latin tribes, those that settled on the hills of Rome, became unified around the city which was, by the time of Allia, to become dominant, exerting authority over a Latin League. These tribes of central Italy were Indo-European in speech, divided between Umbrian and Oscan and Latin dialects.

At the southern end of the Italian peninsula was Megale Hellas (Magna Graecia) consisting of Greek colonies. Many areas had been colonised from the mainland of Greece and the Greek cities of Asia Minor. These colonies were highly civilised and prosperous, having developed a flourishing trade and exploited the fertility of the surrounding territories, and they had created an advanced culture, even establishing their own schools of philosophy and Greek learning. While the peoples of central Italy lived frugal and hardy lives and were engaged in frequent vicious tribal wars with each other, the Greeks led an easier and more luxurious life in their cities, such as Sybaris, Tarentum and Croton. Greek and Phoenician colonies, especially offshoots of the independent Phoenician city of Carthage, were also to be found on the island of Sicily. The growing major Greek power was the city of Syracuse on the south-eastern coast of Sicily, with which the Celts were soon to develop a relationship.

The city that the Celts were to come into conflict with, Rome, lay on the left bank of the Tiber some 14 miles (22 kilometres) from the sea. Founded originally as a small Latin town on the Palatine hill, near the river, the city grew, spreading over adjacent hills. Early historians accepted the date of 753 BC as the time of its foundation. Originally ruled by kings, dominated by the Etruscans, in 509 BC it became an aristocratic republic. The king was replaced by two annually elected magistrates, initially known by the title praetor and later by the title consul. In times of national crisis, a dictator was appointed with supreme judicial and military authority. Officers were elected from the patrician class, or aristocrats. The plebeians had few powers until a law system was introduced in 451 BC, known as the Twelve Tables.

Through the fifth century BC Rome began to exert a growing military power and by the start of the fourth century she had turned to aggressive warfare to dominate her neighbours. As a stock-raising and agricultural economy, producing mainly corn and salt, the city owed its early importance to its position on the chief navigable river on the west coast of Italy and its possession of a bridge across the Tiber facilitating communication between industrial Etruria and the agricultural south of Italy. The sole large-scale commercial enterprise was exporting salt from pans at the mouth of the Tiber (Ostia). Rome could only grow through the conquest of her Latin neighbours' lands, by seizing agricultural areas, metal-working and pottery industries, vineyards, olive farms and orchards. Initially Rome was poor, but once the conquered lands – and, of course, slaves by which to work them – were brought under her control, then she began to achieve dominance. Rome's rise to being an imperial power is the archetypal story of empire. The dynamic is always greed. The short cut to wealth is theft. Primitive tribes, tired of trading to obtain goods, realise that it was easier to simply seize the property of their neighbours. Then greed stirs them to seize more and more property and land until the empire is in place. To justify such theft, a quasi-religious philosophy of the civilising mission of the empire is established. The brutality and evil of such empires are disguised as a vehicle of human progress when the reverse is the grim reality.

As a maritime trading city, it would be hard to believe that Rome, through its links with Massilia, the Greek colony on the coast of southern Gaul, as well as its links with Etrurian seaports, had not learnt something about the Celtic peoples prior to the fourth century BC. The Greeks had written extensively on the Celts from the sixth century BC and Greek was the language of knowledge and literacy used by the Romans down to the mid-third century BC. The Celts had been known to the Greeks for some centuries before they appeared at Rome.

The Celtic people, as all early Indo-European peoples, were a tribal society. The early tribes were based on kinship groups, families claiming descent in the male line from one ancestor who was usually a god or hero. The Greeks had also been divided into tribes (*phylai*) and these tribes sub-divided into 'brotherhoods' (*phratriai*). It had only been in the sixth century BC that Greek society had reformed, dismantling the more prolific tribal system into ten tribes which, in turn, constituted three *trittys* or territorial divisions among which were several communities (*demoi*). Under the reforms of Cleisthenes, Tyrant of Sicyon (*c.*600–570 BC), the tribal system was reformed so that no tribe had a continuous territory nor represented a local interest.

Similarly, the early Romans were divided into three tribes based on kinship. These consisted of related family groups (*gentes*) bearing a common name and descended in male line from one ancestor. Initially the *gentes* were aristocratic or patrician but in early times plebeians also organised themselves into *gentes*. According to Roman tradition, Servius Tullius, the semi-legendary king of Rome (578–535 BC), replaced these with four tribes based on locality (Sucusana, Esquilina, Collina and Palatina). To these urban tribes were gradually added tribes from nearby country regions until, at the time the Celts came into conflict with Rome, Rome consisted of a unit of twenty-one tribes in all. The tribes were the administrative units for the census, for taxation and for the military levy, as well as for representation to the political assemblies.

During Rome's subsequent colonisation of the Po Valley, the form of administration was based on the then thirty-five Roman tribes. Initially, Roman settlers in the Cisalpine Valley could only belong to the Pollia tribe for the purpose of census, taxation and military levies with a few exceptions. In the mid-first century BC, this was broadened so that Cisalpine colonists belonged to any one of the Roman tribes.

The Celtic tribal system, however, had kept more strictly to the original Indo-European concept. Like the early Greeks, the Celts regarded the gods and goddesses as their ancestors. Or perhaps their ancestors had become their gods and goddesses? They maintained the early Indo-European social stratification which still exists in Hindu society. When Julius Caesar noted the division of the Celtic tribes into *druides*, *equites* and *plebs* he was looking at an original Indo-European division, comparable in Hindu society to *brahmins*, *kshatriya* and *vaishya*. He did not include the *sudra*, or menial caste. It would not have occurred to him to mention them because they were apparently self-evident. Therefore, we have the following divisions of Celtic society: the Druids or intellectual caste, comparable to the *brahmins*; the warriors, comparable to the *kshatriya*; and the food producers and tillers of the soil, comparable to the *vaishya*. These would equate with Caesar's *druides*, *equites* and *plebs*. The two groups which Caesar overlooked were, as mentioned, the *sudras* or menials, and the kings, often signified by the term *ri* or *rix*, which is cognate in most Indo-European languages with *rex* and *raja* and derived from the root *reg*, to stretch out the arm as protector and ruler. This word root also gives us the word 'reach'.

It has been a general trend to use the word 'chieftains' when referring to the Celtic tribal rulers, and I have tended to follow this form except where leaders have been specifically referred to as 'kings'. The Romans usually called them *princeps* (prince) or *caput* (chief or head). We see evidence that the Celts themselves used the term *rix* (king), as, for example, in the name or title of the ruler of the Boii, recorded as Boiorix. This translates as 'king of the Boii'. The king or chieftain ruled with his tribal or national council, made up not just from the warrior élite of the society but by 'men of art', the craftsmen and above all the learned classes. Professional judges, doctors, priests of religion, genealogists and historians were all 'men of art'. There are no specific references to Druids in Cisalpine society but that is not to argue that the Druids, who were, after all, only the intellectual caste of society, did not exist. Women, for example, receive only one or two mentions in Cisalpine society but they certainly existed!

Later Roman observers pointed out that the druidic caste was exempt from military service and had several important privileges in society. One aspect of druidic philosophy has had a profound and unfortunate effect on our understanding of the history of the Celts. As we saw in the previous chapter, Caesar noted: 'The Druids believe that their religion forbids them to commit their teachings to writing . . .' An example of the power of the Druids is recorded by Diodorus Siculus who tells us, in respect of war, that 'often when the combatants are ranged face to face, and swords drawn and spears bristling, these men come between the armies and stay the battle, just as wild beasts are sometimes held spellbound.' Of course, the Druids could only arbitrate between opposing sides if both sides knew and respected them. One wonders if these Druids ever tried to arbitrate in a battle between Romans and Celts. Doubtless they would have been given short shrift by the Romans. Strabo had also noticed this: 'They even arbitrated in cases of war and made the opponents stop when they were about to line up for battle.'

The king or chieftain had his retinue, amongst whom were the bards. According to Appian in *Celtica*, when Gnaeus Domitius was campaigning in Gaul in 122 BC,

... an ambassador of Bituitus, king of the Arverni, met him, arrayed magnificently and followed by attendants also adorned, and by dogs, for the barbarians of this region use dogs also as bodyguards. A musician, too, was in the train who sang in barbarous fashion the praises of King Bituitus, and then of the Arverni, and then of the ambassador himself, celebrating his birth, his bravery and is wealth ...

There is the famous account of Poseidonius, quoted by Athenaeus, concerning the father of Bituitus, Lovernius (the fox), who gave a feast for his followers.

A Celtic poet, who arrived too late, met Lovernius [on the road] and composed a song magnifying his greatness and lamenting his own late arrival. Lovernius was very pleased and asked for a bag of gold and threw it to the poet who ran beside his chariot. The poet picked it up and sang another song saying that the very tracks made by his chariot gave gold and largess to mankind.

Sadly, there is little reference in Roman accounts to the women of Cisalpine Gaul. Indeed, it is typical that women are under-represented in the male-orientated Classical sources, although archaeology has done its best to shed light on the female world. Dr James says that it is risky to make simple assumptions about gender roles. However, we can speculate from these Classical comments, and also from the emerging role of women in insular Celtic sources, particularly the law codes of Ireland and of Wales, though the latter is very medievalised.

The same denigration of Celtic men by Roman observers emerges against Celtic women. Ammianus Marcellinus says:

... a whole band of foreigners will be unable to cope with one of the Celts in a fight, if he calls in his wife, stronger than he by far and with flashing eyes; least of all when she swells her neck and gnashes her teeth and posing her huge white arms, begins to rain blows mingled with kicks, like shots discharged by the twisted cords of a catapult. The voices of most of them are formidable and threatening, alike when they are good natured and angry. But all of them with equal care keep clean and neat, and in those districts, particularly among the Aquitani, no man or woman can be seen, be she never so poor, in soiled or ragged clothing, as elsewhere.

In spite of the caricatures, he is at least positive about Celtic cleanliness. The Celts, after all, gave the word 'soap' (*sapo*) to the Latin language. Diodoris Siculus sums up Celtic women: 'The women of the Celts are not only like men in their great stature but they are a match for them in courage as well.'

As I have demonstrated in *Celtic Women: Women in Celtic Society and Literature* (1995), women had a remarkable place in Celtic society compared with their more unfortunate Roman and Greek sisters. There was far more equality and Celtic marriage was much more of a partnership. There are traces of polyandry as well. Some Celtic groups believed in matrilinear descent, an individual status depending on the identity of the mother and not the father. Celtic women scandalised Roman society by their independence, their status in society and their attitudes. There is this famous reply of Argentocoxus ('silver' is the root of this name), the wife of a Caledonian chieftain, to the Empress Julia Augustus. The encounter took place in the third century AD and is recounted by Dio Cassius, who says that the Roman empress criticised the Celtic women for their apparent lack of (Roman) morals. Argentocoxus replied: 'We Celtic women obey the demands of nature in a more moral way than the women of Rome. We consort openly with the best men but you, of Rome, allow yourselves to be debauched in secret by the vilest.'

Although we hear of women attending battles to cheer on their menfolk, there is only slight evidence from Classical accounts that they took part in the battles themselves. Plutarch, in his life of Marius, informs us that when the warriors of the Ambrones started to retreat before the Romans, the women took up weapons and began to fight the Romans and actually used the weapons against their own menfolk whom they deemed traitors for running away. We have evidence from Livy, Tacitus and Cassius Dio that warrior queens did exist, such as Cartimandua and Boudicca. 'We British are used to women commanders in war,' is a statement recorded by Tacitus. Certainly the insular Celtic sources record women warriors in the myths and 'pseudo-history' of Ireland and Wales. But, sadly, in terms of the Celts of Italy we have no glimpses of an Onomaris, a Boudicca, Cartimandua or Chiomara.

Plutarch, however, mentions Celtic women intervening to prevent a war among the Celts in Italy in the early fourth century BC. In *De Virtute Mulierum*, Plutarch says that at this time Celtic women were active in public life and fulfilled the role of mediators. They appeared often as ambassadors and priestesses. Dio Cassius mentions Ganna, 'a virgin among the Celts', who went on an embassy to the Emperor Domitian. Flavius Vopsicus identifies her as being of the Tungri, from modern Tonges, near Liège, Belgium, one of the Belgae tribes. The word *gannas* implies an 'intermediary' and survives in Cornish.

We are privileged in that we have discovered the tombs of several prominent Celtic woman, obviously leaders of their people. In 1953 came the discovery of the tomb of 'the princess of Vix' near Mont Lassois, in France. This lady, who was thirty-five years old, was buried in a four-wheeled chariot in the sixth century BC. She had a warrior's torque made from 480 grams of gold in exquisite craftsmanship. A grave of another such woman at Waldalgesheim dated to the fourth century BC produced an amazing variety of jewellery. A third-century BC chariot burial of a woman at Wetwang Slack, Yorkshire, revealed another prominent female leader. And the 'Reinheim Princess', with her jewellery and, more significantly, her gold torque of office, reinforces the theory that women had a prominent role in Celtic society and its political structures. The wide dispersal of these female graves shows that the prominence of women was not confined to only one section of the Celtic world.

The burials also show what many Celtic women were wearing; their love of jewellery and advanced use of cosmetics are evident. The poet Sextus Propertius (*c.*50 BC–after 16 BC) in a book of poems to his mistress, Cynthia, criticised her for applying her make-up like a Celt, particularly using *belgius color*, which seems to be an imported Celtic eye-shadow or blusher.

Strabo puts forward the Roman view of the Celts in this passage:

To the frankness and high-spiritedness of their temperament must be added the traits of childish boastfulness and love of decoration. They wear ornaments of gold, torques on their necks, bracelets on their arms and wrists, while people of high rank wear dyed garments besprinkled with gold. It is this vanity which makes them unbearable in victory and so completely downcast in defeat.

From the evidence, and particularly from the Celtic sources, the codes of law which were committed to writing in the early Christian period, we can see extraordinary parallels between Celtic society and Hindu society. Professor Myles Dillon has brought together many of these similarities in his fascinating studies *Celt and Hindu* (1973) and *Celts and Aryans* (1975), demonstrating the parallels in language, law, mythology and religious ideas. It would seem that while the other Indo-European cultures, such as Greek and Latin, had rapidly evolved away from many of the common Indo-European ideas, Celtic society had been conservative, maintaining the original concepts, customs and even terminology which can be compared to the language and concepts of the Sanskrit Vedas. Dr Calvert Watkins of Harvard, the leading linguistic expert in the field, has pointed out that of all the Celtic linguistic remains Old Irish represents an extraordinary archaic and conservative tradition within the Indo-European one. The nominal and verbal systems of Old Irish, he says, are a far truer reflection of Indo-European than Classical Greek or Latin and the structure of Old Irish can be compared only with that of Vedic Sanskrit or Hittite of the Old Kingdom.

One Indo-European concept, held in common with the Hindus, was the belief that in the time of primal chaos, divine waters from heaven had flooded downwards and soaked the earth. These waters, which they called Danu (a word also found in Sanskrit, *danu*, rain or moisture), nurtured a sacred oak named Bíle. From the conjunction of the two came forth the pantheon of their gods. Danu, whose name is found in all Celtic mythologies as well as in river place-names, gave her name to what was regarded as the major Celtic sacred river of Danuvius (the Danube) and the myth is similar to the Vedic story of Ganga, the goddess of the Ganges. As we have seen, the Rhône was the Rhodanus (*ro*, great and *Danu*). Even among the Celts of Britain we find the River Don in Durham deriving from the same name. In Irish myth the goddess becomes Dana, also Anu, and in Welsh myth she becomes Dôn. And, as we have also discussed, we find her in the earliest name for the Po – Eridanus.

The names of some 374 gods and goddesses have been recorded by scholars throughout the ancient Celtic world. Most of them seem to be local gods but some, like Danu, Belenus or Bíle, Lugh, Brigit, Ogimos and Cernunnus, were part of the major pantheon and left place-names throughout the Celtic world. Due to the early Romanisation of Cisalpine Gaul after the conquest, most of the old Celtic gods of this area appear in their Latin forms. Caesar put Apollo in second place in his list of the main gods of the Gauls. Unfortunately, he does not give Apollo a native name. However, the popularity of Apollo is reflected among the Cisalpine Celts. Dedications are everywhere.

Diana, in her Celtic guises, was also popular and Cisalpine Gaul ranks only second among the areas of Italy in its acknowledgement of the goddess. She seems to have been identified with the Celtic Matronae and the Silvanae. Minerva was also included by Caesar as a major Transalpine Gaulish goddess and she appears to have been popular in Cisalpine Gaul. She was equated with the goddess of battle by the Insubres, and in her temple, says Polybius, were stored their golden standards called 'the immovables'. Dedications to her are widespread.

There is no lack of attestation, both literary and in dedications, to the Celtic worship of an equivalent of Mars. Dedications occur right across Cisalpine Gaul. He was seen not just as a god of war but as a protector of individuals. Even more popular was Heracles. The majority of dedicants to Heracles were Celts. And Mercury was more popular among the Celts than the Italians. Caesar called him the chief god of the Celts. The fact that he was the god of tradesmen does not mean to say that the Celts worshipped trade but that the first Romans and Greeks to make contact with them were traders and he is doubtless the first Graeco-Roman god whose name they learnt.

Silvanus is also to be found in Cisalpine Gaul, sometimes associated with Mercury and Jupiter.

However, can any trace of the original Celtic gods be found in Cisalpine Gaul? We have mentioned a local deity called Poeninus in the Great St Bernard Pass. But what of the Po Valley itself? There are traces. Epona, the Celtic horse goddess, was celebrated on a feastday on 18 December in Mantua and she was also known at Aquileia. Dedications to the Matronae, the triple Mother Goddess, were found around Milan, Como and the lakes. Belenus seems, from the dedications which have survived, to have been popular in the east and was claimed to be a major god of Aquileia with fifty inscriptions to him as well as places-names, such as Belvedere to the north and Beligna, where there appears to have been a temple to him. The Romans later claimed him as a version of Apollo, which is significant in Cisalpine terms in view of the other Apollo dedications. The name means 'brilliant', and he was a sun deity. He was associated with solar festivals and the great feast on 1 May, Beltane – the fires of Belenus survive in modern Irish, Scots and Manx as the name of the month of May.

In the Val Policella surviving inscriptions imply the worship of Sequana, a river deity who gave her name to the River Seine and was worshipped at its source in the valley north-west of Dijon. Other Celtic gods crop up on numerous dedications throughout the area.

The Celts believed in the immortality of the soul and are regarded as the first Europeans to develop the concept of a life after death. Caesar uncharitably says of the Celtic bravery in battle: 'The Druids' chief doctrine is that the soul of man does not perish but passes after death from one person to another. They hold that this is the best of all incitements to courage as banishing the fear of death.' Pomponius Mela (c.AD 43) echoed this: 'One of their dogmas has come to common knowledge, namely, that souls are eternal and that there is another life in the infernal regions, and this has been permitted manifestly because it makes the multitude readier for war. And it is for this reason too that they burn or bury with their dead things appropriate to them in life . . .'

They believed that the soul was to be found in the head and when those whom they had respected died, they decapitated them and preserved the heads in cedar oil. Roman propaganda painted the Celts as 'head hunters' and it is a picture which some still cling to. It is far from the case. The heads of those the Celts respected were taken only after death in battle. These were the heads of great warriors, even slain enemy warriors. As Diodorus Siculus says: 'They cut off the heads of enemies slain in battle and attach them to the necks of their horses . . . they embalm in cedar oil the heads of the most distinguished enemies, and preserve them carefully . . .' Heads were also made into votive offerings and consigned to sacred rivers, such as the Thames in Britain. Here is another link to Hindu practices via the Indo-European traditions. As the Hindus consigned their dead to the Ganges, so too did the Celts consign their dead to the Thames.

The Thames itself was called in Celtic *Tamesis* and is thus recorded by Caesar. This is cognate with the Sanskrit *Tamasa* which is significantly the name of a tributary of the Ganges, and the two forms mean the same – 'river of darkness', for through the darkness one proceeds to rebirth. The Celts took the bodies out of their settlement at Lugh's fortress (London) through Bíle's gate, the point where the god Bíle, whose role was to transport souls to the afterlife, was said to have waited to transmit the souls through the dark river to the Otherworld. Darkness came before rebirth in both Celtic and Vedic traditions. The spot is still known as Billingsgate today.

Roman writers loved to talk about Celtic savagery, the quality of being fierce, cruel and uncivilised. By Rome's own bloodthirsty standards, any Celtic cruelty seems to have been quite mild. The practice of human sacrifice by the Celts as a deliberate act of religious worship is mentioned by Strabo, Diodorus Siculus and Julius Caesar, all of whom seem to be using Poseidonius as a source. Cicero also mentions human sacrifice among the Celts. 'They thought it right to sacrifice human beings to the immortal gods,' he says, and again, 'they find it necessary to propitiate the immortal gods and defile their altars and temples with human victims'. This is rather an impudent comment coming from the Romans who also indulged in human sacrifice. In 216 BC the Romans actually sacrificed a Celtic man and woman, as well as a Greek man and woman, by burying them alive under the Forum Boarium. Ritual killings were a way of Roman life and in the Tullianum, at the foot of the Capitoline hill, state prisoners were ceremonially executed to appease the gods of war. Among the victims we know of is Jugurtha, the Numidian king, taken prisoner in 107 BC by Rome and put to death in 104 BC as part of Marius' triumphal celebrations. A more famous victim of the celebratory sacrifice was the Celtic king, Vercingetorix, who surrendered himself to Julius Caesar in 52 BC. He was taken to Rome and had to remain incarcerated for six years before being ritually executed to celebrate Caesar's triumph. What else were these executions but human sacrifice?

It has been a curious fashion to view the Romans as advanced and moral and accept their condemnation of human sacrifice among the Celts without examining their own morality too closely. In 264 BC it is said that Marcus and Decimus Brutus, members of a Roman plebeian family, decided to mark the death of their father by having three pairs of slaves fight to the death, which was done with the approval of the priests. Having slaves fight to the death at funerals became a popular event and by 145 BC it was recorded that ninety pairs of slaves fought for three days at one funeral commemoration. Soon it became the custom for rich Romans to stage slave fights and those slaves marked for death were called gladiators – 'swordsmen' from the word *gladius*. Even Julius Caesar in 46 BC, so disapproving of the human sacrifice which he claimed was practised by the Celts, had slaves fight to the death at the funeral of his daughter Julia.

This form of 'human sacrifice' to please the bloodlust of the Roman crowds reached its height in the reign of Trajan when in AD 107, 5000 pairs of gladiators were forced to fight to the death in one contest in Rome. In AD 10 there were four major gladiatorial schools in Rome: the Great School, the Dacian School, the School for Bestiarii (animal fighters) and the Celtic School. In these schools, the condemned slaves from the conquered peoples were sent to train. Marcus Valerius Martialis – the poet Martial (*c.*AD 40–103/4) – who boasted of his Celtic parentage, recounts that 'the games' he watched were held over six days, and opened with some 9000 animals, from deer to bulls, from ostriches to wild horses, being slaughtered.

From the time of Nero, Christians were especially singled out to die in the arena and death came in many different ways. Women and young girls were forced to have intercourse with animals as part of the grotesque spectacle to entertain the Roman masses. Men, women and children were attacked by various animals, burnt or nailed to crosses, or simply forced to fight experienced gladiators. The Emperor Diocletian (AD 284–305) is recorded to have had 17,000 Christians slaughtered in the arena in one month alone. The most terrible persecution of Christians in the arena for Roman entertainment took place under the 'enlightened' emperor, Marcus Aurelius, in AD 166. Marcus Aurelius is better known for his twelve philosophical books of 'Meditations' (*ta eis heauton*), written in Greek, than for his systematic slaughter of men, women and children in the arena in the name of 'games'.

In spite of this history, it is the Romans who are accepted as 'civilised' and the Celts who are condemned for 'human sacrifices'. The truth is, of course, that both peoples lived in what we now perceive to be a barbaric age. If anything, the Celts seem to have had a moral edge over the Romans for they had not developed the systematic form of slaughter and bloodlust that marked the height of Rome's 'civilisation'. Pomponius Mela reported in AD 43, at a time when tens of thousands met their death by ritual slaughter in Rome's arenas, that the Celts had once made human sacrifices but it was a thing of the past.

Another thing that marked the Celts from the Romans was, of course, their differing attitudes to slavery. When Diodorus Siculus made his famous disparaging remark that a Celt would exchange a slave for an amphora of wine he was expressing the popular opinion that the Celts cared for nothing other than alcohol. He was not making the point that Celts had slaves to exchange. We will come to this in a moment.

The institution of slavery had existed in Rome from early times. As in Greece, slaves were the legal property of another who had total control over all their activities. As Aristotle put it, the slave was merely 'a living tool'. Slaves had no rights at all. If they attempted to escape, the owner could have them branded, whipped or killed. In short, they were without any legal protection.

It was as Rome began to dominate central Italy and her empire spread, particularly in the second century BC, that the slave population rose to incredible numbers. L. Aemilius Paullus, after his victory over Perseus of Macedonia at Pydna in 168 BC, is recorded as having sold 150,000 slaves. Julius Caesar on one occasion after his wars against the Celts sold 53,000 into slavery. In the second century BC the Romans used slave labour on a grand scale on their agricultural estates, preferring slaves to hiring free labourers. At this time only the slave bailiff of the estate could marry and have children. But after the rise of the emperors, with Rome occupying most of the free world and few wars to gain them new slaves, slaves became expensive. Roman capitalists began to breed slaves like farmers breeding animals. The high cost of slaves eventually changed the economic situation in Rome; capitalists turn to cheaper free labour in unskilled jobs while slaves were pampered and given professional tasks. Because of their high capital value by the fourth century AD they were also given economic incentives which brought their position close to that of free craftsman.

Curiously enough, a similar situation developed in the West Indies in the mid-seventeenth century. The English had begun transporting slaves to the colonies from Africa. Lord Broghill had suggested to the Lord Deputy of Ireland, Henry Cromwell, son of the Lord Protector, that a means of both solving the 'Irish question' and supplying the need for labourers in the New World colonies would be to send Irish men, women and children to the West Indies as forced labour. English soldiers made dawn raids on Irish villages carrying off captives, men, women and children. They were collected at Irish ports in their thousands and then transported mainly to Barbardos. 'Barbados you!' became an Irish curse.

These unfortunates were placed, at government expense, as 'indentured servants' under the control of local plantation owners. Theoretically, they were supposed to be indentured to the plantation owner for a period of five to seven years. After that time the owner was supposed to free them and provide passage to wherever they wished to go, so long as it was not back to Ireland. The reality was that the 'engagés', snatched from their homes and loved ones and forced into slavery, if they even survived the voyage, were subjected to extreme cruelty. All too often the Irish 'indentured servant', male, female or child, became a mere chattel at the absolute disposal of the master. Most were treated as inferior to the African slaves. The reason for this had been shown in the parallel of the last centuries of the Roman empire. The slave was seen as a permanent possession, a property for which the slave owner had given good money. It was therefore to the advantage of the master to preserve the slave as long as possible by good treatment. The Irish servants were cheaply come by. If they were worked to death, the government would send replacements. They were treated accordingly. It has been estimated that during the Cromwellian period in Ireland some 50,000 Irish were forcibly sent to the West Indies alone. England finally abolished its slave trade in 1807 but it was not until 1833 that slavery throughout the British empire was abolished.

In ancient Rome, slaves were also chattels although a few might be granted freedom for good service or by purchase if they accumulated enough *peculium*. The freedman (*libertus*) continued to belong to the family of the former master (*patronus*) and the two were bound by mutual obligations. The freedman assumed the *nomen* of his liberator, as for example did the Insubrean warrior Caius Caecilius Statius, who was taken prisoner at Telamon in 225 BC and became, as a freedman, Rome's most successful comedy playwright.

By comparison, there is little evidence of any institution of slavery among the Celts. What we know of social institutions from the Celtic viewpoint is confined mainly to the insular Celts. The Celtic peoples with whom Rome first came into contact were essentially kinship groups, a collection of extended families and clans which came together in large tribal units. Often tribes united in multi-tribal confederations but these were constantly reforming according to the political fortunes of the individual tribal members. Tribes were usually governed by kings, or chieftains, often operating in pairs. They were not autocrats but had to conform to the dictates of the clan or tribal assembly. Often these councils were made up of several hundred leading men of the tribe.

There was a class which some observers made analogous to slaves. Dr P. W. Joyce, in examining the Irish law system, uses the term 'non-free' class. He explains:

> The non-free people were those who had not the full right of the free people of the tribe. They had no claim to any part of the tribe-land, though they were permitted, under strict conditions, to till little plots for mere subsistence. This was by far the most serious of their disabilities ... Their standing varied, some being absolute slaves, some little removed from slavery and others far above it.

There were, in ancient Ireland, three classes of 'non-free' people. The lowest class consisted usually of criminals, thieves and murderers. The others were captives taken in battle, hostages, people who had fallen into debt, or those who refused to work, wastrels and such. As there is evidence for similar institutions in ninth-century A D Welsh law, we may hypothesise a common Celtic social system applied throughout the Celtic world. Certainly there is no extensive description from either Roman or Greek sources of the Celts being involved in slave owning, or using slaves as an economic force, as the Greeks and Romans developed slavery.

These, then, were the people who had settled in the Po Valley and, as we have demonstrated, had been settled there for some centuries when the Senones arrived. Because of the density of population in the Po Valley, when the Senones passed through the Alps they found they had to move on south in search of other lands to settle. Their passage through the Apennines into Etruria brought them into conflict with Roman arrogance. They brushed aside Rome's legions, marched on the city, whose gates stood wide open, with most of the citizens fled, and Brennus, king of the Senones, was now about to make himself master of Rome.

[4]

The Fall of Rome

JUST AFTER dawn on the morning of the day which was later to be known as 19 July 390 BC, the advance guard of Brennus' victorious Celtic army began to enter Rome through the Colline Gate at the north-east of the city. They soon reported back to the Celtic king that the only area of the city still fortified and defended was the twin-peaked Capitoline hill whose sides were precipitous and whose great temples were surrounded by walls like a fortress. Situated on the Capitoline, rising above all other buildings, more spectacular and impressive than any, was the great temple of Jupiter Optimus Maximus – 'Jupiter, best and greatest'. The chief temple of Rome had been begun in the reign of Tarquinius Superbus, the second and last Tarquin Etruscan king of Rome, in 509 BC. Temples to Juno and Minerva, Jupiter's companions, and an ancient temple to Jupiter Feretrius, associated with the ancient worship of an oak tree, reputedly founded by Romulus himself, rose in the shadows of the great temple.

On receiving these reports Brennus entered the city together with many of his main body of warriors. He ordered that the Capitoline hill be surrounded. Others of his warriors he allowed to disperse through the city in search of plunder. Livy tells us the story from the Roman viewpoint.

Finding the streets empty, crowds of them broke into the first houses they came to; others went further afield, presumably supposing that buildings more remote from the Forum would offer richer prizes but there the very silence and solitude made them uneasy, separated as they were from their companions, and suggested the possibility of a trap, so that they soon returned, keeping close together, to the neighbourhood of the Forum.

Near the Forum, Livy says, they found the poorer houses locked and barred but the great mansions of Rome's élite had been left open. Livy suggests that the Celts were awed by the great houses and held back. Then, looking in at the gates, they saw, each seated in his own courtyard, on his *sella curulis*, or ivory inlaid chair of office, the old patricians of Rome, still patiently awaiting their fate, clad in their ceremonial robes of office. Livy enthuses that these old men were 'august beyond reckoning, the majesty they expressed in those grave, calm eyes like the majesty of gods. They might have been statues in some holy place, and for a while the Celtic warriors stood entranced . . .'

Livy's account of the patricians each being in his own home is more believable than Plutarch's account in this instance. He has all the old men gathered on their chairs awaiting their fate in the Forum.

Livy now records one of the popular legends of the Celtic sack of Rome. One Celtic warrior entered the courtyard of the house of Marcus Papirius. Papirius belonged to an ancient patrician family which during the previous fifty years had produced five consuls and military tribunes of Rome, including Lucius Papirius Mugilanus who had been appointed *interrex*, an office which had originally been held by an individual appointed by the Senate on the death of a king to rule until the appointment of the next king. Under the republic, if both consuls died or resigned, *interreges*, who had to be patricians and senators, were appointed until the new consuls were elected. It seems likely, and within the time scale, that the Marcus Papirius mentioned by Livy was the same Marcus Papirius Atratinus who had been consul in 412/411 BC, twenty years before these events.

Livy says that the Celtic warrior walked up to the silent Roman patrician as he sat stoically on his ivory seat. Doubtless the Celtic warrior was bemused at the sight of the old man sitting alone and silent in his deserted courtyard. Marcus Papirius wore his white hair long in the Roman fashion of those days and, intrigued, the Celt reached out a hand to the silken beard to touch it. Papirius suddenly moved and struck the Celt on the head with his ivory staff. Livy says:

That was the beginning: the barbarian flamed into anger and killed him, and the others were butchered where they sat. From that moment no mercy was shown; houses were ransacked and the empty shells set on fire.

The story of Papirius and the slaughter of the elderly patricians is repeated by Florus, the author of an abridgement of Roman history until the time of the Emperor Augustus. Florus lived in the second century AD and while some argue that he was writing an epitome of Livy's account, there are certain elements of contradiction which point to the fact that he was drawing on other sources. The poet Publius Ovidius Naso (Ovid, 43 BC–AD 17) in his *Fasti*, written about AD 2, uses the drama of this scene with the old Romans being killed still seated in the *atria* of their houses.

Now was the moment for the imagination of Livy to go to town on the sack of Rome, although, as he was writing for the Romans, he could not allow the Celts to entirely destroy the city. But overcome with rhetoric he is contradictory, saying in one place the city was entirely destroyed by fire (*etsi omnia flammis ac ruinis aequata vidissent*, v. 42) and in another that only half of the city was destroyed (*instruit deinde aciem, ut loci natura patiebatur, in semirutae solorbis*, v. 49). It is unlikely that the Celts would have put the entire city to the torch because they were going to occupy it. We know that several temples and public buildings outside the Roman-held Capitoline were actually preserved down to imperial times.

Livy, in spite of his contradiction, is probably right when he writes:

The extent of the conflagration was, however, unexpectedly limited. Some of the Celts may have been against the indiscriminate destruction of the city; or possibly it was their leaders' policy, first, to start a few fires in the hope that the besieged in the Capitol might be driven to surrender by the fear of losing their beloved homes, and, secondly, to leave a portion of the city intact and to use it as a sort of pledge or security – or lever – to induce the Romans to accept their terms. In any case the havoc wrought by the fire was on the first day by no means universal – or even widespread – and much less than might have been expected in the circumstances.

For the Romans besieged in the Capitol the full horror was almost too great to realise; they could hardly believe their eyes or ears as they looked down on the barbaric force roaming in hordes through the familiar streets, while every moment, everywhere and anywhere, some new terror was enacted; fear gripped them in a thousand shapes now here, now there, the yells of triumph, women's screams or the crying of children, the roar of flames or the long rumbling crash of falling masonry forced them to turn unwilling eyes upon some fresh calamity, as if fate had made them spectators of the nightmare stage scene of their country's ruin, helpless to save anything they possessed but their own useless bodies. Never before had besieged men been in a plight so pitiful – not shut within their city but excluded from it they saw all that they loved in the power of their enemies.

It is obvious that Brennus and his council of chieftains would have attempted to make contact with the Romans holding out in the one remaining part of the city. A demand for surrender would have been rejected. It seems that the consul, Quintus Sulpicius Lagus, was still in overall military control. For most of that day the Celts plundered the city, while maintaining an impregnable ring around the Capitoline hill. Doubtless some skirmishing took place to test the defences of the Capitol. Livy does not bother to give details. He merely says that the Celts were aware that they must reduce the Capitol to claim complete victory over Rome. He also says that after some days they determined to carry the Capitol by a fierce assault.

At dawn, therefore, on a given signal, the whole vast horde assembled in the Forum; then, roaring out their challenge, they locked shields and moved up the slope to the Capitol.

Livy can't have it both ways. At one time he is speaking of 30,000 Celts attacking the city, leaving aside the 70,000 given by other historians, and then he has 'the whole vast horde' impossibly jammed into the Forum. Brennus had probably simply chosen his best warriors to make the assault up the one easy route to the Capitol.

The Roman garrison remained calm, says Livy. Every point of approach had been reinforced. The Roman commanders instructed their men to wait, letting the Celts exhaust themselves in the climb up the hill. When the attackers paused to rest about half-way up, and gather themselves for the assault, the Romans made a sudden counter-attack, driving the besiegers back with great loss.

Brennus realised, from this repulse, that it was going to be impossible to take the Capitol by storm. Nature had created a well-defended
position and Sulpicius Lagus took advantage of the redoubt. After
this rebuff, the Celtic king decided on a lengthy siege, knowing that
there must be limited supplies on the Capitol, and that the alternative
to taking it by storm with unacceptable losses to the Celts was to
starve the garrison into surrender. Livy suggests that 'not having
thought of it before, they had destroyed in the fires all the city's store
of grain'. Once again, as is common with Roman attitudes to the
Celts, they are painted as bungling amateurs in war, childlike savages
who have no idea how to conduct affairs. As Brennus sat down to
a long siege, he certainly had his troops scouring the countryside for
supplies. But this was doubtless due to the fact that the Romans
themselves had taken what they could with them and destroyed as
much of the residue as possible in case it fell into the hands of the
enemy.

The Celts were to hold Rome for seven months, according to
Polybius. Livy and most other sources agree that the Celts would
not depart until the Ides of 'the month of cleansing', that is *Februarius*
– 13 February.

While the siege of Rome's Capitol continued, events were happening at Ardea, a town of the Rutuli in Latium, 20 miles south of
Rome. It was here that Marcus Furius Camillus was living in exile.
A scion of a Roman patrician family, the Furii, Camillus was a
statesman and general whose exploits have been considerably
embellished in later times particularly by the Greek biographer, Plutarch. Between 403 and 399 BC, he had been elected military tribune
three times, and in 398 BC he was appointed *interrex*. He had already
been one of Rome's two leading generals and conducted siege operations at Capena, an Etruscan town at the foot of Mount Soracte
(now Monte di S. Silvestro) near Rome. He was then made dictator
in charge of the siege against the Etruscan city of Veii.

A dictator was allowed supreme judicial and military authority
which was not subject to appeal, and he could not be called to
account for his actions. He was called *magister populi* (master of
infantry) and could appoint as second-in-command a *magister equi-
tum* (master of horse). A dictator could only hold office for six
months before having to relinquish office or be reappointed.

When the city of Veii fell before Camillus' savage onslaught, the richest town in Etruria became his. He had the entire population removed by slaughter or selling the survivors into slavery. He took the statue of Juno, the Etruscan goddess of the town, and had it transported to the Aventine hill in Rome where he built a temple for it. Having completed a successful campaign he resigned his commissions but remained politically active. He opposed Senate plans to send half of the poor population of Rome to repopulate the ruined city of Veii. His opposition became an embarrassment and he was given a command to reduce the city of Falerii, the capital of the Falisci, closely related to the Latins, who lived on the right bank of the Tiber north of Latium. He succeeded in his new military role and his popularity increased. In celebration of the victories he was reported to have dedicated a golden basin to Apollo at Delphi in fulfilment of a vow. Three men were entrusted with carrying his gift to Greece.

Rome had won two more victories at Tusculum and in the Aequian territory. Militarily, Rome's star continued to be in the ascendant but there was internal bickering between the representatives of the patricians and those of the plebeians. The plebeians or 'People's Party' had succeeded in bringing two tribunes to trial for maladministration. They were found guilty and fined. Camillus, as a patrician, threw his support against the plebeians, calling their action 'criminal lunacy of the commons in turning against their own representative magistrates and failing to see that the dishonest verdict robbed the tribunate of the veto and undermined their power'.

Furthermore Camillus continued to oppose the Roman Senate's plans for reinhabiting Veii. 'Religion forbids that a town which the gods abandoned should be inhabited by men; it is a sin to think that our people should ever live on captive soil or exchange victorious Rome for vanquished Veii.' Nevertheless the Senate gave 3.5 acres of land from the estates of Veii to every plebeian, the free-born members of each household, who wished to resettle there.

According to Plutarch, tragedy had struck the Roman patrician in the months before the Celts appeared at Clusium. His young sons had died and, while he was still mourning, a tribune named Apuleius had him legally indicted for misappropriating some of the plunder taken from Veii for his own personal wealth. Camillus' own family would not support him in his claim of innocence. He decided to flee into exile at Ardea and, in his absence, he was fined 15,000 *aera* (lumps of bronze which had no standard weight at this time). According to Livy, as he went into exile he prayed that, as he was innocent and wrongfully accused, the gods should speedily cause his ungrateful city to bitterly regret he had gone. Thus Livy prepared the dramatic way for the Celtic sack of Rome. So, too, did Plutarch, recounting a story that just before Camillus was sent into exile, a centurion named Marcus Caedicius, 'a man who was not conspicuous to be sure but who was esteemed, honest and kindly', was walking down a street in Rome, when he was hailed by a loud voice. He looked around but no one was there. The voice said: 'Listen, Marcus Caedicius; early tomorrow morning go and tell the tribunes that within a little time they must expect the Celts!' When Marcus Caedicius did so, the tribunes laughed at him. 'And a little while after, Camillus suffered his disgrace.'

Now in Ardea, Camillus, we are told, heard the news from Rome with bitter irony. According to Livy, part of the Celtic army had marched as far south from Rome as Ardea itself and were approaching the city. Plutarch says this force of Celts was 'the largest and best disciplined body of them'. Camillus went immediately to the city's Senate and requested permission to speak. Livy puts this speech into his mouth.

'Men of Ardea, old friends – fellow citizens as now you are, for your kindness and my misfortunes would have it so – I beg you not to think I have forgotten my station in thus thrusting myself upon you. We are all of us in peril and every man must contribute what he can to get us out of it. When shall I prove my gratitude for all you have done for me if I hang back now? Where will you need me, if not on the battlefield? At home it was by war that I won my place; unbeaten in the field I was hounded out in time of peace by my ungrateful countrymen. My friends, your chance has come when you can show your gratitude to Rome for all the services she did you long ago – how great you yourselves remember – nay, you do, and I would not reproach you and this town of yours. You can win glory from our common enemy. That enemy is near, his disordered columns are close upon us. They are big men, these Celts, brave men too – at a pinch – but unsteady. Always they bring more smoke than fire – much terror but little strength. See what happened at Rome?; the city lay wide open, and they walked in – but now a handful of men in the Capitol are holding them. Already they are sick of siege, and are off – anywhere, everywhere – roaming the countryside, crammed with food and soused in drink they lie at night like animals on the bank of some stream – unprotected, unguarded, no watches set – and a taste of success has now made them more reckless than ever. Do you wish to save your city – to prevent this country from being overrun? Very well, then: arm yourselves early tonight, every man of you, and follow me – you shall slit their throats as they lie! If I don't give them to you to slaughter in their sleep like cattle, let me be scorned at Ardea as once I was scorned in Rome.'

Here is the typical boastful and prejudiced speech of the Romans. Camillus was wrong. The Celts had not given up their siege of the Capitol. Plutarch makes it clear that Brennus had split his army into sections to raid the surrounding countryside. This section had foraged 20 miles south of Rome within the vicinity of Ardea and was giving alarm to the Ardeans.

That night the soldiers of Ardea, led by Camillus, marched out of the city towards the Celtic encampment. The Roman historians claim the camp was unguarded, without sentinels, and the Ardean soldiers flung themselves on the undefended Celts. 'There was no resistance; unarmed men were killed in their sleep, and in a few minutes the whole place resembled a slaughterhouse.' Plutarch has it that the Celts were asleep and drunk.

A few of them were sobered by fear, armed themselves, and made resistance to Camillus and his men, so that they fell fighting; but most were still mastered by sleep and wine when they were fallen upon and slain without their arms. A few only ran from the camp, under cover of darkness, and when day came, were seen straggling about the fields, but horsemen pursed them and cut them to pieces.

Camillus continued his previous bloodthirsty record by having all the Celtic prisoners, taken by the Ardeans, killed on the spot. Camillus had, it seems, a habit of killing unarmed prisoners.

Now, a night attack, if this took place, obviously threw the Celts into turmoil but, reading between the lines of the biased Roman accounts, it would appear that they recovered and were able to withdraw in good order. Even Livy revised his slaughter story, later admitting that many of the Celts, in fact he uses the word *maximus* (most), reached the town of Antium (Anzio), another Latin city on the sea coast. Unfortunately, he does not tell us whether they went there to capture Antium or merely trade for supplies. It could well be that Antium welcomed the Celts as allies against Rome. Most of the cities of Latium were still very hostile to Rome's dominance in the area. The people of Latium seemed to have looked upon the Celtic victory as giving them a breathing space to recover from Roman imperialism. The Latins at this time rose up against the Romans.

The Celts also found a surprising ally in the Etruscans. Near Veii, the Romans seeking shelter there from the Celtic raiders saw Etruscan columns driving off their cattle and taking what plunder they could. The Romans, under the command of the centurion Marcus Caedicius, the very same man who claimed to have warned the Roman tribunes of the coming of the Celts weeks before, led a counter-attack on the Etruscans and checked their raids. Caedicius slew most of the Etruscans but saved a few prisoners whom he 'persuaded' to lead the Romans to a second Etruscan encampment near a salt works. 'The second surprise attack,' says Livy, 'was equally successful but even more bloody.' The Etruscans now went out of their way to help the Celts against the Romans.

In Rome, the siege of the Capitol was continuing. It is now that the Fabii, whose arrogance had caused the Celtic attack, come back into the picture in the person of Gaius Fabius Dorsuo, who was a priest of Quirinius and presumably had not followed the other priests in the withdrawal from the temples on the Quirinal hill. The story was quoted by Appian of Alexandria from an early historian named Cassius Hemina. Although the annual festival of the Quirinalia was celebrated on 17 February, and we are talking of an event claimed to have occurred around August (then known as the month of Sextilis), Livy says that an annual sacrifice on the Quirinal was due and had to be celebrated by one of the Fabii clan. Determined not to ignore his duties in performing the sacrifice, the young Fabius, wearing a ceremonial toga and carrying the sacred vessels, was said to have walked out of the besieged Capitol and made his way through the Celtic pickets and sentinels, ignoring their challenges and threats. He reached the temple on the Quirinal hill, performed his sacrifice and then returned by the same route; again, through the Celtic besiegers. Says Livy:

> The Celts did nothing to stop him; perhaps they were too much astonished by his incredible audacity, perhaps even touched, for the religious sentiment is strong in them, by a sort of awe.

This rather fabulous tale of the heroism of the Fabii, especially after the disasters of the Fabii brothers as envoys, can be traced to Quintus Fabius Pictor, the Roman historian who was used as a source by both Livy and Polybius. He was a senator who fought in the Second Punic War (218–202 BC) and his history was written in Greek because Latin had not yet become a literary medium. Obviously, Fabius Pictor himself is one of the Fabii so he tells a story which reflects well on his family.

It was the Romans sheltering in Veii who recalled the legendary deeds of the former general Camillus, or so we are told. It would have been impossible to have sheltered in the devastated Etruscan city without thinking of the man who had destroyed it. Caedicius, commanding the Roman survivors there, proposed that Camillus be asked to return as their general and save them from the Celts. It was agreed that the surviving members of the Senate in Rome be asked to agree to the request. A young soldier named Pontius Cominius volunteered to sneak through the Celts' siege lines to the Capitol and put the suggestion to the Roman Senate. The first-century BC historian, Quintus Claudius Quadrigarius, tells the story and this is quoted by Aulus Gellius (c.AD 130–c.AC 180). Cominius, it is said, floated down the Tiber on a raft under cover of darkness at night and climbed up to the Capitol without the Celts seeing him. Plutarch elaborates:

> The greater part of his journey was made by daylight and without fear; but, as night came on, he found himself near the city. He could not cross the river by the bridge since the Celts were guarding it, so he wrapped his light and scanty garments about his head, fastened the corks [which he seems to have carried for the purpose] to his body, and thus supported, swam across [the Tiber] and came out on the other side and went towards the city.
> Always giving a wide berth to those of the enemy who were

watchful and wakeful, as he judged by their fires and noise, he made his way to the Carmental gate, where there was the most quiet, at which the Capitoline hill was most sheer and steep, and which was girt about by a huge and jagged cliff. Up this he mounted unperceived, and finally reached, with great pains and difficulty, the sentries posted where the wall was lowest. Hailing them, and telling them who he was, he was pulled up over the wall and taken to the Roman tribunes.

The senators met and he informed them of the suggestion of the soldiers at Veii. A resolution was then passed by the Senate 'that Camillus by vote of the popular assembly, in accordance with the people's will, be forthwith named Dictator, and the soldiers have the commander whom they desire.' Cominius then returned to Caedicius and the Roman survivors at Veii by the same route and from Veii a mission was immediately dispatched to Ardea to inform Camillus of the news.

The general accepted the charge and began by raising troops at Ardea. True to his class, he appointed as his master of horse, and second-in-command, a member of another old patrician family, Lucius Valerius, who was sent to take over command of the soldiers at Veii. Camillus then instructed Valerius to march his men from Veii and join his forces south of Rome so that together they could begin to train their men into a field army which might hope to meet the Celts on equal terms. Plutarch, on the other hand, says that Camillus had gone to Veii to train some 20,000 men now under arms. But the training took time and the situation on the Capitol was becoming desperate.

At this time, we hear the account of another Celtic assault on the Capitol and the famous warning by the geese of Juno. The Celts, still searching for ways to break the siege quickly, for they must have been well aware that a new Roman army was being trained, saw that the rocky ascent of the Capitol near the shrine of Carmenta was a possible unguarded route. Marcus Terentius Varro (116–27 BC) claims that a Celtic warrior saw the wet footprints of Cominius, where he had climbed out of the Tiber and up the route to the Capitol. Plutarch is more down to earth, saying that the Celts noticed that the plants, earth and rocks had been dislodged. Brennus was called and inspected the route. The king of the Senones decided to make an assault during the night. Plutarch says 'he assembled the nimblest men and best mountain climbers of the Celts and addressed them'.

'The enemy have shown us that there is a way up to them of which we knew not, and one which men can traverse and tread. It would be a great shame for us, after such a beginning as we have made, to fail at the end, and to give the place up as impregnable, when the enemy themselves show us where it can be taken. For where it is easy for one man to approach it, there it will be no difficult matter for many to go one by one, nay, they will support and aid one another greatly in the undertaking. Gifts and honours befitting his valour shall be given to every man.'

The chosen Celtic warriors began to climb up, forming at times a human pyramid, using their large shields as platforms, and passing weapons up from man to man until they reached the top of the wall on the Capitol. Livy admits:

What is more, they accomplished the climb so quietly that the Romans on guard never heard a sound, and even the dogs – who are normally aroused by the least noise in the night – noticed nothing.

We are told by Livy that it was the sacred geese of Juno who started to cackle a warning. Juno, the wife of Jupiter, was goddess of women and marriage and mother of Mars (Ares), god of war. Juno only appears in one Roman myth and it may be that the name is cognate with *iuvenis*, 'young', in the sense of 'young bride'. The Romans recognised *iuno* as a spirit which protected women. She was associated with the moon. Now we are told by Livy and subsequent writers that these geese were kept as a sacred totem in the temple. In fact, originally geese were not sacred to Juno but kept in the Capitol temples for ritual slaughter in the process of divination practices. Hens were used later. If the geese were not sacred to Juno, one cannot help wondering if there is any other reason why Livy introduces them into the epic. It could well be that he is recounting simple fact. On the other hand, as will become apparent later, he was raised in Cisalpine Gaul, and it has been argued that his work is replete with Celtic symbolism. So it should be pointed out that geese were an important Celtic symbol and specifically connected with war.

Dr Miranda Green, in her *Animals in Celtic Myth and Life*, has pointed out: 'In Celtic iconography, geese are most commonly associated with war; thus, because of their watchful and aggressive nature, these birds were perceived as appropriate emblems or companions for warrior-gods.' There is a great free-standing stone goose, gazing alertly from the lintel of the Iron Age cliff-temple of Roquepertuse in Provence, as a symbol of watchful guardianship. Geese were often buried in warriors' graves and are seen on a fourth-century BC Celtic flagon found at Matzjausen in Germany. A first-century BC figurine of a war goddess found at Dinéault, Brittany, shows her with a helmet surmounted by a goose. The goose often accompanies images of Celtic war gods and goddesses. An altarpiece from Vaison shows a Celtic god, presumably of war, with a goose and a raven as his companions. The sacred aspect of the goose was noted by Julius Caesar in Britain when he pointed out that there was a taboo on eating the creatures. This attitude continued in Ireland until medieval times when it was forbidden to eat the *gé ghiúrainn* (barnacle goose) on certain holy days. The exiled Irish soldiers who fought for many foreign lands, such as France, Spain and Austria, were known as *na Géanna Fiáne*, the Wild Geese, a reference to the military symbolism of the goose rather than its migratory habits.

There is a lack of similar symbolism in Latin mythology before the tale of the saving of the Capitol. From archaeological evidence we can be certain that the geese were established in Celtic culture before the sack of Rome. Are we then witnessing the recounting merely of a factual incident or is Livy, with his Celtic background, trying to tell us something else? Have 'the geese of Juno' come into Latin mythology as sacred birds from a Celtic source?

The story of the warning of the geese continues when one of the Roman commanders, Marcus Manlius, was awakened by their hissing, seized his sword and gave the alarm. He hurried to where the Celts were even then climbing over the wall. Racing forward, ahead of his comrades, Manlius smashed the first Celtic warrior back with the boss of his shield, sending him toppling backwards over the wall and headlong down the cliff. His fall dislodged those warriors climbing behind him and carried several of them with him. The

Roman garrison, now roused, threw their javelins and stones down on the attacking force. The Celtic attack was driven off.

At dawn the next morning, the soldiers of the guard were summoned before the military tribunes. Quintus Sulpicius Lagus again appears as the senior commander on the Capitol and he, apparently, in accordance with the Roman attitude of the time, wanted all the members of the guard immediately executed for not spotting the Celtic attack before the warning of the geese. The soldiers of the garrison protested and in the end it was agreed that the poor sentry closest to the Celtic point of assault should be executed. The hapless man was thereby flung from the Tarpeian Rock to his death below. 'The memory of that night of peril led the Romans to keep a stricter watch; the Celts, too, began to tighten their precautions as it was common knowledge that messages were passing between Veii and the Capitol.'

Marcus Manlius was commended for his bravery and allowed to take the *cognomen* of 'Capitolinus' in honour of his exploit. He and his men were given half a pound of flour and a gill of wine each from the dwindling food stores as a reward. Even the geese were not forgotten for, thereafter, the feeding of 'the sacred geese of Juno' was made a charge on the state. They were carried on litters with purple and gold cushions in an annual ceremony while dogs (for the dogs had not barked a warning) were crucified on stakes of elder wood. This ritual survived into Christian times.

Marcus Manlius, however, was to meet his death at the very spot at which he had saved the Capitol. In the political vacuum and uncertainty which followed the Celtic withdrawal from Rome, Manlius, who had been made a consul, fell foul of the new Roman dictator when he supported the poor of the city who were suffering under the stringent laws. He was accused of plotting a revolution and attempting to make himself ruler. He was tried and sentenced to death. Livy says: 'The tribunes threw him from the Tarpeian Rock; so the same place commemorated one man's greatest hour of glory and the supreme penalty he paid.' Not content with Manlius' death they decreed that his house be pulled down and that no patrician henceforth be allowed to live on the Capitol. It was also ordered that no one of the clan of Manlius should henceforth bear the name Marcus. When some years later a plague broke out 'it was attributed by most people to the execution of Manlius; the Capitol (they said) had been polluted by the blood of its saviour, and the gods had been displeased when the man who had snatched their temples from the hands of their enemies had met his punishment practically before their very eyes.' But Marcus Manlius' death was to be some years in the future, in 384/383 BC.

Hunger was devastating the Roman garrison on the Capitol now. Livy makes out that the Celts were also starving which is a rather surprising claim as they were in command of the countryside and supplies. Varro tends to repeat Livy, adding that the Celts were perishing from pestilence and famine and that their bodies were collected and cremated after the evacuation of the city at a spot he calls the Busta Gallica – a *bustum* being the place where corpses were burned. Livy is clearly the source for this for he says:

> The Celts had disease as well to contend with, as the position they occupied on low ground between the hills was an unhealthy one, and rendered more so by the packed conditions of the earth after the conflagrations, and the heat, and the choking clouds of ashes and dust whenever the wind blew. Such conditions were intolerable to a people accustomed to a wet, cold climate; the heat stifled them, infection spread, and they were soon dying like cattle. Before long the survivors had not the energy to bury the dead separately, but piled the corpses in heaps and burnt them. The spot where they burnt them came afterwards to be known as the Celtic Pyres.

Livy says that an armistice was agreed and the opposing soldiers took the opportunity to speak with each other. The Celts told the Romans that they knew they were starving and that they ought to surrender. The Romans, trying to fool the Celts into believing they had plenty of food, would throw bread from the walls of the Capitol to the Celts below. But as the siege continued, the situation was becoming very desperate for the Romans. The Roman garrison realised that Camillus' new army was not going to be trained and ready in time to effect their rescue. The Roman senators realised that they must negotiate with the Celts and seek terms. It seems that the Senate had already put out 'feelers' and, in return, the Celts had let it be known that the sum for abandoning the siege and withdrawing from the city would not be exorbitant.

It has to be remembered that the Celts had only come to punish the

Romans for their arrogance and for breaking 'the law and customs of nations'. Even members of the Roman Senate and the *fetiales*, the patrician priesthood charged with looking after international law, had agreed that the complaint of the Celts was justified.

There were, of course, some Romans who were against any such negotiation. Many years later, in 321 BC, Lucius Lentulus, who had been consul in 328 BC, was making an address to the Senate. He is reported as having said:

'I have often heard my father recall that he was the only man on the Capitol who did not advise the Senate to buy off the city from the Celts with gold; he argued that the Romans were not shut in with ditch and rampart by their enemies, who were always very slow about starting an entrenchment and fortification, and it was possible to break out without inevitable disaster, if not without great danger. They had the chance of running down from the Capitol bearing arms against their attackers, as the besieged have often enough broken out against their besiegers . . .'

But no news had been received from Camillus and the Senate felt Lentulus' advice somewhat foolhardy in the circumstances. After seven months of siege, they authorised negotiations to start. Quintus Sulpicius Lagus and his senior officers conferred with Brennus and his chieftains. An agreement was reached that the city would pay 1000 pounds' weight of gold. The gold was duly brought and the Celts used their own weights which, according to the Romans, were heavier than their own standard. Sulpicius Lagus objected and Brennus flung his sword on to the scale, uttering the cry that was to become famous: *Vae victis!* Woe to the vanquished! In other words, though Livy does not spell it out, the conqueror dictates the terms.

What happened then is the subject of dispute.

According to one early source, Quintus Ennius (239–169 BC), considered one of the greatest and earliest of Roman poets, although he himself was born in Calabria and was part Oscan and part Greek, the Capitol actually fell to the Celtic warriors before the start of negotiations. He was a close friend of the Insubrean Celtic dramatist, Caecilius Statius, so he might well have picked up this story from the Celtic tradition and used it in his *Annales* (fragment 164), his epic history of Rome in eighteen books of which fewer than 600 lines survive.

The tradition that the Capitol actually fell to the Celts is also indicated by Tiberius Catius Asconius Silius Italicus (c.AD 26–c.AD 101) who was from Cisalpine Gaul. In his epic poem *Punica* (i. 525f., iv. 150f., and vi. 555f.) he also indicates that the Celts took the Capitol. Is he thereby recording a Cisalpine Celtic tradition?

To the contrary, according to Livy, Camillus arrived in the nick of time and ordered the gold to be removed and the Celts to leave. He is echoed with minor variations by Plutarch, Appian and Eutropius (AD 364–378). Clearly, Livy's account became popular with the Romans. But, in this account, we are asked to believe that the Celts meekly withdrew from the city and left the gold on the scales. They allow Camillus time to berate the Romans and tell them it is their duty to recover their country not by gold but by the sword. Plutarch says that Camillus arrived at the city during the weighing of the gold and marched in with just a small bodyguard. He simply walked through all the Celtic siege lines and sentinels to where the Celtic and Roman leaders were gathered around the weighing scales.

> These all made way for him in decorous silence, acknowledging him as their dictator. Thereupon he lifted the gold from the scales and gave it to his attendants and then ordered the Celts to take their scales and weights and be off, saying that it was the custom with the Romans to deliver their city with iron and not with gold. When Brennus in wrath declared that he was wronged by this breaking of the agreement, Camillus answered that the treaty was not legally made nor binding since he himself had already been chosen dictator and there was no other legal ruler; the agreement of the Celts had therefore been made with men who had no power in the case.

Even if we can believe this highly implausible account, one wonders if the niceties of the Roman system of government would have meant anything to the Celts in this situation. Plutarch says that the Celtic army, having captured Rome, occupied it for seven months and eventually negotiated an end to the matter, now calmly allowed Camillus and a few Roman soldiers to walk through their battle lines and start dictating in such a haughty fashion. It is utterly nonsensical.

Further we are told that Brennus submissively surrendered the city to a few Roman soldiers and retired outside the city walls to assemble for a battle. Yet this is what Livy and Plutarch would have us believe. The city not being a place for the military manoeuvres of fighting, explains Livy, Camillus led his men out after Brennus and began a battle with the Celts who, obligingly, had marched outside the city walls and waited while the rest of the Roman army arrived and organised themselves. The Celts, we are told, were then 'taken by surprise' and scattered. They regrouped 8 miles on the road to Gabii, half-way to Praeneste, where they also obligingly waited until Camillus marched his army up and fought another battle with them which he also won. Camillus then returned at the head of his victorious troops to be hailed as 'the second founder of Rome'.

Livy is clearly telling the Romans what they wanted to hear and not what actually happened. Polybius contradicts this account by saying that 'at that moment', while the negotiations over the ransom were taking place, 'an invasion of their own territory [in the Po Valley] by the Veneti diverted their attention, and so they made a treaty with the Romans, handed back the city and returned home. Later they became involved in domestic wars, for a number of the neighbouring Alpine tribes often joined forces against them and made raids on their territory when they saw what prosperity the Celts had achieved compared with their own situation.'

Polybius also has to be treated cautiously if we accept that the Senones who captured Rome were not settled in the Po Valley at this time. They had no territory there to be attacked for they had crossed the Apennines in search of land to settle and, as we shall later see, spent the next four decades in the vicinity of Apulia and Rome before settling in Picenum.

Then we have the Sicilian Greek historian, Diodorus Siculus, informing us that the Celts withdrew *with the gold* from Rome but were defeated in Sabine territory by an army of Etruscans from the city of Caere. Strabo also has the Celts evacuating Rome after the treaty and taking the gold with them.

The argument that the Celts took their ransom of a 1000 pounds' weight of gold and were able to withdraw without further conflict at the end of seven months is supported by other historical references. According to Greek historians, Massiliot ambassadors had been sent to Delphi just before the Celtic attack on Rome, to offer gifts to

Apollo. This was for their own safe delivery from an attack on Massilia by a Celtic army led by Catumandus. While returning to Massilia, they heard the news of the attack on Rome and the details of the ransom. The news of the Celtic capture of Rome certainly spread through the Greek world. Aristotle (384–322 BC) had, according to Plutarch, accurate knowledge of the capture of the city, although he referred to Marcus Camillus as Lucius. He confused him with Lucius Furius Camillus who was a consul in 349 BC and also fought against the Celts. Heracleides Ponticus, who was a contemporary to these events or lived shortly after, wrote a treatise 'On the Soul', and says that there was a story current of how 'an army of Hyperboreans' had come from afar and captured a 'Greek city' called Rome, situated somewhere on the shores of 'the Great Sea'. Could he have been confusing the stories of Catumandus' attack on Massilia and the sack of Rome? It seems likely.

The Greek Massiliots, who enjoyed an expanding trade with Rome, established public and private funds to help raise the money to pay the Roman tribute. For this act of friendship, Rome later concluded a treaty with the city, granting them trade immunities and a senatorial seat in the auditorium for the games. This is reported by the Celtic historian, Pompeius Trogus.

If Camillus had arrived and somehow retrieved the ransom and beaten off the Celts, such concessions to the Massiliots would have been irrelevant as would have been the raising of money to help the Romans pay the ransom. And if money had to be raised in Massilia to help pay the ransom, it would indicate that the negotiations and the time given for the Romans to come up with the money must have lasted a minimum of several weeks. Contrary to the idea that Camillus had stopped the gold being handed over, there are many speeches by Roman officials, recorded later, referring to their forefathers having to buy Rome's freedom with gold; something which would not be alluded to if Camillus had arrived before the Celts had taken the gold off the scales. Indeed, Camillus' subsequent victories over the Celts were not mentioned before the second century BC. Early sources all indicate that it took Rome fifty years before they could even begin to start to re-establish their domination over the communities of Latium who had taken the opportunity to reassert their independence. The Etruscans also enjoyed a resurgence of freedom thanks to the Celts. Even Plutarch says that fresh wars now broke out against Rome: the Aequians, Volscians and Latins rose against Rome while the Etruscans laid siege to Sutrium (Sutri), an Etruscan city which had attempted to maintain an alliance with Rome.

Over the next four or five decades, Celtic armies were still active within a few miles of Rome's walls and another battle was fought within sight of the Colline Gate itself. According to Polybius the Celts conducted no fewer than sixteen serious campaigns within the vicinity of Rome. Indeed, it seemed that the Senones were able to move into Apulia (Puglia) where they maintained a base through the mid-fourth century B C.

Professor Rankin believes that we can consign the account of Camillus' victories to historic myth and that we have in Livy merely a literary act of face-saving. The same may be said of Plutarch's account.

> ... after a long and fierce battle, the Romans routed the enemy with great slaughter and took their camp. Of the fugitives, some were at once pursued and cut down, but most of them scattered abroad only to be fallen upon and slain by the people of the surrounding countryside.

The evidence of what subsequently happened to the Senones weighs against the Roman account of their withdrawal from Rome. They were eventually able to establish themselves in a permanent tribal territory along the Adriatic coast between Ariminium (Rimini) and Ancona. The *Periplus* of the pseudo-Scylax, written about 350 B C, certainly puts the Celts on the Adriatic seaboard. Sena was considered to be their main city and takes its name from the tribe (modern Senigallia).

Livy believed that the Senones advanced not only to the outskirts of Ancona but into the valley of Chieti. Archaeological evidence supports this: Celtic remains and tombs have been found in the region of Filottrano and Osimo. The graves are surprisingly wealthy, with Celtic gold ornaments and Etruscan artifacts as well. A grave at San Paolino at Filottrano revealed a rich sword scabbard, dated to the late fourth century B C. This was found in 'Grave XXII' and its style of craftsmanship is comparable to decoration in the best 'Waldalgesheim style'. Both sword and scabbard were ritually bent to 'kill' the weapons so that no unworthy hand would bear this warrior's arms again. They are now in the Museo Nazionale delle Marche in Ancona.

At Montefortino, in the hinterland of Ancona, excavations have revealed Celtic graves that are well furnished with pottery and bronze containers of Greek and indigenous character, in addition to dice and gaming pieces and other objects showing that the Senones Celts took part in sports and even athletics. It was here in 1871 that the archaeologist Gabriel de Montillet first recognised the style of brooches and weapons and realised that this proved the Celts had settled in Italy. Celtic weapons occur in many graves. As we get into the third century BC the helmets are decorated in a mixed style, showing Celtic and Italic ornamental features. Drs Stead and Meeks refer to the fact that the type of helmet found at Montefortino was 'introduced to Italy by the Celts in the fourth century BC, adopted by the Etruscans and eventually developed into the Roman legionary helmet'. Celtic fibulae and rings resemble styles of La Tène art from Transalpine Gaul. In the grave of a woman at Filottrano we find a traditional Celtic gold torque. At Moscano di Fabriano, near Ancona, a warrior buried with his horse was discovered. Unfortunately, it is only the Celtic graves in this area which show the settlement of the Senones here. All traces of their towns and fortress have long since disappeared under new settlements. Dr Venecelas Kruta's work is the latest essential archaeological study in this area.

A point of interest is that many of the early Senones tombs are rich in gold objects – could these possibly have been manufactured from the gold paid to them by Rome? It is only a romantic thought for other stories appear in Roman history as to the recovery of the gold ransom. Gaius Suetonius Tranquillus (c.AD 70) mentions in his life of Tiberius (one of his 'Lives of the Caesars') a story about one Livius Drusus, a maternal ancestor of the Emperor Tiberius. This Drusus was said to have recovered the money paid for the redemption of Rome during the conquest of Gaul. It is an unlikely story, as if the 1000 pounds of gold had somehow been taken to a spot in Transalpine Gaul and remained preserved intact for over three centuries until, incredibly, identified and recovered.

For centuries the Romans were fascinated by the gold ransom paid to the Celts for the freedom of their city. Sextus Julius Frontinius (c.AD 30–c.104), who conquered the Celtic Silures of western Britain,

wrote about the gold, as did Marcus Junianus Justinus (Justin), in
the second or third century AD, and Polyaenus in the second century
AD. The Roman gold ransom took on an aspect of mystical pro-
portions, even more than the lost treasure of Delphi, looted by the
Celts in 279 BC.

Pliny the Elder (AD 23/4–79) repeats a tale of Marcus Licinius
Crassus (115–53 BC), consul in 70 BC and the general who defeated
Spartacus. During his second consulship with Pompey in 55 BC,
Crassus is said to have taken 2000 pounds' weight of gold from
under the throne of the Capitoline Jupiter where it had supposedly
been placed by Camillus. Half of the gold was said to be that recovered by Camillus from the Celts. However, the temple had been
destroyed by fire after the Celtic sack of Rome, notably in 83 BC.
It seems odd that any gold which Crassus took from the temple after
its rebuilding could have remained in the temple from the time of
Camillus. Even if it were so, we have no evidence that any of this
gold was recovered from the Celts.

I think we can accept part of the statement of Polybius in this
case. The treaty was made, the ransom in gold paid to the Senones,
at which time they then evacuated the city, having taught the Romans
a severe lesson for their arrogance and lack of respect for international law. The Romans were left to piece together their shattered
imperial illusions. Where Polybius is wrong is in the story of them
returning north of the Apennines to the Po Valley for they clearly
did not do so.

When the Celtic army had withdrawn, however, the Senate proposed that, with Rome having been almost destroyed, the entire
population should remove to Veii and establish themselves there.
Camillus, who had not given up his office as dictator, was not
pleased. He had opposed a colonisation of Veii by a group of Roman
plebeians before his exile. He was even more opposed to the aban-
donment of Rome by its entire population. According to Livy, Camillus made a long speech to argue against the idea. He argued that
he had not changed his feelings on the matter. He had always been
against the colonisation of Veii. The question was now whether
Rome should remain in existence.

'Why did we save Rome from the hands of the Celts, if we are to
desert her now? When the victorious Celts had the city in their

power, the gods of Rome and the men of Rome still clung to the Capitol and the Citadel – and shall we now, in the hour of deliverance, voluntarily abandon even those strongholds which we held through the days of peril?'

Camillus pointed out that if the people of Rome deserted Rome to colonise Veii it would be

'. . . a wretched and shameful thing – the Celts, not we, will glory in it, for it will be only too clear that we have not left our native city as conquerors, but lost it by defeat. The world will think that the rout on the Allia, the capture of Rome, and the siege of the Capitol have forced upon us the bitter necessity of deserting our beloved homes and of condemning ourselves to flee as exiles from a spot we had not the strength to defend. Must it be seen that the Celts could tumble Rome to the ground, while Romans are too weak to lift her up again? And suppose the Celts came back with another army? Suppose the Celts want to settle here, in this city they captured and which you deserted – what could you do but let them? Or maybe your old enemies the Aequians or Volscians might take it into their heads to do the same – and how would you like to change nationalities with them? Surely you would rather Rome were your own wilderness than built again to house your enemies?'

Camillus' oration is said to have moved his hearers. Livy had, of course, to add a portent. Some soldiers returning from guard duty were passing through the Forum where the Senate was gathered. The centurion in charge ordered them to halt. 'We might as well stop here,' he cried and his voice was heard by the Senate. The senators accepted the words as the omen that they might as well stop in Rome. The proposal to abandon the city and migrate to Veii was rejected and the Senate ordered the rebuilding of Rome.

Livy reports that the rebuilding work was ill planned. Permission to cut timber and quarry stone was granted without restriction and all the work was hurried. No one ever bothered to see that the streets were aligned properly. Individual property rights were ignored and buildings went up simply wherever there was room for them. 'This explains why the ancient sewers,' comments Livy, 'which originally followed the line of the streets now run in many places under private houses and why the general layout of Rome is more like a squatters' settlement than a properly planned city.'

Rome had paid dearly for the arrogance of the Fabii and for the further arrogance of supporting the Fabii when the Celtic envoys had arrived to ask for justice and restitution. The defeat of the Roman army at Allia and the subsequent capture and devastation of the city, the fact (in spite of Livy's propaganda) that Rome had to pay a ransom for her freedom, left an indelible racial hatred towards the Celts. No other people encountered by Rome were viewed with such bigotry and intolerance nor described with such venom and repugnance. The root of this was that Rome feared the Celts. The Greeks, on the other hand, although they too had encountered the Celts in battle, generally showed a more dispassionate approach, and even admired much about the Celts in warfare; they so respected Celtic philosophies that members of the Alexandrian school claimed the ancient Greeks had borrowed much of their philosophy from the Celts. Of course, some Greeks followed the Roman line but inevitably these were Greeks employed in Roman service. The Roman writers invariably painted the Celts as one step above the animal. Not only the Celts of Cisalpine Gaul were to suffer from the Roman prejudice and vindictiveness but Celts in whatever part of the world they were to be found. The reported words of Bennus, *Vae victis*!, were to be used by the Romans to destroy Celtic society wherever they encountered it.

[5]

Celtic Warriors

F OR THE next two centuries the Romans only knew the Celts of northern Italy as military adversaries who filled them with *terror Gallici nominis*. Dr P. F. Stary comments: 'For nearly 200 years the Celto-Italic wars determined Italian history.' Unlike the Greeks, who were interested in recording information on Celtic culture and had social contacts with the Celts as well as trading relationships, the Romans only met the Celts in war. And when the Romans described the Celts in terms of war, they did their best to disparage and degrade not only their abilities as fighting men but even their weapons.

Polybius, although a Greek, generally tends to please his Roman audience by dismissing the Celtic warriors as savage and lawless, no more than bands of marauders who were willing to join whichever side presented the best opportunity. The Romans painted the Celts as treacherous and claimed that the Carthaginians also found them untrustworthy allies. In spite of this, writers agreed on the courage of the Celtic warriors and on their enthusiasm during the initial actions of a battle. But they dwelt on the lack of stamina of the Celts. If the Romans could stand up to the first initial charge, then, they argued, the Celts became disheartened and exhausted and were quickly defeated.

Anyone who has read the accounts of the charge of the Scottish clans at Culloden in 1746 will see that the old Celtic style of fighting survived nearly 2000 years but it was hopeless against a ruthless, disciplined enemy. At Culloden the clansmen, armed with swords and bucklers, stood for twenty minutes under an horrendous cannonade which severely depleted their ranks before they were given permission to charge. When they did charge, they ran straight into both deadly cannon fire and fusillades from the muskets of the Duke of Cumberland's artillery. More than 2000 clansmen were slaughtered on the field. That charge, a ferocious impact from men carrying only swords and small shields, was the tactic witnessed by the Romans and once the legions learnt to withstand it, they stood a good chance of winning a set battle.

However, Rome did lose many battles to the Celts of Italy. Entire Roman armies were annihilated, even consular armies commanded by the most experienced of Rome's generals. The Celtic warriors were no easy pushover as most Roman accounts try to portray them. Dr Stary says: 'It seems that their [the Celts'] unconventional [to the Etruscans and Romans] warfare posed a real problem and compelled the reorganization of the native military systems. The Etruscans were not able to adapt completely to the new situation while the Romans . . . adapted to the new conditions.'

At the time when the Romans first met the Celts in battle, the Roman citizens had a duty to give military service as and when needed. A legion consisted of 6000 foot soldiers divided into sixty companies or centuries. Only later was the legion reduced to 5000 men and then, with the reforms of Marius at the start of the first century BC, returned to a strength of 6000 or more. The tactical formation at this time was to advance into battle in three lines of heavy armed infantry. Each line had ten *manipuli* or maniples of two centuries each. The first line were the *hastati* (spearmen – *hasta*, a spear), the second were the *principes* (men in prime of life) and the third were the *triarii* (third-liners). It was not until later that new weapons such as the *pilum* (throwing spear) replaced the *hasta*, and soldiers were given a *gladius* (sword) and a *scutum*, a long shield to replace the short buckler type.

In spite of Livy's and Polybius' biased views on Celtic weaponry, the Romans, though better organised, were not initially better armed which accounts for the many Celtic loan words in Latin connected with weapons and armour. 'Fortunately,' says Dr Stary, 'many Celtic weapons are known from graves, mainly in eastern and northern Italy, which give a good picture of the Celtic warrior's equipment and point to a longer occupation in these regions. Further, several Etruscan representations of Celtic warriors are known and form the basis for a better understanding of the Celtic influences on the superior [sic] Etruscan and Roman military systems.' One is obliged to point out that had the Etruscan and Roman military systems been superior, then there would have been no need for the massive upheavals caused by military reorganisation and the Romans' adaptation of Celtic weapons for their own use.

Celtic warriors were certainly well armoured. Iron helmets had ousted the weaker bronze war helmets by the fourth century BC. Some of these helmets had fabulous decorations, often with extraordinary crests, hinged cheek pieces, internal neck guards and other embellishments. Diodorus Siculus says:

> On their heads they wear bronze helmets which possess large projecting figures of enormous stature to the wearer. In some cases horns form one part with the helmet, while in other cases it is relief figures of the fore parts of birds or quadrupeds.

The style of the Celtic helmet was new to both Etruscan and Roman. It was a round cap surmounted by a knob with neck and cheek guards. According to Dr Stary:

> This type of helmet was a Celtic invention, which the Celtic tribes brought to Italy during their invasions from the late fifth century onwards, and which were rapidly adopted by the Etruscans and Romans. The Celtic tradition is also evident in a chamber tomb from Perugia, where a knob helmet was associated with a typical Celtic two edged sword.

Dr Stary amplifies:

> The Etruscans and also the Romans adopted these helmets from the Celts, a phenomenon which may astonish us . . . The knob helmet was very suitable for flexible warfare, and was therefore taken over by the Etruscans and Romans, as is shown by representations such as those in the Tomba dei Rilievi in Cerveteri and finds from warrior graves.

The astonishment would only be caused by an acceptance of Roman propaganda about the Celts. Dr Stary adds:

> The knob helmet was used by the Romans with . . . variations for many centuries. One technological improvement seems to have been invented by the Etruscans; the sickle shaped cheek piece

which is known from former Greco-Etruscan types and which replaced the traditional Celtic cheek piece formed of three rounded discs in the shape of a trefoil.

The Celts also had a better shield than the early Romans, one which protected them more efficiently. Diodorus Siculus observed: 'For arms they have man-sized shields decorated in a manner peculiar to them. Some of these have projecting figures in bronze, skilfully wrought not only for decoration but for protection.' Dr Stary observes:

Most of the representations of Celts are characterised by another arm, the oval shield with spindle shaped boss, as on warrior slabs from Castiglioncella, on figures of warriors in the miniatures from Telamon, associated with knob helmets, and also on representations of Celtic warriors and battles from northern Italy . . .

It seems that the Latin word for shield, *scutum*, has its origin in the word which provides the basis of the Irish *sciath* and the Welsh *ysgwyd*, meaning both shield and shoulder. Attempts to explain the word *scutum* from a Latin root *obscurus* or even a Greek root do not ring true. It is noted that *scutum* was a word especially used for a large tall shield; the sort of man-sized shield which Diodorus Siculus describes. What is also interesting is that the innovation of the longer Roman shield, the *scutum*, is attributed to Camillus after the Celts had withdrawn from Rome. According to Plutarch, in his biography of Camillus, the military changes came with the second Celtic attack on Rome.

Knowing the prowess of the Barbarians lay chiefly in their swords, which they plied in true barbaric fashion, and with no skill at all, in mere slashing blows at head and shoulders, he had helmets forged for most of his men which were all iron and smooth of surface, that the enemy's swords might slip off from them or be shattered by them. He also had the long shields of his men rimmed round with bronze, since their wood could not of itself ward off the enemy's blows. The soldiers themselves he trained to use their long javelins like spears – to thrust them under the enemy's swords and catch the downward strokes upon them.

Polyaenus (second century AD) seems to quote Plutarch in his *Strate-gemata*, on military strategy, but says that Camillus had the Roman 'shields sheathed with copper, as wood alone was no protection against the blows' thus indicating that the early Roman shields were just wooden bucklers. Speaking of the large, oval shield, Dr Stary says:

> Whether the Etruscans adopted these shields is impossible to say: the only known Etruscan representations are of Celtic warriors. But it is possible that this shield type was used by some Etruscan troops and it is evident that it was adopted by the Roman army. A modified type of Celtic knob helmet, together with the Celtic oval shield with spindle shaped boss, represented the typical Roman equipment of the last centuries BC; the Roman expansion and conquest distributed these types over many parts of the eastern Mediterranean including Egypt.

Both Polybius and Plutarch say that Camillus observed that the strength of the Celtic warriors lay in their swords. But Polybius, apparently quoting Quintus Fabius Pictor, says the Celtic swords were inferior to the Roman swords since they only cut.

Yet Henri Hubert observed: 'It is generally accepted today that the Latin world *gladius* for sword is of Celtic origin.' This was also claimed by Joseph Vendryes. The word is certainly cognate with the Irish *claideb* and the Welsh *cleddyf* meaning sword. Some ancient historians say that the Romans adopted this sword from the Celtiberians because it had the advantage for cutting and thrusting. It seems that if this happened the *gladius* was not adopted until the third century BC. A suggestion that the word developed from a common Indo-European root has also been argued but without much support.

The observations of later Roman or Roman-orientated writers seem at odds with the evidence. Polybius says of the Celts: 'Their shields were worse in terms of protection and their swords were worse for attack because the Celtic sword has only the cutting edge.' Later he adds: 'The Roman shields, it should be added, were much more serviceable for defence and their swords for attack, the Celtic sword being good only for a cut and not for a thrust.' Could it be that most of the later Roman writers had forgotten, or wished to forget, the military innovations forced on the Romans by the superiority of Celtic weapons of the fourth century BC?

According to Dr Stary: 'It is evident that the Celtic invasions were not merely a short-lived episode within the military development of Central Italy, but were a major influence on the Etruscan and Roman military systems.'

F. Vegetius Renatus (fourth century AD) is quite clear that the Romans had to learn new methods to combat the tactics and equipment of the Celtic warriors.

The ancient Romans were likewise taught not to cut but to thrust with their swords. For the Romans not only made a jest of those who fought with the edge of that weapon, but always found them an easy conquest. A stroke with the edge, though made with ever such force, seldom kills, as the vital parts of the body are defended by both the arms and armour. On the contrary, a stab, although it penetrated but two inches is invariably fatal.

No authority seems to comment on the Celts using the thrusting technique although many of the Celtic swords have been found to have long parallel cutting edges and prominent points. Polybius says: 'The Celtic sword could only be used with the cutting edge and then only from a distance.' The results of the new Roman short sword opposing a Celtic long sword were predictable. Dionysius says:

Agile their foes were, still raising their swords aloft, but the Romans would duck under their arms, holding up their shields, and then stooping and crouching low, they would render vain and useless the blows of the others, which were aimed too high, while waiting for their own part, holding their swords straight out, they would strike their opponents in the groin, pierce their sides, and drive their blows through their breast into their vitals.

The Celts gave to the Romans the words for a variety of spears and javelins. The word *lancea* described a light spear and this has come into English as lance. The *mataris*, from which come *matara* and *materi*, was a pike. A *gaesum* was a strong and heavy javelin; the root *gae* for spear is still easily recognisable in Irish. There was also a *tragula*, originally meaning a light javelin but which Pliny uses as a name for a Celtic sledge.

Strabo summed up the general view of the Celtic warrior when he said: 'Their arms correspond in size with their physique; a long sword fastened on the right side and a long shield and spears of like dimension.'

Dr Stary comments:

> . . . elements of the Celtic warrior's equipment were adopted by the Etruscans and more especially by the Romans . . . The Etruscans were finally unable to adapt completely to the new military phenomena of the Celtic wars, and were forced to hand over their cultural and military hegemony to the Romans, who read the signs of the new age and introduced effective foreign arms and tactics, which they developed to perfection. Their feeling for ability to adapt and develop them, of which they were proud, as Roman sources show, made them finally into the rulers of the ancient world in the late first century BC and early first century AD.

It is impossible to agree with Dr Stary that Rome acknowledged, or was proud of, its debt to Celtic technology in any field.

The Celts fought as a tribal army and were probably divided into septs or sub-divisions of the tribe just as they were over 2000 years later at Culloden. It might even be, judging from the divisions of the Scottish clan army of 1745, that each sept had a hereditary place in the line of battle. The MacDonalds of the Isles always fought on the right of the army and it was their complaint at Culloden that they had been placed on the left wing. Their chieftains claimed descent from Conn of the Hundred Battles. There were a hundred or more septs within the MacDonalds.

The Celtic military system, as it survived in Scotland in 1745, was that every male over the 'age of choice', usually seventeen years old, and fit enough to carry arms was automatically part of the 'regiment' of his clan or tribe. The chieftain was the automatic commander. Brother fought with brother, father with son. Each clan had its own badge, not the tartans of Sir Walter Scott's nineteenth-century imaginings, but a piece of heather, oak, myrtle, holly or other plant fastened on a man's bonnet. Each clan rallied with its own *sluagh gairm* or war cry, the words now adopted into English as one –

'slogan'. They marched into battle with pipes playing, drums beating and voices raised in war songs or battle cries. They were not much different from their ancestors who went into battle against the Romans.

Livy describes how the Celts of earlier times used such noise and tumult to throw their enemies into confusion and terror. 'They are given to wild outburst and they fill the air with hideous songs and varied shouts.' Further, 'their songs as they go into battle, their yells and leapings, and the dreadful noise of arms as they beat their shields in some ancestral custom – all this is done with one purpose, to terrify the enemy.' Diodorus Siculus says that the Celts had trumpets (*carnyx*) that were peculiar to them. 'When they blow upon them, they produce a harsh sound, suitable to the tumult of war.'

Archaeology has shown many examples of Celtic trumpets. The mouthpiece of one trumpet, in the shape of a boar's head, was found in Banff; this shape may be compared with representations on the Gundestrup Cauldron. There are early representations of trumpets on a triumphal Roman arch at Orange in southern France where a few fragments of actual trumpets have been discovered.

Diodorus adds that the Celts had particular shouts of victory and triumph: 'They shouted "Victory! Victory!" in their customary fashion and raised their yell of triumph [*ululatus*].' At the battle of Alesia, Julius Caesar records, 'they encouraged their men with shouts of triumph [*clamore et ululatu*].' The word actually chosen, *ululatus*, means more a howl or wail.

In sharp contrast to the tumult and noise of the Celtic mass charge, we hear of the silent, orderly advance of the Roman soldiers. The contrast is carefully made by the Roman writers to show their 'civilised' superiority.

In the initial encounters between the Romans and the Celts, it was the fact that the Celts used war chariots which attracted the Romans' attention. The Celts, being highly mobile, had developed the use of transport and constructed roads which ranged through Europe long before the Romans. The Celts moved vast distances and this, of course, meant they had developed an advanced system of transport. It is ironic that the Romans now take credit for being the road builders of the ancient world. Even the Greeks had a network of roads, levelled and some of them paved and designed to serve the purposes of trade and communication. The first roads constructed by the Romans, and created for military and political purposes rather than economic and trading ones, appeared nearly a hundred years after the first Celts arrived at the gates of Rome. According to tradition such roads were initiated by Appius Claudius the Censor in 312 BC.

Dr Anne Ross observed in *Everyday Life of the Pagan Celts* (1970):

> That some provision for all this activity and coming and going must have been made in the way of roads is clear; and it is an aspect of Celtic life which cannot simply be ignored. But it is an extremely difficult subject because the evidence for roads is scant and unsatisfactory in the Celtic countries as elsewhere in the barbarian world in pre-Roman times. It was not until the first and second centuries AD, under the Roman Emperors, that the great network of roads in Europe took shape. It has been claimed that this was possible because there was already an existing and efficient system of native roads which the Romans proceeded to improve upon . . .

Certainly the evidence, scant as it is, is there. Diodorus Siculus, in talking about merchants taking heavy goods wagons into the Celtic country, implies the existence a system of roads, as does the use of chariots. It is interesting that the Celtic god Taranis, the thunder god, is symbolised in the Celtic world by a wheel.

Many of the words connected with roads and transport in Latin are, in fact, Celtic loan words. The late Professor Stuart Piggott estimated that there were no fewer than nineteen Celtic words connected with roads and transport, which the Romans received into pre-empire Latin. In his study *The Earliest Wheeled Transport*, Professor Piggott points to 'the rich vocabulary of Celtic loan-words' in Latin in this area. 'The Celtic vehicle words in Latin seemed roughly divisible into two groups, the majority being those absorbed in the language at a relatively early date and then used for a variety of Roman wagons, carriages and two-wheelers; a plausible origin would be among the Cisalpine Gauls.'

Livy seems to be one of the first to record the Celtic *carpentum*, a two-wheeled carriage, later used specifically as a baggage wagon, from which a number of European languages developed words such as carpenter, car, cart and so forth. The word comes from the Celtic root *carbanto*, which emerged in such place-names as Carbantorate, Carpentorate and Carbantoritum. By the time of Propertius, Juvenal and Suetonius it was in general use in Latin to mean a civil vehicle built especially for women. Florus uses the word to describe the silver-mounted vehicle in which the Arverni chieftain Bituitus was paraded after his defeat in 121 BC. Florus also uses it to describe the Cimbric vehicles.

There was the *carruca*, a four-wheeled carriage, and the *carrus*, which was a four-wheeled goods wagon. The *essedum*, a Celtic war chariot, was also adopted into Latin, and the warrior who fought from this chariot was known as an *essedarius*. This comes from the Celtic *ensedo*, implying something for sitting in. The *essedum* became a Roman pleasure carriage and during the time of Seneca they were all too common in Rome. But, as Professor Piggott points out, 'we are in a world where foreign names are in use for wholly Roman vehicles, like nineteenth-century London when gentlemen might discuss the relative comfort of the beline or landau as against brougham and tilbury.'

The *reda* or *rheda*, a four-wheeled carriage used for journeying long distances, driven by a *redarius*, was also taken from Celtic into Latin, as was the *petorritum*, an open four-wheeled Celtic wagon. It was Martial, an Iberian Celt, who introduced a new Celtic loan word – *covinus*, a war chariot, which eventually became a Roman *covinarius* or travelling cart. The word comes from the Celtic *co-vignos*, implying a shared transport. But Martial has it as scythed or with *falces* fitted to its axles.

Another Celtic term was *plaustrum* or *ploxenum* of which Quintilian, quoting Catullus, noted that '*ploxenum circa Padum invenit*' – showing that this wagon came from Cisalpine Gaul. Cato, Varro and Virgil all describe it as a heavy-duty wagon drawn by oxen, asses or mules with disc wheels and iron tyres and an axle turning with the wheels. Curiously, Ovid uses the word *plaustrum* as a name given by the Celts for the constellation of the Great Bear (Ursus Major).

Piggott writes: 'To the dozen or so words for vehicles can be added others associated with horses, including *caballus* itself and *badius* a chestnut bay colour . . .' *Caballus*, which Horace and Juvenal used as meaning a pack horse, gives English the words cavalier, cavalry, cavalcade. The word also finds its way into place-names such as

Cabillonum, a town of the Aedui, now Châlons-sur-Saône. Other words imported from Celtic include *equus*, a horse, *mannus* and *mannulus*, a small type of horse, and *leuga*, borrowed into Latin as a measure of distance on a journey equivalent to 1.5 Roman miles. From this word comes the English 'league', now used mainly as a poetic form.

It should be pointed out that not all the rich vocabulary of Celtic words in Latin was simply the result of Roman contacts with the Cisalpine Celts. Dr Bonfante has observed: 'When Caesar opened up the north . . . Celtic styles and artifacts became fashionable . . . this fashion for northern styles was an ephemeral fad, soon supplanted by the rage for Egyptian antiquities.'

Chariots in battle were something new to the Romans. Chariots as war machines had fallen into disuse in the ancient world centuries before the Roman-Celtic collision. They were used, by the Celts, mainly on the flanks with cavalry. In the initial stages of a battle they would drive against the enemy at speed for the purpose of causing panic. A thousand Celtic chariots took part in the battle of Sentium (295 BC) and chariots were used at Telamon (225 BC). In one conflict Livy notes: 'Many of the first line [of Romans] were trodden underfoot by the rush of horses and chariots.' But after that first charge it seemed that the chariot became a means of transporting the warriors to their combat positions as foot soldiers, just as they had done in Homeric Greece.

Diodorus Siculus commented: 'When going into battle, the Celts use two-horsed chariots which carry the charioteer and the warrior. When they meet with cavalry in war, they throw their javelins at the enemy, and, dismounting from their chariots, they join battle with their swords . . . They also bring freemen as servants choosing them from among the poor, and these they use as charioteers and shield bearers.'

Gradually, the use of chariots as war machines among the Celts gave way to their use as ritual carriages for chieftains. Chariots seem to have fallen out of use among the Continental Celts after the battle of Telamon. Julius Caesar seemed surprised when he found that they were still in use in Britain during his invasions. He wrote:

> In chariot fighting the Britons begin by driving all over the field hurling javelins, and generally the terror inspired by the horses

and noise of the wheels is sufficient to throw their opponents' ranks into disorder. Then, after making their way between the squadrons of their own cavalry, they jump down from the chariots and engage on foot. In the meantime their charioteers retire a short distance from the battle and place the chariots in such a position that their masters, if hard pressed by numbers, have an easy means of retreat to their own lines. Thus they combine the mobility of cavalry with the staying power of infantry; and by daily training and practice they attain such proficiency that, even on a steep incline, they are able to control the horses at full gallop, and to check and turn them in a moment. They can run along the chariot pole, stand on the yoke, and get back into the chariot as quick as lightning.

Caesar confesses that the soldiers of his VII Legion were unnerved by the British Celtic chariots. Remains of such chariots have been found in Parisii Celtic graves in Yorkshire and are usually of the two-wheeled type drawn by two horses. These are also found in Celtic graves in France and Germany and date back to the fifth century BC.

The chariot motif was common on Celtic coins. Archaeologists have found that the construction of early chariots showed advanced craftsmanship. Wheels were strengthened by iron rims or tyres made in one piece and set round the wheel while it was still hot; this compressed the wood as it cooled, so strengthening it. The spokes were lathe-turned, usually of willow, around a similarly turned hub of elm. The yoke had a series of bronze rings through which the reins were threaded to allow the charioteer greater control of the horses. The leather harnesses were elaborate and well made, with richly decorated ornamental pieces usually of bronze and inlaid with coral or enamel.

Another formidable aspect of a Celtic army was the cavalry. The Celts developed a reputation for excellence in mounted warfare. Like the chariots, Celtic cavalry combined mobility and staying power for the cavalryman would not only unnerve the enemy by shock charges but would also dismount and fight. The Celtiberians were noted for having small pegs attached to their horses' reins. They rode into battle, then dismounted and fixed the pegs into the ground so that the horses would not stray until they returned. Pausanias, describing

Celtic cavalry in Greece, talks of groups of three horsemen called a *trimarcisia – marca* was a Celtic word for a horse. One of the riders would be the warrior and he would be attended by two others. He would ride into battle and the two others would stay behind the ranks. If the warrior needed a fresh horse they would be ready to supply him. If he were wounded or killed, then one of them would take his place while the other took his body back to camp. Diodorus adds that 'when they have defeated [the enemy] cavalry, they dismount and assuming the role of infantry, they stage marvellous battles . . .'

At the other end of the Celtic world, in the Iberian peninsula, Poseidonius tells us that the Celtiberians possessed horses of fine quality and that their cavalrymen and horses were trained to such a degree that, in case of necessity, at a word of command from the rider, the horses would sink to their knees. They had a tactic of mounting two men on one horse so that in the event of an engagement one might be at hand to fight on foot. Strabo and Pliny mention the fleetness of Celtiberian horses. While the Romans came up against them during their conquest of the Celtiberians, they probably first encountered such horses during Hannibal's invasion of Italy. The names of two Celtiberian breeds of horses found their way into Latin: *celdones* from Gallaecia (Galicia) and *asturcones* from Asturias.

Livy, of course, has much to say about the tactics of Celtic cavalry. The Spartans respected Celtic cavalry when they fought for them against the Thebans. The Hellenic kingdoms were among the first to hire the services of Celts as mercenaries, in particular as cavalry. The Carthaginians also used cavalry to good effect and even the Romans, in spite of their sneering criticisms, employed Celtic cavalry as auxiliaries in their army after they had conquered the Cisalpine Celts, the Celtiberians and Transalpine Gaul. Celtic cavalry became an essential part of the empire of the Caesars. While the Germanic tribes did not develop a saddle, the Celtic saddles were very intricate. In fact the Celts made a key technical innovation by introducing a four-pommel saddle. Archaeologists once thought that cavalry had only limited effectiveness until the invention of the stirrup but the saddle used by the Celts in the late La Tène period provided a firm seat by means of the four pommels, two behind the rump and one angled out over each thigh. The rider sat in, rather on, this saddle.

Early Rome did not seem to develop any strong feelings for the use of cavalry in battle. Initially Roman cavalry was a small group of wealthy Roman citizens, the *equites*, who were the 'knights'. This social class was drawn from the wealthiest families. Each was given a horse from state funds. By the second century BC the cavalry was raised from the levies of the conquered peoples, such as the Celts, while the equestrian order served as staff officers in the army and not as a cavalry unit. Strabo, expressing his admiration of the Celtic cavalry, says that during his day the best cavalry in the service of the Roman empire was the Celtic cavalry. 'Although they are all fine fighting men,' he says, 'yet they are better as cavalry than as infantry, and the best of the Roman cavalry is recruited from among them.'

Another Greek observer, from Nicomedia in Bithynia, who made a successful career in the Roman army, Flavius Arrianus or Arrian (b.*c.*AD 85–90), was deeply impressed by Celtic cavalry and says that the Romans even borrowed cavalry tactics from them and that later the Celts were an important element in the army. He describes military manoeuvres.

Those [Celtic cavalrymen] who are conspicuous ... for skill in horsemanship ride into the mock battle armed with helmets made of iron or brass and covered with gilding to attract the particular attention of the spectators. They have yellow plumes attached to the helmets, not to serve any other useful purpose than for display. They carry oblong shields, unlike the shields for a real battle but lighter in weight – the object of the exercise being smartness and display – and gaily decorated. Instead of breastplates, they wear tunics, made just like real breastplates, sometimes scarlet, sometimes purple, sometimes multi-coloured. And they have hose, not loose like those in fashion among the Parthians and Armenians, but fitting closely to the limbs.

Perhaps one of the most significant tributes the Romans could make to the effectiveness of Celtic cavalry was the adoption of the Celtic horse goddess Epona (from the Celtic *epos*, a horse) as part of the official Roman religion. Epona was worshipped throughout the Roman empire and even in Rome where she had her own official feast day in the Roman calendar on 18 December. That the Romans themselves would recognise a Celtic deity is a rare occurrence. The cult of the divine 'horsewoman' was found throughout the Celtic world and one fascinating portrayal of her, indicating the symbolism of geese in the Celtic world, shows her astride a goose.

Epona became particularly popular among Romans between the first and fourth centuries AD. Many Roman writers incorporate stories of her into their works, including the greatest of Rome's satirical poets, Decimus Junius Juvenalis (Juvenal), who flourished in the early second century AD and who mentions her in *Satires* VIII, Lucius Apuleius (*c*.AD 155), the author of the only Latin novel that survives entire – *Metamorphoses* III – and Marcus Minucius Felix (flourished AD 200–240), who was an early Latin Christian and who mentions her in *Octavianus* XXVII. Epona even appears in an anonymous Greek text which recounts a myth in which a man named Phoulouios Sellos copulates with a mare, the result of the union being a beautiful baby girl whom the mare names Epona. There is an echo here of the symbolism of the Irish kingship ritual referred to by Gerald of Wales (Giraldus Cambrensis) in his *Expurgatio Hibernica*. In this he describes the inauguration of an Irish king. A mare was ritually slaughtered and the king-elect ate the flesh of the beast, then drank and bathed in a broth made from the carcass. It was a ritual in which the king sought fertility for himself and his people. This ritual of horse sacrifice appears in another Indo-European culture, the Hindu ritual of *asvamedha*.

The main point, of course, was that Epona would have been the patron of all cavalrymen. As a deity she was the protector of their horses and themselves, and would thus have easily infiltrated into Roman religious worship. As Dr Miranda Green points out: 'Celtic cavalry was renowned throughout the known world, and Gaulish horses were an integral part of the Imperial Roman Army.'

There is evidence that the Celts used bows and slings but usually as defensive weapons. Caesar reported that the Gauls would place their archers among the cavalry to support them; if the cavalry had to fall back, archers would cover the withdrawal. As in all armies, however, the mainstay was the foot soldiers who were usually armed with javelin, sword and shield.

The warriors wore clothing that the Romans found colourful and striking. According to Diodorus Siculus, the Celts 'wear colourful clothing, tunics dyed and embroidered in many colours, and garments which they call *bracae* [breeches]; and they wear striped cloaks, fastened by a brooch, thick in winter and light in summer, worked in a variegated, closely set pattern.' The trousers were in particular worn by Celtic cavalrymen; being such a strange garment to the toga-wearing Romans, they were quickly noticed and adopted by the Romans whence the Celtic word *bracae* came into the Latin language and from it made its way in local form to many other languages including English (as 'breeches'). Irish still has the word *bríste* for trousers. Linen shirts and tunics were also used and shoes of leather. The Celts liked wearing ornaments, including gold bracelets, and brooches, with which their cloaks were fastened; leading warriors and chieftains wore a gold necklace, a torque, around their necks.

It later became fashionable in Rome to wear a *sagus* (later *sagum*), a Celtic warrior's cloak of coarse wool. The word was used symbolically by Cicero in the phrases *saga sumere*, or *ad saga ire* – to take up arms or prepare for war – and *saga ponere*, to lay down arms. Another Celtic cloak used by the Romans was the *caracallus* (hooded cloak). The word became *cacullus* and eventually gave English the word 'cowl' with cognates to be found in many other European languages. The *cadurcum* was a fashionable linen coverlet made by the Cadurci Celts of Aquitania who became famous in Rome for their linen products.

What particularly fascinated the early Romans was the fact that some Celtic warrior bands fought naked. Appian claims that Camillus captured some of these Celts and 'showed them naked to the Romans, saying: "These are the creatures who assail you with such terrible cries in battle, bang their swords and spears on their shields to make a din, and shake their long swords and toss their hair."' These warrior bands were later wrongly identified as a tribe called the Gaesatae. Polybius describes a contingent of Gaesatae at Telamon. They went into battle with only sword and shield. As we will see when discussing Telamon, the Gaesatae were not a tribe at all but a group of élite professional warriors who fought naked for religious purposes as they believed it enhanced their martial karma, their spiritual vibrations in battle. Dionysius of Halicarnassus also observed these naked warriors: 'Our enemies fight bare-headed, their breasts, sides, thighs, legs are all bare, and they have no protection except from their shields; their weapons of defence are thin spears and long swords. What injury could their long hair, their fierce looks, the clashing of their arms and the brandishing of their arms do us?'

But he does add that not all Celts fought naked for he goes on to describe others in clothing and armour.

The fact was that the majority of the Celts did not fight naked, only these élite groups. The use of body armour among the Celtic tribes is confirmed by archaeological finds and even by Roman representations of the Celts. Indeed, one of the Celtic technical innovations was the invention of chain mail around 300 BC. Didorus Siculus mentions this, and shirts of interlocking iron rings have been found at Celtic sites. These were labour intensive products and so only leading chieftains could probably afford to wear them. These chain mail shirts became highly prized among the Romans who soon adopted the idea. The Latin word *cataphractes* for a chain mail shirt has been argued to come from the Celtic root *cat* for war or battle rather than Latin *catena* meaning a fetter or chain. Similarly, the word *caterva*, first used for a company of 'barbarian' (Celtic) soldiers, uses that root. Cicero, oddly enough, later applied the word to a company of actors.

When the Celts won victories over the Romans, Roman historians would dismiss their prowess as simply being the outcome of sheer ferocity. Diodorus talks of their 'senseless bravado':

> Thus, at one moment, they would raise their swords aloft and smite after the manner of wild boars, throwing the whole weight of their bodies into the blow like hewers of wood or men digging with mattocks, and again they would deliver crosswise blows aimed at no target as if they intended to cut to pieces the entire bodies of their adversaries, protective armour and all . . .

We find similar references to the Celts being ferocious and wild in battle in the works of Livy, Florus and others. They talk of the Celts 'fighting like wild beasts', without leadership, without discipline and manoeuvring in battle unintelligently. Yet Livy can, in contradiction, then speak of the closed defensive ranks of the Celtic warriors at Sentium and the fact that they deployed a *testudo* – a battle tactic called a 'tortoise' in which fighting men locked shields together to form an impregnable wall. The Romans copied this manoeuvre, once having adopted the Celtic shield – for it is clear that such interlocking could not be achieved with the original Roman round shield or buckler – and now the *testudo* is regarded as a Roman battle tactic.

Polybius also admired the defensive formations of the Gaesatae at Telamon as well as their gallantry in battle.

If the Celts were initially able to teach the Romans a thing or two about warfare, why is it that the Celts, with the exception of those in Ireland and northern Britain, were eventually defeated and conquered by the expanding empire of Rome? The reason has been clearly stated by Dr Simon James who says it lies in the contrasting natures of the two societies. They thought about war and waged it in different ways. War to the Celts was a matter of honour, of individual courage. Celtic armies tended to be fragile because they were a group of individuals, competing with each other to display valour as much as to secure a victory over the enemy. The Celts rejected authority and discipline. They thought as individuals and were natural anarchists. In modern times the attributes are seen as laudable. Unfortunately, they can be observed, throughout Celtic history, as the reason for the downfall of the Celtic peoples.

As we shall later discuss, war for the Celts could begin and end with a personal single combat. As Diodorus Siculus remarks, it was the Celtic custom, when gathered for a battle, for a warrior to step out of the ranks and challenge the most valiant champion among the enemy to a single combat, brandishing his weapons, boasting of his deeds and those of his ancestors in order to break the nerve of his opponent. Depending on the results of the combat the entire battle could be decided.

For the Romans, war was a cold-blooded profession. The legionaries had been trained to fight as units, unquestioningly obeying the commands of their officers, relying on their fellows to act with them as a cohesive force. Roman generals wrote and studied military treatises, and planning and method became important. That planning, that ruthlessness, finally gave Rome the military advantage. Indeed, a certain lack of humanity, a devotion to discipline, and a severity of punishment to any who transgress that commitment to the will of a central power, appear necessary for the growth of an imperial regime. The Roman legionary had to be more frightened of his superiors than he was of the enemy. The same principle has often applied in modern armies.

[6]

The Return of the Celts

THE ANNALIST, Quintus Claudius Quadrigarius, says that a
Celtic army reappeared near Rome in the year 367 BC. To
counter this threat, the then ageing Camillus was appointed
dictator for the fifth time. Who were these Celts? It seems obvious
that they were further war bands from the Senones who were still
carrying the war to Rome. At this early stage of the conflict between
Rome and the Celts, the major tribes in the Po Valley, the Boii,
Insubres and Cenomani, appear to have been pursuing a more peaceful agricultural life, while the Senones were more restless. It is reason-
able to suppose that the Senones had not yet settled in the area of
Picenum. The tribe seem to have been constantly on the move. We
have to ask ourselves the question why, when they had received their
gold from Rome and concluded a treaty with the Senate, the Senones
kept reappearing over the next decades. The answer is that they
returned not simply on their own terms but as allies of the Latin
cities opposed to Rome.

Had the words of Brennus to the Fabii brothers before Clusium
been prophetic? 'Cease, therefore, to pity the Clusians when we
besiege them, that you may not teach the Celts to be kind and full
of pity towards those who are wronged by the Romans.' Had their
experience with Rome demonstrated to the Celts that not even
Rome's close neighbours, the cities of Latium, accepted Roman dominance, and had these cities offered friendship and alliance to the
Celts? We also know that within two decades of their defeat of the
Romans, the Celts were joining forces with the Greeks of southern
Italy against Rome. We will come to this shortly.

The Celts reappear in a battle recorded as having taken place near
the River Anio, a tributary of the Tiber. This engagement is reported
by some authorities as having been settled by a single combat between
Titus Manlius and a Celtic warrior. However, Livy thought Quad-

rigarius mistook the date of this combat when he recorded it as 367 BC. Livy was inclined to believe that the Manlius combat took place later and the battle in 367 BC was fought in the vicinity of the city of Alba, not near the Anio. Plutarch, however, says that a battle took place at the River Anio 'thirteen years after the capture of Rome' thus placing it either in 377 or 374 BC, depending whose dating you use. Are we talking about several different battles or one at the Anio and one in the Alban hills?

We know that Plutarch says that the Romans 'mightily feared these barbarians who had conquered them in the first instance . . . so great had their terror been that they made a law exempting the priests from military service *except in the case of a Celtic war* [my italics].' Of this second war with the Celts, Livy says that this was where the ageing Camillus met a Celtic army in the vicinity of the city of Alba, 13 miles (20 kilometres) south-east of Rome. 'The Romans won a victory which was never in doubt, without much difficulty, although they were in great terror of the Celts through the recollection of their earlier defeat.'

Plutarch confirms that Camillus was 'now quite old, lacking little of eighty years; but recognising the peril and the necessity which it laid upon him, he neither made excuse, as before, nor resorted to pretext, but instantly took upon him the command and went to levying his soldiers.'

Livy claims that the Celts were killed in their thousands, their camp was captured and the few survivors were dispersed, fleeing towards Apulia. This 'victory' has the sound of a Roman boast again because a few months later, early in the following year, Livy admits that there was panic in Rome with widespread rumours of an impending Celtic attack from their bases in Apulia. If the Celts had suffered such a devastating defeat as Livy suggests, they would hardly have been in a position to cause the Roman citizens fly into a panic a few months later. Livy, I believe, is just whistling in the dark.

Archaeological evidence confirms the presence of the Celts in Apulia. One of the most interesting finds was a rich burial vault in Canosa di Puglio, the site of ancient Canusium, in 1897. It appeared to be of a Celtic warrior with a rich assemblage of gold, bronze and glass objects dated to the late fourth century BC. Among the objects, including spears and armour, was a bronze and iron war helmet of typical Celtic work, made of an iron cap or crown covered by two sheets of bronze with symmetrical patterns of S-scrolls, peletae and coral infill. Bronze tubes would have supported plumes on this helmet and it seems that there might have been cheek pieces which no longer remain. This is now in the Staatliche Museen, Antikenabteilung, Berlin.

Plutarch provides more details of the battle which he places near the Anio. He admits that the Romans flew into 'terror' when the news of the approach of the Celts reached them. When Camillus' newly trained and equipped army sallied forth they found the Celtic army encamped by the Anio. He placed his forces in a gently sloping glade in which there were many hollows and thus concealed the majority of the Romans so that the Celtic warriors would not see them.

> Then, while it was yet night, he sent his lightly armed troops forward to hinder the Celts from forming their battle lines and throw them into confusion, as they marched out from their camp. Just before dawn, he led his men down into the plain and drew them up in formation, many in number and full of spirit, as the Celts now saw, not few and timid. To begin with, it was this which shattered the confidence of the Celts, who thought it beneath them to be attacked first.

Camillus' hidden skirmishers, the lightly armed troops, began their attack, putting the Celts into disorder. However, the Celtic lines continued to advance on the main Roman positions, swords upraised and attempting to get to close quarters. The Romans brought up their long javelins, with which Camillus had now armed them. It is here that Plutarch curiously says that the Celtic weapons were soft and weakly tempered so that the swords bent against the superior Roman weapons. He actually says that the swords were bent double while the Celtic shields were pierced and so weighed them down that many Celts had to drop sword and shield.

> Therefore they actually abandoned their own weapons and tried to possess themselves of those of their enemies, and to turn aside the javelins by grasping them in their hands. But the Romans seeing them thus disarmed, at once took to using their swords, and there was a great slaughter of the foremost ranks, while the

rest fled every whither over the plain; the hill tops and high places had been occupied beforehand by Camillus and they knew that their camp could easily be taken, since in their overweening confidence, they had neglected to fortify it.

As this was the last military exploit of the ageing Camillus, doubtless Plutarch has to make it a significant victory. However, the description of the poorly tempered weapons, a theme which a few Roman writers have dwelt on, does not really accord with the archaeological reality of Celtic technology at this time nor with the fact of the Roman adoption of Celtic weapons, armour and loan words. Could Plutarch have been reversing the true position, and was it the Romans who had the problem against the superior armaments of the Celts? It is not unlikely. To reiterate, the terror felt by the Romans in the following year at rumours of another approach by a Celtic army does not really support the idea of such a devastating defeat of the Celts by the Romans, nor of the gross inferiority of their weaponry.

Another Celtic threat eventually materialised in 362/361 BC. 'An immense army' of Celts marched to within 3 miles of Rome. By now, Camillus was dead. Titus Quinctius Poenus had been made dictator to face this new Celtic threat while Servius Cornelius Maluginensis was appointed his master of horse or second-in-command. Livy confirms that Quinctius was made dictator for one reason only: because of the new Celtic threat to Rome. The Celts drew their army up on the far bank of the River Anio where the Via Salaria (the Salt Road) passed over a bridge. The Senate and courts of Rome were suspended, shops were closed and every man of military age was called up into the muster of the army. Quinctius then moved his legions out and took up positions on the opposite bank, facing the Celtic positions.

The two armies, Celt and Roman, encamped opposite each other on the banks of the Anio. A number of skirmishes took place for control of the single bridge which separated them. It is then that the first detailed description of a Celtic single combat is recorded. Single combat to resolve an entire battle was a matter of honour among the Celts and a chosen method. Rather than mass slaughter, it was better that the chosen champions of either side fought it out. The Celts were prepared to stand by the decision of whoever proved their skill. Unfortunately, the Romans were not. If a single combat was won by a Roman, the Celts were prepared to withdraw. But if a Celt bested a Roman, the Romans would fall in fury on the Celtic warriors. It was a conflict of cultural attitudes that was never resolved.

Diodorus Siculus says of the Celts:

> It is also their custom when they are formed for battle, to step out of the line and to challenge the most valiant men from among their opponents to single combat, brandishing their weapon in front of them to terrify their adversaries. And when any man accepts the challenge, then they break forth into a song of praise of the valiant deeds of their ancestors and to boast of their own achievements.

Poseidonius, quoted by Athenaeus, also mentions such combats, adding:

> The Celts sometimes engage in single combat at dinner, assembling in arms they engage in a mock battle-drill, and mutual thrust and parry, but sometimes wounds are inflicted, and the irritation caused by this may lead them to the slaying of the opponent unless the bystanders hold them back.

According to Livy, a Celt of enormous size advanced to one end of the empty bridge and shouted across to the Roman lines: 'Let the bravest man Rome has today come on and fight, so that the two of us can show by the result which nation is superior in war!' It was a typical Celtic challenge. In other words, the entire battle was to be settled by means of a single combat.

Aulus Gellius in *Noctes Atticae*, quoting from the lost *Annales* of Q. Claudius Quadrigarius, says the Celt was gigantic and naked, adorned only with his gold necklace, the traditional torque showing his rank as a warrior and chieftain, and bracelets, shield and two swords. However, Livy contradicts this description by saying that the Celtic warrior 'was remarkable for his stature, resplendent in multi-coloured clothing and painted armour inlaid with gold.'

The Romans, it is said, were at first unwilling to accept the challenge of this Celt. Then Titus Manlius, the son of Lucius Manlius Imperiosus, who had been dictator in the previous year of 363/362 BC, and who was, of course, of the same family as Marcus

Manlius Capitolinus, came forward. He went up to Quinctius and said: 'Without an order from you, sir, I would never fight out of my company, even if I were certain of victory; but if you permit me, I want to show that monster strutting about so boldly in front of the enemy's standards that I belong to the family which threw the Celtic army down from the Tarpeian Rock.'

Quinctius is said to have replied: 'Blessings on you, Titus Manlius, for your courage and loyalty, and with the gods' aid you will show that the name of Rome is invincible.'

Titus Manlius took an infantryman's shield and an Iberian sword and went to the bridge. We are told the Celt was delighted at finally having an answer to his challenge and Livy says the ancient historians recorded every detail of the engagement, even to the fact that the Celt stuck out his tongue at the Roman. He brandished his weapons and sang a war song. The singing of war songs either on the march or just before a battle, when lined up on the field, was, as we have seen, a common Celtic warrior tradition.

One of the Celtic loan words to be adopted into Latin is *alauda*, a lark. According to Gaius Suetonius Tranquillus, the Roman biographer (b.*c*.AD 70), when Caesar formed a Celtic legion after his conquest of Gaul, they were called the Alaudae ('The Larks'), presumably because they sang as they marched or went into battle singing. Cicero even used the word in a wider context to mean 'the soldiers of the legion'.

Livy presents the Roman version of the combat. Alas that we do not have a Celtic counterbalance.

When they took up their stand between the two armies, the hearts of the many men standing round them were on tenterhooks of hope and fear. The huge bulk of the Celt towered over the Roman; holding his shield in his left arm in front of himself, he brought his sword down with a slashing stroke and reverberating clang on to the arms of his oncoming opponent but to no effect. Manlius struck up the lower rim of the shield with his own, and, raising the point of his sword, slipped between his enemy's body and weapons, coming too near for any part of his person to be exposed to a wound. He gave one thrust followed immediately by another, gashed open the belly and groin of his enemy and threw him headlong to the ground to lie stretched out over a large area.

Aulus Gellius quoting Quadrigarius adds:

> Manlius, armed with an infantry shield and Hispanic sword, advanced against the Celt . . . according to his customs, the Celt held up his shield singing. Manlius, relying more on his courage than his skill, dealt him a blow shield to shield and upset the Celt's stance. While the Celt tried to regain his balance, Manlius once more struck his shield against that of his opponent, again knocking the man from his position. In this way he got under the Celt's guard and stabbed his Hispanic sword into his breast.

Livy takes up the story:

> He then spared the corpse any abuse, despoiling it only of a torque, which blood-spattered as it was, he put round his own neck.

Aulus Gellius, again quoting Quadrigarius, says that Manlius cut off the Celt's head to remove the torque. There was silence in the Celtic ranks. Perhaps, at first, the Celts thought Manlius was removing the head of a respected enemy, as was the Celtic custom. One wonders what their thoughts were when he, removing the torque, then tossed the head aside, the ultimate sacrilege in their eyes. The Romans rushed forward to greet their hero and promptly named him 'Torquatus' for his deed in taking the Celt's badge of heroic chieftainship. Henceforth this became a title among the Manlius family. Quinctius praised Manlius and gave him a gold chaplet.

For the Celts the result of the single combat had decided the encounter and during the night they evacuated their encampment and withdrew. The Romans, not understanding the significance of the combat, thought the Celts had fled in fear. In fact, the Celts made their way to Tibur (Tivoli), a city some 17 miles (28 kilometres) north-east of Rome, with whom they had agreed an alliance against Rome. The people of the city supplied the Celts with provisions and the Celtic army moved on into Campania. As a punishment for this alliance, the Roman decided to make a punitive expedition against Tibur. The consul, Gaius Poetelius Balbus, commanding two legions, marched on the city. On hearing this news, the Celtic army hastened back to the defence of their Latin allies. They were successful in skirmishes in the neighbourhood of Labici, Tusculum and Alba. Was it these successes which caused Polybius to claim: 'Thirty years after their occupation of Rome, the Celts again advanced with a large army as far as Alba. On this occasion the Romans did not dare to meet them in battle...' This would place the attack, by Polybius' reckoning, in 356 BC. But other later Roman historians were still claiming victories over the Celts by that time. Was Rome merely revising the historical record in its favour?

The Romans, we are told, had learnt that the Celts were not so fearful and invincible. Manlius' defeat of the unknown Celtic champion had demonstrated that. Even a couple of hundred years later the Romans were still boasting about the exploits of Manlius.

However, the successes of the Celts in defending their allies of Tibur had forced the Romans to appoint another dictator. This time Quintus Servilius Ahala was elected and named Titus Quinctius as his master of horse. He order the consul, Poetelius Balbus, to continue to lay siege to Tibur while he raised another army, calling up all Romans of military age. The Celts had once again marched their army along the Via Salasa and were within sight of the walls of Rome. Livy reports:

> Not far from the Colline Gate the entire manpower of the city fought a battle in sight of their parents, wives and children. These can provide a strong incentive to courage even when soldiers are far from home, but being then in full view they stirred their menfolk's sense of honour and tender feelings. Much blood was shed on both sides, but in the end the Celts were turned back.

The battle is not given a name but if it occurred, as Livy says, within sight of the Colline Gate, then the city of Rome should name the battle. The brevity of the account indicates it was no easy victory, especially as Livy admits 'much blood was shed on both sides'. We are told that the Celtic survivors withdrew to the city of Tibur again where the townspeople came out to help them. The consul, Poetelius Balbus, allowed the Celts, presumably many of them wounded, to flood into the city before closing his siege lines again, thus locking them inside. Rome celebrated this as a triumph.

However, it was not long before a fresh army set out from Tibur, leaving the city in the early hours under cover of darkness, brushing through Poetelius Balbus' besieging army, and reaching Rome by dawn. Yet another battle was fought under the very walls of the city. However, the Romans were able to turn back this attack.

News came in 358 BC that a fresh Celtic army was at Praeneste, now Palestrina, in Latium, a town famous for its roses, nuts and a temple housing the oracle of Fortuna. We are told that the people of Praeneste eventually had their lands confiscated 'because they had once joined forces with the Celts, a race of savages, out of disgust with Roman rule'. The city lay scarcely more than 20 miles from Rome. Gaius Sulpicius was named dictator with Marcus Valerius as his master of horse. Sulpicius selected the best veteran soldiers from the two consular armies and set off at their head to meet the Celtic threat.

The Celts were eager for battle but Sulpicius, of the same family as the general who had lost at Allia to them, was reluctant to risk his army. His policy was to wear the Celts down by blockades and skirmishes without attempting a pitched battle. But he found his own troops were the ones being worn down. The Celts, with their cavalry and chariots, had great mobility and were well supplied. Sulpicius kept his Roman troops confined to a fortified camp which was then surrounded by the Celts who carried off his supplies and stopped reinforcements getting through. The Roman soldiers began to grumble. They even questioned Sulpicius' ability as a general and some began to say that they would either take the fight to the enemy or retreat to Rome. The centurions also began to side with the soldiers and the rumblings of mutiny could even be heard in Sulpicius' tent before which the soldiers assembled, demanding action.

A centurion named Sextus Tullius became spokesman for the soldiers. It was the seventh time that he had served as senior centurion in the Roman army and he had won many battle honours. He, and a group of soldiers appointed for the purpose by their fellows, went to meet with Sulpicius. We are told that Sulpicius was surprised to see Tullius as spokesman. Livy puts these words into Tullius' mouth:

'By your leave, sir, the entire army thinks you have condemned it for cowardice and practically deprived it of the right to fight the enemy as a mark of disgrace. The army has begged me to plead its cause with you. For my part, even if we could be reproached for abandoning our posts anywhere, turning our backs to the enemy, of shamefully losing our standards, I should still think it right for you to grant what we ask, and allow us to redeem our fault by our courage and wipe out the memory of our shame by winning new glory.

'Even the legions which were routed at the Allia, subsequently marched out from Veii and regained, by their valour, the very city that they had lost when they panicked and fled. In our case, thanks to the gods' generosity, your own good fortune and that of the Roman people, our fortune and our glory are unimpaired though I hardly dare to speak of glory, when the enemy keeps us cowering like women behind our ramparts, to be taunted with every kind of insult! And you, our general – which is harder for us to bear – think of us as an army without spirit, without arms or hands to hold them, and before you have even tested us, have such low expectations of us that you count yourself in command of an army of cripples and weaklings. What other reason can we suppose there is for an experienced general as you are, and one so fearless in war, to be sitting, as they say, with hands folded? For, whatever the truth of the matter, it is more likely that you should appear to have had doubts about our courage than we about yours. But if that is official policy, not your own, and some agreement among the Senate and not the Celtic War is keeping us away from the city and our homes, I beg you to take what I am going to say as addressed not by soldiers to their general but by the plebeians to the patricians – and if we proposed to have our own policies, as you have yours, who can blame us? I say that we serve you as soldiers not as your slaves, and were sent to war, not to exile; that if anyone gave the signal and led us out to battle we would fight like men and Romans; but if there is no need of our arms, we would rather spend our leisure in Rome than in an army camp. This is what we would say to the patricians. But we implore you, our general, as your soldiers, to give us a chance to fight. Victory is what we want, but even more, to win victory led by you, to crown you with the laurel of glory, to escort you into the city in triumph, to march behind your chariot and approach the temple of Jupiter Best and Greatest shouting our exultations to him with joy.'

The soldiers' voices rose in approval of Tullius' speech. Sulpicius publicly assured the soldiers brusquely that their wish for battle would soon be granted. He then took Tullius aside and demanded to know what prompted this mutiny. Tullius, realising that Sulpicius, in spite of his assurances to the soldiers, could have him executed immediately, pointed out that he was still a loyal serving officer and respected his general. However, Tullius argued, he realised that if the soldiers became a mob, a mob took direction from a leader. If he had not taken over the leadership someone else would have done so and they might have led the army to disaster. He had taken command of the mutiny in order to save the army and keep it loyal to Sulpicius. However, unless Sulpicius devised a plan to meet the Celts in battle, then the men would choose the time and place for the battle themselves and their choice might not be wise.

In the middle of this conversation, some Celts made a daring attack on the supply base of the Roman encampment and a Celtic warrior was able to drive off some of the pack animals. Two Roman soldiers attempted to stop him and came under attack by other Celts. The guard was turned out and there was a skirmish which might have developed into a pitched battle as the Roman soldiers wanted to rush forward on to the Celtic lines. The centurions managed to restore discipline. Sulpicius realised that he could prevaricate no longer. He issued orders for a full-scale engagement on the following day.

Sulpicius was worried, however, believing his army to be out-numbered by the Celts. He devised a ruse by which he hoped that his enemy would think themselves outnumbered instead. He gave orders for the pack saddles to be taken off the mules and was able to muster one hundred mules and their drivers. To the drivers he gave weapons either captured or taken from the sick so that from a distance they looked like cavalry. He added to this force 1000 infantry. Then he ordered this column to move at night into the forests across the nearby lower slopes of the mountains behind his encampment. They were to conceal themselves among the trees and not to move until his prearranged signal.

At dawn he moved his main legions from the camp and set up his battle lines on the lower slopes of the mountain near a spot called Poestini so that the Celts had to take up their lines in the valley below, a position which placed them at a disadvantage. The Celtic war chieftains, instead of attacking up the slopes as Sulpicius hoped they would, simply waited. Obviously, they were too experienced to

This carving from Pasparido (see pp 26-27) seems to be the earliest known representation of the Celtic god Cernunnos, equated with the Irish The Dagda, father of the gods.

From the third century BC another representation of the god Cernunnos showing the god wearing the traditional Celtic torque and sitting in the 'yogi' position.

This bronze head of a Celtic war goddess of the first century BC from Dineault, Brittany, shows a warning goose on her war helmet. A typical Celtic motif.

This Celtic warrior with helmet, shield and sword, is part of a 4.5cm gold brooch. It dates to the second century BC and has been considered to be of Iberian Celtic workmanship. It might represent either an Iberian Celtic warrior of Hannibal's army or one of the Po Valley Celts.

A horde of Celtic silver coins of the second century BC from the Cremona area.

A selection of coins of the Taurini from the second/first century BC. The Taurini whose capital was initially Turin were driven out by the Roman conquest of the Po Valley eastwards towards what is now Slovenia where these coins were found.

This is one of the earliest known Celtic coins from the third century BC minted by the Insubres, whose capital was at Milan, in the Po Valley.

A gold leaf crown found in a Celtic grave at Benacci di Bologna, in Boii territory, and dated to the late fourth century/early third century BC.

A bronze figure (55cms high) of a second century BC Celtic warrior, during the period of the last Punic War.

Epona, the horse goddess, was one of the few Celtic deities which became a cult in Rome. This figure of Epona is one found in Alesia (Mount Auxois) after it was sacked by Rome in the first century BC. Alesia was a main centre for the Epona cult.

A lot of Celtic statues have not survived vandalism. This one from the first century BC shows what appears to be a leading Celtic warrior with a typical long Celtic shield which the Romans later adopted with modifications.

(Below) Figures of Celtic warriors from the second century BC. It has been suggested these might come from a rendering of the battle of Telamon and depict the Gaesatae.

One of the earliest known Celtic inscriptions dated to the fifth century BC with the name 'Tivalei Belleni'. Bellenus was a major Celtic god.

(Right) From the fifth century BC this Etruscan stone found at Bologna shows Etruscans and Celts at war. The bottom section shows a Celtic warrior on foot engaging an Etruscan horseman.

Stones inscribed in Celtic and Latin from the Todi area of northern Italy and dated late third or early second centuries BC.

A Celtic helmet from the late fourth century/early third century BC found in a burial ground at Benacci di Bologna, the territory of the Celtic Boii. The Celts brought many innovations into Italy which were later adopted by the Romans.

Two Celtic war helmets of the type worn by the Senones when they captured Rome. Both are from the fourth century BC. The first is bronze with cheek pieces found at Amfreville-sous-les-Monts, Eure in France. The second was found in Canosa di Puglia, Bari, in Italy, and seems to have been worn by a Celtic warrior of the Senones.

The Romans frequently remarked on the fearsome aspect of Celtic war helmets and the emblems carried on them. This magnificent Celtic helmet dates to the third century BC and has a bronze raven, symbol of death and battles on it, which has eyes of coloured glass.

The Celts of the Po Valley lived well; they were a
highly advanced civilisation but intermarriage and
intermixing with the people they displaced, such
as the Etruscans, is demonstrated in many parts.
This Etruscan style flagon of the third century BC
was found in a Celtic grave at Ceretolo (Bologna).

accept the Roman invitation to certain disaster. Finally, and presumably irritated that he had underestimated the intelligence of his enemy, Sulpicius gave the order for the Roman legions to march downhill to the attack. Only as the legions charged down the slopes did the Celts prepare to meet them.

The Roman right wing began to crumble against the Celtic defence. It would not have held had not Sulpicius himself galloped over to them. Sextus Tullius was commanding this wing and Sulpicius called him by name, demanding to know if this was how he fulfilled his promise that his men would fight? Where was the clamour for battle, sneered Sulpicius? 'Where are their threats that they would start a battle without their general's order?' Sulpicius galloped forward, sword in hand, ahead of the standards. Was there no one to follow him from those who had declared that they were ready to lead – fierce fighters in camp but cowards on the field?

The soldiers, stung by his abuse, rallied against the Celtic lines. They regrouped and charged again, this time with such fury that the Celtic lines began to crumble in their turn. Then Sulpicius waved in his cavalry support. The Roman cavalry was commanded by Marcus Valerius. Once the right was strengthened and was pushing back the Celtic left wing, the Roman general turned to his own left wing where the enemy was now concentrating. It was at this time that he gave the agreed signal to his men hidden in the forests on the mountain. A fresh Roman battle cry was heard and the Celtic leaders saw what they thought was a new army with fresh cavalry moving through the forests directly towards the Celtic encampment. The Celtic leaders did not want to be cut off from their base camp and ordered a withdrawal in that direction. This was their undoing. Marcus Valerius and his cavalry had been able to decimate the Celtic left wing and those survivors who fled to the mountains were caught by the oncoming muleteers and infantry and 'horribly massacred', according to Livy.

Was the battle a Roman victory? Not even the Roman historians claim it was for they say 'the battle petered out'. Sulpicius, however, was able to collect a considerable weight of gold from the fallen Celtic warriors – presumably their golden torques or neck bands – which he subsequently dedicated on the Capitol. That the battle was not decisive can be seen by the fact that Rome continued to be threatened by the allies of the Celts, the people of Latium. Two more battles were fought with the Hernici of Latium and the Tarquinii of Etruria. The consul Gaius Fabius, of the ill-fated Fabii clan, had been defeated by the Tarquinii who had taken 307 Roman soldiers prisoner and then sacrificed them in a special ceremony. In addition Roman territory was laid waste many times by raids from forces from the Latin towns of Privernum (Piperno) and Velitrae (Veletri).

The Celts still remained within a short distance of Rome. Why? Why had the Celts returned to Rome to attack it not once but many times? No reason seems to be given by Roman historians. It is wrong to adopt the Roman prejudice that the Celts acted on whim, that they were without reason or planning. They had only attacked Rome initially because of Rome's arrogant treatment of them and then only after envoys had been sent to address the Senate. There is no record of any Celtic envoys going to Rome and stating their case now. But there must have been a reason.

One answer is suspected by Livy and made clear by the Greek Theopompus of Chios (c.376–323 BC) who claimed that the Celts had, during this period, offered an alliance to Rome's enemy, the Greek city of Syracuse (Siracusa) in Sicily.

In the south of Italy, beyond the land of the Samnites and Latium, lay what had become Magna Graecia (Megale Hellas), the collective name for the Greek cities of southern Italy which had been founded by colonisation from Greece. They had, as has already been mentioned, become prosperous through the fertility of their land and through trade. They had their own schools of philosophy and centres of artistic and scientific thought. Elea (Velia) was famous for its school of philosophy founded by Parmenides in the sixth century BC. Pythagoras, though born in Samos, had settled in the town of Croton in the sixth century BC, and founded his own school there.

At the time that the Celts first attacked Rome, most of the Greek cities of southern Italy acknowledged themselves to be part of the empire of Syracuse (Syrakousai) and its ruler Dionysius I. Syracuse, on the south-east coast of Sicily, had been founded by colonists from Corinth in 733 BC. Dionysius had established himself as sole ruler in Syracuse in 405 BC and was to rule until 367 BC. His rule, though regarded as oppressive, brought wealth and power to Syracuse. He had checked the aspirations of the empire of Carthage, a Phoenician city in north Africa, which controlled most of the trade in the western Mediterranean, and made himself ruler of most of Sicily. He then turned his attention to the Italian mainland. Many cities of southern Italy initially united against him under the leadership of Croton, on the west coast of the Gulf of Tarentum. Dionysius defeated an army of 15,000 infantry and 2000 horse commanded by Heloris near the River Elleporus in 389 BC. Soon city after city fell or surrendered to him.

By 379 BC Dionysius captured Croton itself and his rule and suzerainty extended across southern Italy even along the Adriatic coastline into Apulia. The empire of Syracuse had become the dominant power in southern Italy. Dionysius had, significantly, about this year, planted a Syracusean colony at Ancona where the merchant ships of Syracuse would trade and revictual *en route* to the ports near the mouth of the Po, particularly Venetian Hadra, a city of marshes and canals, which was also colonised by Dionysius. This city became the market and port of exchange for supplying Greek merchandise not only to the Celts of Cisalpine Gaul but to their fellow Celts beyond the Alps.

In his rise to power, Dionysius had realised that naval power was the prime factor in securing an empire. His fleet consisted of some 300 ships and he is credited with the invention of the *quadriremis*, a war vessel with four banks of oars, and the *quinqueremis*, which had five banks of oars. These were the most powerful vessels afloat in his day. He is also said to have introduced the catapult into military operations, engines which hurled stones of two or three hundredweight for a distance of 200–300 yards. It revolutionised warfare at the time.

Dionysius encountered the Celts either during his military expansion in southern Italy or, more likely, when he started to establish trade links along the coast of Apulia and north to Ancona. Livy and other historians frequently refer to the Celts withdrawing to Apulia after their attacks on Rome. Why Apulia, in the south-east of Italy? It would surely have been more logical for them to have withdrawn north across the Apennines to the Celtic lands of Cisalpine Gaul. Apulia was a region which had been extensively Hellenised. It had a dry fertile soil and was famed for its wool, for it was renowned as sheep-breeding country. If the Celts were in alliance with Syracuse, then Apulia, as part of Dionysius' territory, would be a natural base of operations. And in such an alliance might also lie the reason why, in the mid-fourth century BC, the Senones settled along the coastline of Picenum around Ancona. Had Dionysius, as repayment for their services, allowed the Senones to establish their settlements here?

As has already been outlined in *Celt and Greek* (1997), Dionysius I and his son Dionysius II employed Celtic mercenaries. In the summer of 369 BC Syracuse sent military aid to help the Spartans and Athenians against Theban attack. In his fleet there were some 2000 Celtic cavalry troops as well as Celtiberian troops. The Celts are recorded as being crucial in turning the tide against the army of Epaminondas. More contingents of Celts were sent from Syracuse in the following year. The historian Xenophon was enthusiastic in describing the Celtic prowess as cavalry and Plato himself, an eyewitness to the events, described the Celtic warriors as hard-drinking and fearless. The Greek attitude towards the Celts was, as we have seen, more admiring than that of the Romans. Xenophon remarked that they were worthy soldiers and Diodorus Siculus indicated that even the Spartans admired the Celtic fighting qualities. Livy is one of the few Roman historians who admitted, when speaking of the Etruscans, that 'there was no other nation (except the Celts when they invaded) more formidable under arms'.

The idea that the Celts, attacking Rome during the fourth century BC, were, after their initial attack, doing so as allies or mercenaries in the employ of Syracuse makes more sense than the idea of bands of nomadic Celtic raiders wandering Italy and seeking booty whenever the opportunity arose. The Celts were only interested in one enemy in Italy and that was Rome. There is no evidence of attacks on other cities. In fact, the reverse is true for other cities of Latium and Etruria were in alliance with the Celts against Rome. The Celts also made agreements with cities and towns among the Samnites. Tibur, Antium and Praeneste are recorded as supplying and helping the Celts against Rome.

The fact that Syracusean coins, as well as other Greek coins, are to be found in significant numbers among Cisalpine Gaul and elsewhere in the Celtic world might indicate that many young Celts saw mercenary work, offered by Syracuse, as a means to collect wealth and return to their homelands thereby boosting the native economies. On the other hand, trading links must not be entirely dismissed. The Greek colony of Tarentum, a prosperous town striking coinage, also seemed to have links with the Celts. Tarentine coins of the period c.334–272 BC have been found even in the former Belgic Celtic territory of Picardy. The coins of Syracuse from Dionysius to Aga-thokles, who assumed the title king in 303 BC, particularly gold staters and drachmas, have been found in abundance among the Celts of the western shore of Gaul. Even coins of Hiketas (288–279 BC), who succeeded Agathokles, have also been found distrib-uted throughout the Celtic world. The distribution of such coinage demonstrates, claim Dr Daphne Nash and others, that Celts from many areas, not just the Senones and the Cisalpine Celts, sought service in the armies of Syracuse. But the phenomenon of Celtic mercenaries serving the Hellenic states occurs in the years after the Senones ceased to be a threat to Roman security.

Rome's eventual conquest of Tarentum in 272 BC and then of Syracuse in 263 BC closed two Greek city markets for Celtic mercen-aries and probably opened the way for the development of auton-omous Celtic coinage. Certainly the Insubres of Cisalpine Gaul were among the first to start minting their own distinctive coinage – beat-ing the introduction of Rome's own coinage by a short head.

Celtic activity against Rome continued, as we have seen, after the death of Dionysius I in 367 BC, and went on during the troubled reign of Dionysius II and the reign of his brother-in-law, Dion, who was assassinated in 353 BC. After the liberal Timoleon of Corinth became ruler in 344 BC, the Celtic attacks on Rome seemed to recede and we hear of a peace treaty being made between the Celts and Romans. But there are, unfortunately, no details as to what was involved. This coincides, however, with the time that we can safely place the Senones as settling around the Syracusean ports and colonies along the Adriatic coast of Italy from Ariminum to Ancona. Syracuse itself later became a more moderate oligarchic state on the Corinthian model and was eventually crushed by Rome in 211 BC.

The picture that emerges is that the Senones Celts who had attacked Rome, once in the vicinity of Rome, had discovered that their enemy was almost universally disliked, even by the other Latin cities. The Etruscans and the Samnites and many hill tribes were also sworn enemies of Rome. The arrival of the Senones, and their victory over Rome in 390 BC, had acted as a catalyst in the struggle of these people against Roman domination. The Celts were nothing loath to make alliances against Rome including an alliance with Syracuse.

The Senones Celts enter history as an entire nation who had crossed the Apennines in search of land to settle. After they withdrew from Rome, they found that land in Picenum on the eastern seaboard of Italy. Here they settled down, the main part of the tribe resorting to agriculture, like the rest of the Celts, raising livestock, fishing and even constructing fortified towns.

The Celtic armies that continued to plague Rome were doubtless raised from the young men of the tribe during the 'fighting seasons', that is the summer months. The Celts had no such thing as a standing army. Indeed, nor was there a professional army in Rome until the first century BC. It would appear, as the fourth century progressed, that the Celtic army which kept returning to Rome and its environs was not simply comprised of Senones but, judging from the dispersal of Greek city coinage of the period among the Celts, included young men who had volunteered from all parts of the Celtic world. This is accepting Dr Nash's theory that the Greek cities were paying the Celts for their military services and that the coin dispersal did not come from merely trading. Dr Nash's interpretation would have it that, from the late fourth century BC, Rome was not facing a single tribal army but an army consisting of contingents from various tribes.

[7]

'The Celtic Terror'

ITHIN a decade of Sulpicius' battle near Praeneste, the *terror Gallici nominis* was continuing to alarm the citizens of Rome. In 351 BC the threat was so alarming that Marcus Fabius was elected dictator to meet a Celtic army which was reported to be massing in Latium. Marcus Fabius, another of the Fabii clan, chose Quintus Servilius to be his master of horse and second-in-command. However, it was the consuls who confronted the Celts. Lucius Cornelius Scipio had been appointed consul for the patrician party while Marcus Popilius Laenas was the consular choice of the plebeians.

The Celts were less than 15 miles from Rome. A large army was reported to be gathered to the south-east of the city in the Alban hills, now called the Castelli Romani. They were assembled within the shadow of Mons Albanus (Monte Cavo), the second highest summit of the Alban hills, on whose slopes was Alba Longa, the most ancient town in Latium. Here was situated the sanctuary of Jupiter Latialis built by Lucius Tarquinius Superbus (534–509 BC), the last king of Rome. It was regarded as a holy mountain by the Latins.

That a large Celtic army was about to get as near as this forty years after the original sack of Rome demonstrates the support that the Celts were receiving from the cities of Latium and indicates how little faith one can put into the accounts of continuous 'great victories' over the Celts by Rome.

The patrician consul Cornelius Scipio was taken suddenly ill and Popilius Laenas was given command of the consular army. He was able to equip and train four full-strength legions which were encamped outside the Capena Gate. Popilius Laenas suggested to the Senate that the praetor for that year, Publius Valerius Publicola, raise a second army as a reserve. Popilius Laenas appears a more conscientious commander than his predecessors.

The consular army then marched towards Monte Cavo, traditionally along what is now the Via dei Laghi, and approached the Celtic positions with care. The consul sent a small detachment of troops to a hillock in order to learn the enemy strength. The Celtic commanders, having observed the position of the Roman standards, began to deploy their men ready to meet the approaching Romans. Popilius Laenas ordered his men to dig in on the hills, thus being protected by their position on the rising ground before the Celtic lines.

A charge from the Celts surged upwards to where the third line of Roman soldiers were still in the process of digging in. The first and second lines stood ready in front of their working parties. As they were on rising ground above the Celts, their javelins and spears were used to good effect and the Celts suffered many casualties from the falling missiles. While the force of their charge did carry them up to the enemy lines, the Celts found a determined defensive position. After fierce hand to hand combat, they found that they were being pushed slowly back down the hill. Many of the Celts were pushed back on each other. Some of the wounded were trampled to death in the fierce fighting as the Romans drove them back.

The Romans, believing victory was in their grasp, came charging down on to the plain only to find large numbers of Celts assembled in battle lines. 'It was,' admits Livy, 'as if a new army had sprung up again. The Celtic chieftains were urging on fresh troops against their enemy in spite of the Roman victory.' They advanced quickly but ground to a halt at the foot of the hill. The Romans were exhausted and the consul, Popilius Laenas, had been run through the left shoulder by a Celtic javelin, and carried off the battlefield to have his wound tended. The Roman lines began to waver. Hearing this news, the consul rose from his bed, where the physicians were still attending him, remounted his horse and rode back to the standards.

Livy says he appealed to his men in the following terms.

'What are you stopping for, men? This is no Latin or Sabine enemy you deal with, one whom you can turn into an ally once defeated in battle. We have drawn sword against wild beasts, and must either shed their blood or spill our own. You have forced them back from the hill, driven them headlong downhill to the valley and you stand on the prostrate bodies of your foe; now cover the plains with butchered corpses as you did the hills. Don't wait for them to run away while you stand still; you must press the attack.'

Thus encouraged, the Romans began to push slowly forward, fighting fiercely every step of the way, until they finally broke through the leading companies of Celts by forming a wedge formation. The Celtic lines eventually disintegrated and they began to withdraw towards Monte Cavo itself, which Livy calls the Alban Citadel. It is thought that the ancient Latin city of Cabum was situated here, which became Rocca di Monte Cavo and is now Rocca di Papa due to the proximity of the Pope's summer palace at Castel Gandolfo. Livy turns the withdrawal into a panicked retreat and accords the Romans, as usual, another overwhelming victory.

If this was such a devastating victory, as he claims, why did Popilius Laenas not pursue the Celts to Monte Cavo? Livy has his excuses ready. We are told that the consul's wound was paining him. Presumably he could have delegated command of the pursuit? To forestall this inevitable rejoinder, Livy tells us that Popilius Laenas did not want to take his army into the hills occupied by the enemy. He therefore gathered some spoils from the abandoned Celtic encampment, and marched back to Rome. He was too ill to receive the official triumph and, as both consuls were ill, new consuls had to be elected: Lucius Furius Camillus and Appius Claudius Crassus. They were both patricians yet the custom had been that one of the consuls should be a plebeian. This election caused much dissension between plebeians and patricians.

Popilius Laenas' 'triumph' had hardly been celebrated when the Celts came out of the Alban hills during the severe winter weather and began a series of raids on outlying farmsteads around Rome. We are told this was during the winter of 349/348 BC. If this is so, and we accept the same source giving the date of the battle at Monte Cavo in 351 BC, we would have to assume the Celts had been holed up in the hills around Rome during the winter of 351/350 BC and during the whole of the summer and autumn of 350 BC. What had they been doing? Roman historians are quiet on this matter.

What is interesting about the raids by the Celts from bases in the Alban hills that winter was the fact that harrying fleets from the

Greek city states of southern Italy also began raiding along the west coast and even into the mouth of the Tiber itself. Livy believed that these Greek sea raiders had been sent by Dionysius II of Syracuse. It is reported, on one occasion, that the Greeks from the ships and the Celts from the hills encountered each other 'and fought an indecisive battle, so that the Celts returned to their camp and the Greeks to their ships, both uncertain whether they had lost or won'. Polybius, a source for this clash, does not make clear what the cause of this battle was. If the two were, indeed, allies, then it was probably a confusion of identification.

As spring ended the severe winter in 348 BC, the Latin cities once more defied the Romans. They again refused Roman demands for tribute, especially the order to send levies to fight for Rome. 'The Latins,' says Livy wryly, 'would rather bear arms for their own liberty than for another's dominance.' The Latin League began to prepare for war against Rome making Ferentinum, modern Ferento, a town of the Hernici, the headquarters of the league. This was just south of modern Ariccia. In the meantime, the Celts were still the only army in the field which really worried Rome and they were still in the vicinity of the city.

The consul, Lucius Furius Camillus, who had been re-elected, raised ten legions. Each legion had a strength of 4200 infantry and 300 cavalry. He left two legions behind to protect Rome and divided the remaining eight legions between himself and his fellow consul Lucius Pinarius. Pinarius was instructed to march to the sea in order to confront any landings from Greek ships while Camillus himself marched towards the Celtic positions.

Camillus must have been aware of the dangers of uprisings from the Latin cities and the possibility of a Latin army, now being hurriedly trained, attacking him in strength. However, he seems to have discounted the Latin threat for the more pressing problem of defeating the Celts. He marched south to the Pomptine marshes, now Pontine, roughly 40 miles south of Rome in the modern area of Latina. It was a low-lying marshy district, 30 miles long and 12 miles wide, exposed to the inundation of the Rivers Amasenus and Ufens on the Appian road. Livy and other Roman sources tell us that the consul did not want to meet the Celts in open battle, rather as Gaius Sulpicius had in 358 BC. He wanted to constrain them because he was sure that their army had to subsist on what they could forage.

If he could cut off these supplies then he would weaken and defeat them. The Celts were certainly not subsisting on pillage. They were being supplied by their allies, the cities of the Latin League.

Livy says that during this campaign a Celt approached the Roman picket lines and announced himself by striking his spear on his shield. He was a man of outstanding size and wore armour. This time Livy says that the Celt used an interpreter to issue his challenge for any Roman to come and take part in single combat with him. There was a twenty-three-year-old tribune named Marcus Valerius in the army and he went to Camillus and sought permission to answer the Celt's challenge.

It is now that Livy recounts a combat which has remarkable resonances with Celtic mythology.

The duel proved less remarkable for its human interest than for the divine intervention of the gods, for as the Roman engaged his adversary, a raven suddenly alighted on his helmet, facing the Gaul. The tribune first hailed this with delight, as a sign sent from heaven and then prayed for the good will and gracious support from whoever had sent him this bird, were it god or goddess. Marvellous to relate, not only did the raven keep the perch it had once chosen, but as often as the struggle was renewed it rose up on its wings and attacked the enemy's face and eyes with beak and claws, until he was terrified at the sight of such a portent; and so bewildered as well as half blinded, he was killed by Valerius. The raven then flew off out of sight towards the east.

Valerius began to strip the body of the Celt, at which the Celts moved forward threateningly. The Romans also came forward. There began a skirmish over the body of the Celtic warrior which developed into a fierce battle. Camillus ordered his legions to engage the enemy, knowing them to be elated by the tribune's victory. 'Copy him, soldiers,' he cried, pointing to Valerius, 'and cut down the Celtic hordes around their fallen leader!'

For Livy 'gods and men took part in the battle'. Inevitably the Celts, having seen the portent, are said to have fled. It is interesting where Livy has them fleeing: south to the Volscians in the Falernian district, from where they made once again for Apulia.

We are told that Camillus called a military assembly, officially praised Valerius and bestowed on him ten oxen and a golden crown. Valerius took the *cognomen* Corvus, which means 'raven' or 'crow'. He was shortly to be elected consul.

Although Cassius Dio (*c.*AD 150–235) also mentions this combat, he seems to use Livy as an authority. But we have to remind ourselves again that Livy was raised in Cisalpine Gaul. Camille Jullian, in his *Histoire de la Gaule*, suggested that Livy was influenced in his work by Celtic epics for this is unlike any straightforward Roman story. Henri Hubert goes so far as to suggest that it is straight from Celtic mythology and points to the fact that the raven or crow is one of the personae of the Celtic war goddess, a creature which symbolises death and battles. Dr Hubert says the episode is remarkably like one in the *Táin Bó Chuailgne* in which the Ulster champion Cú Chulainn is fighting in single combat. He has rejected the advances of the war goddess, the Mór-Ríoghain (Mórrígán or great queen). In some versions she assumes the form of a raven of battle and attacks him, hindering his single combat against the champion Lóch. Cú Chulainn knows that when the goddess, in the form of a great crow or raven, stands before him and croaks of war and slaughter, the portent means one thing. 'My life's end is near; this time I shall not return alive from the battle.' And when Cú Chulainn, mortally wounded, ties his bleeding body to the pillar stone so that he can die standing up, the goddess, in the form of a raven or crow, comes and sits on his shoulder.

Rather than a story specifically from mythology, this could be merely a recounting of Celtic symbolism for the raven was the chthonic emblem, a symbol of death and battles. It was also a bird associated with oracles. Ravens warned the god Lugh of the approach of the Fomorii. Lugdunum (Lyon), named after the god Lugh, once issued a coin with a raven on it. The Celtic goddesses Nantosuelta and Epona are sometimes accompanied by, or depicted as, ravens. Even in the thirteenth-century Welsh myth, the *Dream of Rhonabwy*, Owein ap Urien raises a raven army to attack Arthur's men. In fact we have at least one Celtic warrior's helmet – found in Ciumesti, Romania; a bronze war helmet from the third or second century BC – which has a bronze crest in the form of a raven which is 25 centimetres high. However Livy came by the idea of introducing the raven into his story, he knew that the symbol of the raven or crow was of special significance to the Celts. It is almost as if he is addressing a Celtic audience. Its appearance in support of the Roman warrior in this single combat foretold the Celt's doom.

The Roman historians mention several single-handed combats which, inevitably, involve mainly Roman successes. One wonders how many Celtic successes there were in these combats. Perhaps an indication occurs in 340 BC when Titus Manlius Torquatus was consul with Publius Decius Mus. He issued a decree that no Roman officer should accept any challenge to single combat. 'It was time to recall military discipline to its former ways,' comments Livy. Manlius Torquatus' own son, a headstrong young man, it is recorded, then disobeyed his father's commands and accepted a challenge from Geminus Maecius of the Tusculum (Frascati) cavalry. Although he killed his opponent, his father had him beheaded in front of the army as punishment so that it could be demonstrated that he was prepared to sacrifice his own son to enforce the law. 'The commands of Manlius not only caused a shudder at the time but were a grim warning for the future.'

Polybius says that 'the Celts made another attempt to invade in force', placing the date at 344 BC. But we have no details of this campaign. 'After this alarm they kept quiet for thirteen years, and then as they saw that the power of the Romans was growing fast, they concluded a formal treaty with them and faithfully observed its terms for thirty years.'

It seems that around 334 BC Rome did conclude a treaty with the Senones. Unfortunately we know nothing of its terms and the reasons behind it. But rumours of possible Celtic attack continued for a long period afterwards. In 332 BC, in fact, the rumour of a Celtic invasion so unnerved the Romans that Marcus Papirius Crassus was chosen as dictator and scouts were sent out to check up on the stories. They returned 'to report all was quiet amongst the Celts'. Yet more rumours followed a few years later in 330 BC when Lucius Aemilius Mamercinus was one of the consuls of the year. Reports spread to Rome of an approaching Celtic army. The Senate ordered him to raise an army and march out to meet them before they could reach Rome. We are told that an immense Roman army gathered at Veii from where the campaign was to be mounted against the Celts. However, it was decided not to move from Veii in case the Celts should outflank the Romans. A few days later scouts reported that 'all was quiet amongst the Celts'. The rumours had been inaccurate.

Rome's consciousness of the Celtic threat seemed paramount at all times; the Celtic sack of Rome was frequently mentioned in speeches in the Senate and it was used as an icon, a rally standard against Rome's enemies. The event clearly had a strong impact on the Roman collective psyche. It is this fact, I believe, which contributed to the continual denigration of the Celts at every opportunity by Roman and Romanised writers, resulting in many of their descriptions of the Celts being totally at odds with what we have subsequently learnt from archaeology or insular Celtic writings. The Roman view of the Celts in warfare, of the supposed inferiority of their weaponry and tactics, is one aspect that has been demonstrated. Polybius' depiction of the Celts merely as vagrant savages in a pre-agricultural stage of development, who roamed with their cattle herds and preferred to keep their property in movable gold is, as has been mentioned, far from the reality.

The Roman fear of the Celts had been a real fear in the early years of their relationship, especially because the Celts had easily pricked the bubble of Roman conceit and arrogance with their victory at the Allia and subsequent capture and occupation of Rome for seven months. Yet this real fear vanished after fifty years of conflict. We should remind ourselves that the Celts had a valid reason for their initial attack on Rome. Rome had broken international law when its ambassadors, instead of taking a natural stand in a dispute, joined forces against the Celts. When the Celts, quite correctly, sent envoys to protest to the Roman Senate, they were not only sent away in dismissive terms but the same ambassadors were elected to high office as an additional 'slap in the face'. The Celts did not attack Rome for some whim or on an unwarranted impulse.

However, it appears that a neurotic fear replaced the real fear after the Celtic threat receded. The root of the real fear remained in that the Romans could not forgive the Celts for 'cutting them down to size'. The neurotic fear brought about an almost instinctive urge to denigrate the Celts at every opportunity. Thus a prejudice towards the Celts, an antipathy based upon faulty and inflexible generalisations and stereotypes, was propagated by Roman writers and those wishing to appease their Roman audiences. This type of neurotic prejudice may have its root in the frustration felt by any imperialist power in the face of a people who will not meekly accept dominance – particularly, in this instance, a frustration at not being able to

understand the Celtic mind and attitudes which were so at variance
with Roman attitudes. This frustration can lead to displaced hostility
and aggressive attitudes. Above all, the hostility is accompanied by
attempts to justify the prejudice that accompanies it. Thus, as we
have seen, Caesar and Cicero would wax indignant against reported
Celtic 'human sacrifice' when there were probably more ritual killings
going on in Rome.

As Professor Toynbee realised, 'the Romans are not unprejudiced
witnesses when they are testifying about the Gauls.' The French
philosopher Jean-Paul Sartre (1905–1980) once described the need
of the conqueror to denigrate the conquered, or, indeed, the people
who refuse to be conquered, in these succinct words: 'How can an
élite of usurpers, aware of their mediocrity, establish their privileges?
By one means only: debasing the colonised to exalt themselves, deny-
ing the title of humanity to the natives, and defining them simply as
absences of qualities – animals, not humans. This does not prove
hard to do, for the system deprives them of everything.'

This sort of denigration has been seen in other empires apart from
Rome especially in the empires of England and France because they
have been the heirs to Rome's attitudes towards the Celts whose
modern descendants, the Irish, Manx and Scots, the Welsh, Cornish
and Bretons, they have sought to conquer and incorporate. Victorian
English attitudes to the Celts, especially to the Irish, find an eerie
echo from Roman writers. John Emerich Edward Dalberg, first Baron
Acton (1834–1902), professor of modern history at Cambridge,
writing in 1862, could argue:

> The Celts are not among the progressive, initiative races, but
> among those which supply the materials rather than the impulse
> of history, and are either stationary or retrogressive. The Persians,
> the Greeks, the Romans and the Teutons are the only makers of
> history, the only authors of advancement. Other races possessing
> a highly developed language, a speculative religion, enjoying lux-
> ury and art, attain to a certain pitch of cultivation which they are
> unable to either communicate or to increase. They are a negative
> element in the world ... The Chinese are a people of this kind
> ... So the Hindoo ... So the Slavonians ... To this class of natives
> also belong the Celts of Gaul ... The Celts of these islands, in
> like manner ... Subjection to a people of a higher capacity for

government is of itself no misfortune and it is to most countries the condition of their political advancement ... Theorists who hold it to be wrong that a nation should belong to a foreign state are therefore in contradiction with the law of civil progress.

Lord Acton, although he never completed a book, was not a maverick outside the mainstream of serious scholarship. He was a highly influential historian, influencing English attitudes to empire through his essays and Cambridge lectures. He devised the *Cambridge Modern History* series. Curiously, Lord Acton claimed to be a liberal in philosophy and politics.

Representative of the French attitude to the Bretons are Honoré de Balzac's comments, in *The Chouans* (1827):

... they strive to preserve the traditions of the Celtic language and customs; thus their lives retain deep traces of the superstitious beliefs and practices of ancient times. There the feudal customs are still respected. There the antiquarian finds druidical monuments still standing, and the genius of modern civilisations stands aghast at the very thought of penetrating immense primeval forests. Incredible ferocity, brutal obstinacy, but unswerving fidelity to one's oath; utter ignorance of our laws, our manners, our customs, our new coins, our language, but patriarchal simplicity and heroic virtues unite to make the inhabitants of these country districts poorer in intellectual combinations than the Mohicans and redskins of North America, but withal as grand, as crafty and as unforgiving.

As the ruling classes of both these nineteenth-century empires justified their economic greed and legitimised the conquering of other peoples and the forging of 'the wheel of empire' as 'civil progress', so too did the ancient Roman ruling class.

[8]

Celt, Etruscan and Samnite

FTER the Celts, or rather the Senones tribe, had 'concluded a
formal treaty' with Rome, says Polybius, they 'faithfully
observed its terms for thirty years'. The treaty was concluded
around 334 BC and thus the last three decades of the fourth century
BC ended in 'the Celtic terror' having diminished. It is at this time
that the Senones settled down to a life of agricultural and pastoral
farming on the eastern seaboard of the Adriatic between Ariminun
and Ancona. With the Celts having disappeared as a threat in the
vicinity of Rome, the Roman military strength began to renew.
Finally Rome set off in a new attempt to subdue its neighbours.

Latium was first to, once again, feel the *pax Romana*. Latium
had, just before the Celtic arrival, been forced to accept Roman
overlordship. The Celtic intervention in the area had given them
several decades of renewed independence. With the Celtic victory at
the Allia, the cities of Latium seized the chance to break free of
Rome. But now, with the Celtic withdrawal from the area, Rome
was able to start a new war of conquest. This lasted between 340
and 338 BC and was known as the 'Latin War'. It reasserted Rome's
dominance and the Latin League of cities was dissolved. Those cities
who had supplied and helped the Celts during the previous fifty years
were severely punished.

Soon Rome had control from the Cimmian forest in Lower Etruria,
which formed her northern frontier, south to the Pomptine marshes,
which she also annexed and colonised. Beyond these lowland
marshes lay the Volscian hills and beyond them was Campania with
the richest plains of Italy. The Volsci were another Indo-European
people occupying central Italy; their three main cities were Arpinum
(modern Arpino, the birthplace of Cicero), Antium (modern Anzio)
and Terracina. They were a continued threat to Rome's ambitions
and were next in line to be annexed. Rome was able to make a treaty

with Neapolis (Naples) in 326 BC. After successfully dealing with a threat from the Samnites, the first Roman military road, the Via Appia, the Appian Way, from Rome to Neapolis, was constructed in 312 BC.

Apart from the Etruscans, the most powerful threat to Rome's growing power in central Italy was now the Samnites who occupied the hills of Abruzzi. These were part of the Sabelli, a collective name given by Rome to the Indo-European tribes of central Italy such as the Sabines, Umbrians and Apulians – the last being the non-Hellenic natives of the area. Of these peoples, the Sabines had lived north-east of Rome from early times. They were famous for their bravery, morality and strong religious feelings. The Rape of the Sabines is one of the traditional stories from the early period of Rome. Livy records many stories of wars between Rome and the Sabines. From 343 BC there had begun what was to be a series of three Roman-Samnite Wars over the next seventy years. And it was towards the end of the fourth century BC that the Celts reappeared in Roman history as allies of the Samnites.

The reason why the Celts re-entered the scene was because of the perceived growing threat from Rome. Skirmishes with the Etruscans and battles against the Samnites had resulted in an uneasy peace in 304 BC. Seizing this opportunity Rome planted colonies and fortified townships to secure control of the central Apennines, at Sora, Alba, Fucens, Carisioli and Narnia.

In 299 BC the Etruscans decided that Rome's growing military and economic strangle-hold must be broken. The Etruscans made an alliance with the Celts in Picenum. Once again, these Celts were the Senones, who were also worried about the increasing nearness of the new Roman colonies along their borders. Watching the encroachment of Rome the Senones appear to have allied themselves with the Etruscans for mutual defence. Livy puts matters differently, of course. He says the Etruscans offered the Celts money. 'The barbarian Celts did not refuse an alliance; it was only a question of the price.' He says a sum was agreed and the money changed hands. The Etruscans prepared to march to war against Rome. He then claims that the Celts backed out of the alliance, insisting that the payment had been made not for making war on Rome but for not destroying cultivated Etruscan land while the Etruscan army was away. 'However, they were willing to take up arms if the Etruscans really wanted them to do so, but only on condition that they received a share of Etruscan lands where they could settle.' According to Livy, the Etruscan Senate met and discussed the matter but in the end refused to grant them any land. The Celts then returned to their own territory 'with an enormous amount of money which they had acquired without effort or risk'.

Polybius has a different story to tell. He says that there was a new influx of immigrants from the northern Celtic homelands at this time. The Celts were fearful that the new tribes would cause overpopulation and war. Therefore, by pleading ties of kinship, and giving them some bribes, they encouraged their distant kinsmen to join them in the alliance with Etruria. Is Polybius right? It is not until 283 BC that we hear specifically of Celts other than the Senones moving south of the Apennines and this was when the Boii joined an alliance with the Etruscans. Could the Senones have persuaded the Boii into the alliance earlier than the date in which they are first mentioned? It is, of course, possible.

One point of significance in Polybius' story is that he seems to indicate it was the Celts who instigated the Etruscans' defiance of Rome. The stories of Livy and Polybius are at variance. Given Rome's expansionist policy, I see nothing which would contradict a mutual Celto-Etruscan alliance for the defence of their respective territories. Polybius, however, continues to present the Celts in the blackest terms:

> They marched first through Etruria where they were joined by the Etruscans, and after they had seized great quantities of plunder they returned safely from Roman territory. But no sooner had they arrived home than they began to quarrel about obtaining a larger share of the spoils, and in the end destroyed the greater part of their own army and even the plunder itself. This is a common occurrence among the Celts after they have appropriated a neighbour's property, and it usually arises from their undisciplined habits of drinking and gorging themselves.

The consul Titus Manlius, obviously a descendant of Manlius Capitolinus, had been dispatched with a Roman army to confront the Etruscans and their allies but he had fallen off his horse and died from his injuries three days afterwards. Marcus Valerius was elected consul in his place and set off to take command, destroying Etruscan lands and burning their towns and farmsteads. The Samnites seized the opportunity to commence their third war against Rome.

The Samnites made an alliance with Etruria. Envoys told the Etruscan Senate:

> ... how for many years they had been fighting the Romans for their freedom; how they tried everything to see if they could bear the heavy brunt of the war by their own unaided strength, and had also made trial of help from their neighbours, which had proved of little use. They had sought peace from the Roman people when they could not keep on the war, and turned to war again because peace with servitude was harder to bear than war with liberty. The only hope left them lay with the Etruscans; them they knew to be the richest people in Italy, in arms, men and money, and they had for neighbours the Celts, a nation born to the clash of arms, fierce not only by nature but also in their hatred of the people of Rome, of whose defeat and ransom for gold they could boast, naming no empty brag.
>
> If the Etruscans still had the spirit which fired Porsenna [Lars Porsenna the Etruscan king of Clusium] and their forebears, there was nothing to prevent their driving the Romans out of the whole region north of the Tiber, and forcing them to fight not to maintain their intolerable tyranny over Italy but for their own self-preservation. The Samnite army was there ready for them; it had come fully armed and prepared to follow at once even if the Etruscans led them to attack the city of Rome itself.

The Etruscan Senate decided to join with the Samnites. Supreme command seems to have been given to Gellius Egnatius, a Samnite, who began to prepare the resistance in Samnium itself. The Celts also emerge as part of the new alliance. Roman historians once more reserve their sarcasm for the enemy who had almost destroyed them, saying that 'the Celts were being offered pay in return for their support'. Livy remarks on the enormous size of the Celtic army when it joined with the Samnites and Etruscans. The Umbrians also joined the alliance and Rome was faced with a grave challenge to its imperial aspirations.

Livy says it was the Celtic Senones who arrived 'in great hordes' in the neighbourhood of Clusium. Two Roman legions commanded by Lucius Scipio were sent to the Latin town of Cameria in order to hold a pass through the mountains through which the Celts were expected to advance. Livy is full of excuses, as usual, for what happened. 'He [Scipio] was in a hurry; he had not properly investigated the route, and reached a ridge which was already taken by the enemy. Thus the legion was heavily attacked in the rear and completely surrounded.' Indeed, Livy puts it delicately when he says that 'some authorities say that the legion there was even totally destroyed'. Indeed, one of Scipio's legions, some 6000 men, had been cut to pieces and the battle of Cameria became a Celtic victory almost as shocking for Rome as the Allia.

Livy tries to make light of the matter and even says that some authorities claim the Romans were defeated not by Celts but by Umbrians, although he quickly adds that 'it is more probable that defeat was suffered at the hands of the Celts than the Umbrians . . .' He mentions that the legion which had been annihilated was commanded by Lucius Manlius Torquatus, possibly a son of Titus Manlius who had been killed after the fall from his horse.

The legions of the Roman consuls, Quintus Fabius Maximus and Publius Decius Mus, were approaching Clusium when their advance scouts came in contact with cavalry units of the victorious Celts. 'Celtic horsemen came in sight, carrying heads hanging from their horses' breasts and fixed on their spears, singing their customary song of triumph.'

The two consular armies did not engage them but marched for Sentium, modern Sassoferrato, 35 miles from the Adriatic coast just across the Apennines. The Romans encamped with four legions some 4 miles from the town. Three Etruscan deserters from Clusium arrived at the Roman camp that night to inform the consuls that, while the Celts and Samnites were to attack in a set battle the next day, the Etruscans and Umbrians planned to outflank the Romans and attack the rear. Messages were sent to Gnaeus Fulvius and Lucius Postumius Megallus, the two pro-praetors, to move their armies to the area around Clusium and destroy as much of the Etruscan lands as possible. This would have the effect of causing the Etruscan contingent of the allied army to withdraw in defence of their own territory. It seems unlikely that within the space of twelve hours messengers reached Fulvius and Postumius, their armies moved to Clusium and began to ravage the country and, finally, word reached the Etruscans for them to withdraw their armies to protect Clusium: more probably this all took several days.

For two days skirmishes took place before Sentium and, indeed, the Etruscan contingents did withdraw. The Samnite-Celtic-Umbrian alliance refused battle with the Romans until they had rearranged their plans. Livy is fond of recording omens.

As they stood in battle formation, a hind in flight from a wolf, which had chased it down from the mountains, ran across the plain between the two armies. Then the two animals turned in opposite directions, the hind towards the Celts and the wolf towards the Romans. The wolf was given a way through the ranks but the hind was struck down by the Celts. At this one of the soldiers from the Roman front ranks cried out, 'That is how flight and bloodshed will go – you see the beast sacred to Diana lying dead, while here the wolf of Mars is the winner, unhurt and untouched, to remind us of the race of Mars and of our Founder!'

The Samnite general Gellius Egnatius was in command of the combined army and had placed the Samnites on the left wing with the Celts on the right wing, mainly with their war chariots and cavalry. Fabius had placed the I and III Legions on the Roman right, facing the Samnites, while Decius with his V and VI Legions lined up against the Celts. Lucius Volumnius, the pro-consul, had taken the II and IV Legions to Samnium itself. Livy suggests that, had the Etruscans and Umbrians been there, the Romans would have had a disastrous result but they had been drawn away by the Roman ruse.

The battle opened with the war chariots of the Celts giving an initial advantage on the right wing. The Romans staggered under the weight of the massed charge from the horses and heavy vehicles. Again Livy has excuses for what happened.

Decius was more impatient, being young and high spirited, and let loose all the resources he had at the first encounter. And since the infantry battle seemed to be going rather slowly, he called on the cavalry to attack, and riding himself amongst the bravest of his youthful squadrons, summoned the young nobles to join him in a charge; they would win double glory, he said, if victory came first to the left wing and the cavalry. Twice they forced back the Celtic cavalry, but the second time they were carried on too far and then found themselves fighting in the midst of companies of infantry, where they were alarmed by a new style of fighting.

What was this new style?

The Celts, standing up and holding their weapons in chariots and wagons, bore down on them with a fearful noise of horses' hooves and wheels and terrified the Romans' horses with the unusual din. Thus the victorious cavalry were scattered by assorted panic frenzy, their blind flight overthrowing them, both horses and riders. Their confusion spread to the standards of the legions, and many of the first line were trampled underfoot by the horses and vehicles sweeping through the army. As soon as the Celtic infantry saw their enemies in disorder they came at them, not leaving them a moment to regain breath and recover themselves. Decius shouted to know where his men were fleeing or what hope had they in flight; then he tried to stop them as they broke away and called them back when they ran. Then when he found himself powerless to stem the rout, he called on the name of his father Publius Decius: 'Why do I longer delay,' he cried, 'the destiny of our house? Our family was granted the privilege of being sacrificed to avert dangers to our country. Now it is my turn to offer myself to the legions of the enemy as victim to Earth and the gods of the Underworld.'

He told his aide, Marcus Livius, the pontiff, to leave the field and report what he had said, raising him to the rank of praetor, in command of his division of the army. Decius's father had similarly sacrificed himself at the battle of the River Veseris, at the foot of Mount Vesuvius, where Titus Manlius Torquatus had won a victory in the Latin War in 340 BC. Having prayed to the gods, Decius turned and galloped towards the Celtic lines where he saw the fighting at the thickest and thus met his death.

The death of the consul Decius apparently had the effect of rallying the Romans instead of adding to their panic. Marcus Livius assembled the dispirited troops as, at the same time, reinforcements arrived under the command of Lucius Cornelius Scipio, who had survived the destruction of one of his legions. Gaius Marcius was second-in-command of the new force.

The Celtic lines were advancing close packed in a *testudo*. The Romans fought desperately and finally managed to break the formation, holding their ground.

On the right wing Fabius had been holding back. Now he ordered his cavalry to make a sortie around the Samnite flank and, at a given signal, attacked it, while his legions charged the front ranks. The Samnites began to crumble before the advance and when needed, Fabius brought up his reserves to keep up the momentum on their lines. Gellius Egnatius, the Samnite commander, was killed and the Samnites were swept away, leaving the Celtic flank undefended. The Celts stayed close packed behind their *testudo*.

Fabius ordered a squadron of 500 cavalry to swing behind and to attack the Celtic rear. As soon as their formations were shattered, the commander of the III Legion was ordered to charge in with his men. Livy gives the alliance casualties as 25,000 killed and 8000 taken prisoner and Roman casualties as 8700 men killed, 7000 of whom had been with Decius' wing of the army. The remains of the Samnite army, 5000 men, suffered the loss of a further 1000 men killed as they were trying to withdraw. These are, of course, the Roman estimates of the casualties.

While this battle was taking place, Gnaeus Fulvius had been carrying out his campaign in Etruria. He killed over 3000 of the citizens of Perusia, modern Perugia, and Clusium and captured twenty military standards.

'Great is the fame of that day,' Livy records with satisfaction. Indeed, it was the first significant victory recorded by the Romans over the Celts in battle. In spite of it, there was still no peace in either Samnium or Etruria. The battle had been won but not the war. Battles, skirmishes and raids continued. However, after several other defeats, the Samnite army ceased to exist. The Romans carried out a campaign of reducing each Samnite city, killing the citizens, ruthlessly and methodically, until they established their dominion over the Samnites.

Only the Etruscans and the Celts now stood in the way of total Roman supremacy in central Italy. In 284 BC the Celts had some success in a battle at Arretium (Arezzo). This Etruscan town had surrendered to the Romans and been forced to agree a peace treaty.

The Senones laid siege to the town. Polybius simply records: 'The Romans went to assist the town, attacked the enemy before the walls and suffered a defeat.' In this battle the commander of the Roman army, the praetor Lucius Caecilius, was killed. The news of this victory caused many Etruscan cities, which had made agreements with Rome, to renounce their treaties and the unrest spread once again through Samnium and Lucania.

Polybius goes into some further detail by saying that the survivors of the defeated Roman army had appointed Manlius Curius, presumably the senior surviving officer, to negotiate a truce with the Celts. This officer is said to have been the same person as Manlius Curius Dentatus. As this Curius Dentatus had been an army commander in the campaign against the Samnites, he would hardly have now been a junior officer to the praetor Caecilius at Arretium. Perhaps Polybius slides several events together and this Manlius Curius was the son of Curius Dentatus? Polybius says: 'The Celts treacherously broke the truce and massacred the envoys, whereupon the Romans were roused to such anger that they immediately took the offensive and invaded the enemy's territory, where they were confronted by the Celtic tribe called the Senones. They defeated them in a pitched battle in which the greater number of the Celts were killed . . .'

The defeat of Lucius Caecilius' army and his death would have been a severe blow: severe enough for the survivors to seek terms from the Celts. Yet we are now asked to believe that these defeated men suddenly ended the negotiations, regrouped, brushed aside the very army that had defeated them, and went rushing off into the territory of the Senones and defeated them again in a devastating battle. Several events are obviously run together here.

Firstly, the envoys of Manlius Curius are said to have been slain by the Celts. Why? Once again the Romans irritatingly do not explain, leaving one to think this is just normal behaviour from the 'barbarian' Celts. It has been argued that perhaps the Celts killed the Roman ambassadors in remembrance of the partisanship of the Fabii at Clusium a hundred years before. I doubt it. The Celts, as we have already discussed, held ambassordorship, the very word being Celtic, as a sacred trust, so much so that it was the breaking of such a trust which had caused their initial descent on Rome. Was this slaughter of Roman envoys at Arretium merely a Roman excuse for the subsequent ill treatment of the Senones? Or were they indeed killed while trying to out-manoeuvre the Celts or repeating the partisanship of the Fabii? Once again, we can only pick up half of the story and a biased half at that.

The descent of a punitive expedition into the territory of the Senones in Picenum took place in the following year, 283 BC. Suetonius is clear about the date and confirms that another battle was fought in which the Senones were defeated. We are told that Curius Dentatus – there is no doubt about his identity now – burnt and pillaged the country to such an extent that it was made into a desert. He destroyed the Celtic towns and began to drive out the inhabitants from the coastal main tribal town, now called Senigallia (town of the Senones Gauls). The town was later to be occupied by Roman colonists who retained the place-name of the previous occupants.

With the defeat of the Senones, the other Celtic tribes of the Po Valley emerged clearly into Roman history. The Boii were the first to be identified for they joined an alliance with the Etruscans and marched south. They reached the Vadimo lake, now the Lago di Bassano, near the Tiber, between Volsinii and Falerii, just 42 miles north of Rome. A Roman army commanded by Publius Cornelius Dolabella hurried north to meet them and arrived to find the Etruscan forces crossing the river near the lake. Dolabella immediately launched an assault and practically annihilated the Etruscans before they could regroup. Then he turned on the Celts as they were marching to relieve the Etruscans.

In spite of Roman claims, even those of Polybius, that the Etruscan army and the army of the Boii were 'wiped out', we find Polybius having to admit that 'the two peoples again joined forces in the very next year'. One wonders how this miracle occurred. Polybius makes an attempt at explanation by saying that they were young adolescents. An army of young boys would surely have drawn more attention than the Roman historians give to the incident. They merely say that the Celts and Etruscans met another Roman army in 282 BC and suffered another defeat. In the wake of this defeat we find the Etruscans suing for peace and this year is generally seen as marking the final collapse of any Etruscan independence. Rome became dominant throughout Etruria. The Celts apparently were included in this peace treaty. The Boii returned back north of the Apennines as their part of the bargain. Did Rome assure them that she would not venture over the mountains into their territory? There was surely some *quid pro quo* to encourage them to leave Etruria.

Rome devised a policy of establishing colonies among its conquered northern lands. The Senate still saw the Celts as a threat and turned an anxious gaze north of the Apennines to the *ager Gallicus*, the territory of the Celts. In 268 BC, a Latin colony was established on the eastern seaboard at Ariminum, at the northern end of the Senones' territory. For many years this military colony, whose population was estimated at about 4000 people, would remain Rome's northern defence post, closing the gap between the Apennines and the sea to prevent the Celts moving into Picenum and Umbria. Some fifty years would pass, before the role of Ariminum would change from a defensive sentinel to a springboard for the Roman offensives against the Celts of the Po Valley.

Rome's growing empire had spread to the control of all central Italy. Would she now turn north into the land of the Cisalpine Celts or south to the rich cities of Magna Graeca? Rome was hungry for land, wealth and power. Professor Rankin makes a very accurate summary when he says that a new phase in Celto-Roman relationships was developing at this point. 'The Romans were weary of living in fear, not merely of intrusive raids but of the risk of being overwhelmed and destroyed by the numbers, vigour and ferocity of tribes who now occupied the valley territory of northern Italy.'

Celtic incursions into the Etruscan empire had destroyed the former power and, ironically, by these actions, the Celts had contributed to the growth of the power of Rome. Rome, having united all central Italy, could now call on vast reserves of manpower, even though these forces came from allied cities and states who might defect if an advantageous prospect were set before them. Professor Rankin observes that the Celts had made themselves the 'menace' on the northern boundaries of Rome's sphere of influence. Inevitably, Rome, in her quest for domination of the known world, would have to remove that menace.

Pyrrhos, Carthage and the Celts

A s the dynamic of Rome's empire was to acquire land, wealth and power, it was obvious that she would turn first to the rich Greek city states of southern Italy rather than to the unknown quantity of the Po Valley behind the Apennine barrier. The Roman Senate could look with confidence at the wealthy cities which had emerged from the Syracuse empire as small warring factions once again. The Greek city states of Megale Hellas, becoming aware of Roman intentions, decided to combine against the inevitable onslaught. The city of Tarentum was the principal organiser of this defensive alliance. According to Plutarch:

> The Romans were at this time at war with the people of Tarentum, who were neither strong enough to carry on the struggle, nor, because of the reckless and unprincipled nature of their dema- gogues, inclined to put an end to it. They therefore conceived the idea of making Pyrrhos their leader and inviting him to take part in the war, since they believed that he was the most formidable general of all the Greek rulers and also that he was more free to act than the others.

A formal invitation called upon Pyrrhos, king of Epiros, to come to their aid and command their armies. Pyrrhos (319–272 BC) was a second cousin to Alexander the Great. He had been ousted from his throne in Epiros after the battle of Ipsus in 301 BC but had, with the aid of Ptolemy I of Egypt, been restored in 297 BC. He was a good organiser and an ambitious military adventurer. His ambition was to retrieve the empire of Alexander under his rule. Plutarch says that 'as for Pyrrhos' knowledge and mastery of military tactics and the art of generalship, the best proof is to be found in the writings he left on those subjects.' It is said that when Antigonus (Gonatus) was asked who was the best general, he replied, 'Pyrrhos, if he lives to be old enough.' In a later age, Hannibal of Carthage once observed that Pyrrhos was the greatest of all generals. Unfortunately, Pyrrhos' writings have not survived.

Pyrrhos landed in Tarentum in 281 BC, with 20,000 infantry, 3000 cavalry, 2000 archers, 500 slingers and twenty elephants. The elephant as a war machine had not been used in Italy before. The Romans were to call it the *Luca bos*, the Lucanian ox, because it was in Lucania that they first saw elephants in action. Pyrrhos had already sent a Thessalian named Cineas with an advance guard of 3000 men.

The news of the coming of Pyrrhos was probably looked on with interest by the Celtic chieftains of the Po Valley. The Celtic world, generally, had had good relationships with the Greeks until this time. Contingents of Celts had served in the Greek armies of Syracuse, which had once dominated these southern Italian Greek city states, and had also served with distinction in the army of Sparta. The Celtic tribes on the northern borders of Macedonia had made treaties of friendship with the formidable Alexander the Great. Soon, three great Celtic armies would erupt into the Greek peninsula, defeating the Macedonians, the Thessalians and even the Athenian army. But these events were a few years away and would not concern the Celts of Italy.

The main concern in 281 BC was whether Pyrrhos and the Greeks of southern Italy could counter the imperial designs of Rome. It was not long before Rome sent an army to test Pyrrhos' resolve. The consul Laverius Laevius marched against Tarentum with an army of 35,000 men. Pyrrhos was an astute politician and sent envoys to the Romans asking them if they would be prepared to agree to a treaty respecting the independence of the Greek city states of southern Italy. If so, he assured them, there was no need to have recourse to warfare. The Romans, after their victories over the Samnites, Etruscans and Celts, were in the first flush of success in the creation of their empire. They would give no such guarantee.

Pyrrhos advanced to the plain between Pandosia and Heracleia in Lucania. It was his first victory. Roman losses were placed by Dionysius of Halicarnassus, quoted by Plutarch, at 15,000 dead with Pyrrhos losing 13,000. Hieronymus of Cardia seems more accurate with 7000 Roman dead and 2000 captured with Pyrrhos losing 4000.

Pyrrhos was now looking for allies against Rome and was joined by the Lucanians and Samnites. These Samnites appear to have recovered from their defeat with the arrival of a strong ally. To buy time to train his new army, Pyrrhos sent Cineas as ambassador to Rome to start new negotiations. Cineas laid a number of proposals before the Roman Senate by which the conflict could be ended. Basically, all Rome had to do was agree to leave the Greek cities of southern Italy unmolested. The Senate refused and sent Gaius Fabricius to negotiate the release of Roman prisoners. Fabricius and Pyrrhos became good friends on a personal level although they remained enemies politically. Fabricius even warned Pyrrhos of a plot to assassinate him because he did not want Pyrrhos' downfall to bring reproach on Rome by history saying that his end was brought about by treachery. It is to Pyrrhos' credit that he tried several times to make a just peace with Rome, his one condition being that Rome should respect the independence of the Greek cities.

Fabricius, now elected consul, marched a new army to engage Pyrrhos in Apulia. By this time the chieftains of the Insubres, the Boii and the remnants of the Senones had decided to send contingents to join Pyrrhos' army. The Celts did not join him as mercenaries. They were fighting the old enemy, Rome, as allies of Pyrrhos on an equal footing in order to stop the inevitable movement of Rome across the Apennines into the Po Valley. If Rome succeeded in subduing the southern Italian cities, the Celtic chieftains realised it would only be a matter of time before the Roman legions crossed the Apennines into the Celtic homeland.

However, it has been argued that Pyrrhos did enlist Celtic mercenaries from as far afield as what is now Picardy, the territory of the Belgae federation. Daphne Nash has shown that various coins from Tarentum of the period *c.*334–272 BC were used in that area; coins, she claims, which returning veterans would have brought back with them having been paid for their services. Dr Nash discounts the idea that any of these coins might have arrived by way of trade with Greek merchants, a suggestion, I believe, which is unfairly ignored.

At Asculum, modern Ascoli Satriano, Pyrrhos was faced with a new Roman army commanded by Sulpicius Saverrio. Once again, the Greek general pushed the Romans back but only after a fierce battle which lasted from sunrise to sundown. Pyrrhos was wounded in the arm by a javelin. Hieronymus, echoed by Plutarch, estimated

Roman losses at 6000 dead, compared with 3500 dead from Pyrrhos' army. Pyrrhos is said to have commented: 'One more victory like that over the Romans will destroy us completely!' Hence the term 'pyrrhic victory'.

Most of his commanders and friends had been killed in this battle. No reinforcements could be summoned from Greece. It is an irony that this was due to the Celtic invasion of Greece which had swept through the peninsula. Plutarch comments: 'And from Greece messengers reported that Ptolemy, surnamed the Thunderbolt [Ptolemy Ceraunnos, king of Macedonia] had been killed in a battle with the Celts and his army annihilated, and this was the moment for Pyrrhos to return to Macedonia where the people needed a king.' While Pyrrhos pondered his response, a delegation from Sicily arrived to offer him command of the armies of the cities of Agrigentum (Agrigento), Syracuse (Siracusa) and Leontini (Lentini) on condition that he help them against the Carthaginians.

The republic of Carthage had become the dominant colonial and trading power in the western Mediterranean. The city occupied a strong strategic position on the Tunisian coast of North Africa and had been established by Phoenician colonists from Tyre traditionally in 814 BC. During the sixth century BC it began to grow as a trading power and its interests began to conflict with the Greek colonies and settlements throughout the Mediterranean. Forming an alliance with the Etruscans, the Carthaginians were able to drive the Greeks from Corsica and gain control of Sardinia. Cities in Sicily and several coastal towns on the Iberian peninsula, such as Gades (Cadiz), became part of the Carthaginian empire. In their settlements in Iberia, the Carthaginians had come into conflict with the Celtiberians, Celtic tribes who had crossed the Pyrenees and were established in the Iberian peninsula as far south as Gades by the seventh century BC.

The Carthaginians were a Semitic people. Their government was oligarchic, with two chief magistrates answerable to an assembly called the Suffete. They were elected annually from among the rich and aristocratic. The religion was oriental in origin, worshipping the gods Melkart, Baal-Hammon and Eshmoun and practising human sacrifice. The art of Carthage was a combination of Greek and Egyptian styles. Her wealth of cornlands was proverbial and her fleets dominated the seas, connecting the city with her various colonies. The Carthaginians were known as Poeni, the adjective being Punicus;

hence the word Punic to describe the various Carthaginian wars with Rome.

Pyrrhos seems to have made a curious decision. Had he returned to Greece he would have undoubtedly been welcomed by all the Greek states as their saviour from the Celtic invasion as I have outlined in *Celt and Greek*. However, he decided to go to Sicily. He left a garrison in Tarentum and moved into Sicily in 278 BC. Carthage, having concluded a peace treaty with Rome, was now threatening the Greek trading ports in Sicily. Pyrrhos met with indifferent successes.

Three years later, in 275 BC, Pyrrhos became frustrated that he was making no gains in Sicily. He recrossed the Straits of Messina, having to fight a sea battle with the Carthaginians as he did so. Back on the Italian mainland he managed to gather a combined army of Greeks, Celts, Samnites, Lucanians and Bruttians. At the Hirpini town of Beneventum, modern Benevento, 130 miles south-east of Rome, he was met by an army commanded by consul Manlius Curius Dentatus, who had also conducted the campaign against the Senones. Pyrrhos opened the battle with a night attack, but the Romans drove the advance guard off with heavy losses which included eight of Pyrrhos' war elephants. Encouraged, Curius Dentatus launched a counter-attack on the main body. The first Roman legion crumpled against Pyrrhos' defence. A second legion, following immediately on, broke his phalanxes and put an abrupt end to the battle.

Plutarch says: 'This manoeuvre gave the victory to the Romans and finally established their superiority in the struggle against Pyrrhos. These battles not only steeled their courage and their fighting qualities, but also earned them the reputation of being invincible; the result was that they at once brought the rest of Italy under their sway, and soon after Sicily as well.'

The Roman victory at Beneventum saw the end of Pyrrhos' campaign in Italy and he decided to leave the cities of Magna Graeca to their inevitable fate. In fact, he left the Greek cities completely to the mercy of the Romans without even nominating a commander to replace him. Within a few years the Greek city states fell to Rome and Rome became the master of the Italian peninsula as far north as the Apennines, the border with the Cisalpine Celts. Pyrrhos' withdrawal had another important effect on the Celtic world, according to Dr Nash. When Rome conquered Tarentum in 272 BC and formed an alliance with Syracuse, the two most important western Greek markets for the recruitment of Celtic mercenaries soldiers were closed. As an offshoot of this, the Celtic tribes of the remoter areas, who had sent their young men to serve as mercenaries to bring back the gold and silver coins, according to Dr Nash, began to concentrate on producing their own coinage.

A final effect of these events was to bring the new Roman empire into a collision course with Carthage over the matter of trade and involvement in Sicily. According to Plutarch, Pyrrhos had already seen the danger signs and, as he was leaving Sicily, he is said to have looked back at the island and remarked to his companions: 'My friends, what a wrestling ground we are leaving behind for the Romans and Carthaginians.' The first war between Rome and Carthage, the First Punic War, commenced in 264 BC.

As Rome continued to rise in power and influence, it was inevitable that a military conflict would occur over trade dominance. The war started with a squabble over control of the city of Messana, now Messina, in Sicily. In 263 BC a strong Roman force under the consul Manlius Valerius failed in an attack on the Carthaginians at Syracuse, which they now controlled. The following year, the Romans attacked the Greek city of Agrigentum on the Italian mainland. Their subsequent decision to conquer the whole of Sicily cost the Romans twenty more years of warfare although in 260 BC their victory over the Carthaginian fleet at Mylae, modern Milazzo, 17 miles west of Messina, gave Rome command of the Sicilian waters. The newly organised Roman battle fleet of 140 ships acquitted itself well against the 130 ships of Carthage. Carthage lost fifty ships and 3000 men killed with 7000 taken prisoner, according to Roman sources.

A new phase of the war opened in 256 BC with the battle of Ecnomus, near Licata, on the south coast of Sicily, acknowledged as the hardest fought ancient naval action in western waters, involving 350 Carthaginian ships and 330 Roman ships. The aggressive Roman fleet shattered the Carthaginian formations and sank thirty ships, capturing thirty more. The Roman commander Marcus Atilius Regulus was able to land unopposed on the shores of Africa and secure a base against Carthage. The following year he was able to march four Roman legions to within a few miles of the city of Carthage itself. There were no defensive walls because Carthage had always relied on its fleet for defence.

Xanthippus, the Spartan general, had been given command of the

Carthaginian forces, 12,000 infantry, 4000 cavalry and 100 elephants. The result of the engagement was that only 2500 Romans, out of the 17,000 men who comprised the legions, managed to escape back to their ships and most of these were lost when a storm devastated the Roman ships on the return journey. Atilius Regulus himself was captured but paroled to negotiate peace terms on behalf of Carthage. Sent back to Rome to negotiate, he was rewarded with torture and death by the Roman Senate. Rome did not like her generals to fail her.

In 255 BC Rome seemed no nearer success than at the start of the war. She had however grasped the importance of sea power and spent a great deal of money building a new fleet. In 254 BC Rome launched a new offensive and her army managed to capture Panormus (Palermo), Carthage's principal town in Sicily. In 251 BC Hasdrubal, son of the Carthaginian commander Hanno, and son-in-law of Hamilcar Barca, attempted to recapture the city. However, the Carthaginians were defeated by Lucius Caecilius Metellus. The Romans went on to capture Lilybaeum (Marsala) but the Carthaginian fleet was able to resupply the garrison and virtually annihilate the Roman fleet commanded by Publius Claudius Pulcher off Drepanum (Trepani).

Hamilcar Barca, the father-in-law of Hasdrubal, who was to be the father of Hannibal, assumed command in 247 BC with his headquarters on Mount Eryx (Monte San Giuliano), 22 miles north of Lilybaeum. Rome had once again rebuilt a battle fleet and now 200 *quinqueremes* commanded by Gaius Lutatius Catalus met the Carthaginian fleet during a heavy storm on 10 March 241 BC, off the islands of the Aegates, modern Egadi. The Roman fleet devastated the Carthaginians, sinking fifty ships and capturing seventy.

With his naval force wiped out, Hamilcar Barca reluctantly accepted peace terms for Carthage. He agreed to the payment of 3200 talents and the surrender of Carthage's claim to Sicily. Sicily became the first official province of the new Roman empire. When Hamilcar Barca evacuated his stronghold on Mount Eryx he took with him his six-year-old son, Hannibal. Hannibal was later to claim that he had become a hater of all things Roman from that day onwards.

Polybius claims that Rome negotiated a favourable treaty with Carthage only because of the 'Celtic threat'.

For the present they did not venture to impose conditions or to make war on Carthage, because at this time the threat of a Celtic invasion was hanging over them and an attack was expected almost from day to day. They therefore decided to try to mollify and conciliate Hamilcar in the first place, and then to attack the Celts and put the issue to the test of war, for they were convinced that so long as they had an enemy such as the Celts threatening their frontier, not only would it be impossible to control the affairs of Italy, but they would not even be able to live in safety in Rome itself. So they first sent envoys to Hamilcar and concluded a treaty. According to its terms nothing was said about the rest of Spain, but the Carthaginians undertook not to cross the Ebro under arms. Then the Romans at once threw themselves into the struggle against the Italian Celts.

When Hamilcar returned to Carthage, the mercenaries he had brought back mutinied over a dispute about the amount of money they felt was owing to them and they fomented an insurrection among the Numidians who served as the main cavalry units. Numidia was a country bordering Carthage in North Africa, the equivalent of modern Algeria. Carthage, still smarting under its defeat, had to recruit fresh mercenary troops from outside for which it was dependent on Roman goodwill. Hamilcar Barca was given overall command, put down the mutiny, and restored Carthaginian dignity.

Rome, however, had seized this opportunity to capture Sardinia from Carthage and when Carthaginian envoys were sent to Rome to protest, they were met with a new declaration of war by Rome and a refusal to even arbitrate. To add insult to injury, Rome then demanded the surrender of Corsica from Carthage and an additional indemnity of 1700 talents. This land grabbing was a miscalculation – a final insult which could not be ignored. It showed that Rome's claim for 'fair dealing' was part of her self-propaganda and festered the spirit of vengeance among the Carthaginians. The seeds of the Second Punic War were sown hardly had the First Punic War ended.

For the moment, however, Rome, aggressive, confident, and once again filled withy her former pre-Allia arrogance, was unconcerned about what her Mediterranean neighbours thought.

[10]

Telamon!

POLYBIUS, ignoring the Celtic involvement with the campaign of Pyrrhos, claimed that the 'Celts remained quiet and at peace with Rome for forty-five years'. However, Polybius is right when he says that the Cisalpine Celts 'interpreted the slightest action of the Romans as a provocation'. Following Pyrrhos' departure for Greece, and during the First Punic War, Rome had been putting pressure on the Senones, following their defeat in 283 BC. This included not only the establishment of military garrisons in their territory but punitive raids. The Boii were certainly keeping a wary eye on Rome's activities, especially as Rome had entered a policy of actually clearing the Senones from the land – a piece of ancient 'ethnic cleansing'.

Polybius says that the Boii 'invited the Alpine Celts to join them in an alliance'. We do not know precisely whether these were Celtic tribes from the Alpine foothills or valleys or Transalpine Celts. We do know the names, for the first time, of the kings of the Boii. Polybius names them as Atis, interpreted as 'he who seizes', and Galatus, 'the Gaul' or 'the Celt'. In 242 BC an army of Celts, led by Atis and Galatus, arrived at the Roman garrison colony of Ariminum in what had been Senones territory. However, Polybius tells us that the rank and file of the Boii were not happy with the alliance and he relates that dissension between the Boii and their Alpine or Transalpine comrades erupted into physical conflict. The Celts fought a pitched battle before Ariminum in which both factions suffered heavy losses. The Boii kings, Atis and Galatus, were killed.

The Romans, receiving word of the arrival of the Celtic army at Ariminum, had dispatched an army to the north but hearing the news that the Celts were fighting one another, they returned to Rome.

By 232 BC, the consul Marcus Aemilius Lepidus had completed the expulsion of the Senones from Picenum and the confiscated lands

were allotted to Roman citizens to settle. The Senones finally disappear from Italy. Dr Ursula Ewins represents popular opinion when
she says that 'the Senones had been defeated and the tribe extermi-
nated'. It is more likely, however, that the defeated remnants of the
tribe decided to move north, retracing the journey that their ancestors
had made over 150 years before. When Julius Caesar set about the
conquest of Gaul, he found a tribe called the Senones living in the
area south-east of modern Paris, in the neighbourhood of Agendicum, modern Sens. It is true that they might have been a people with
the same tribal name but it seems doubtful. Caesar described them
as 'a very powerful tribe with great influence over the others'. They
sent 12,000 warriors to Vercingetorix, 'over-king of the world', to
fight against the Roman invasion of Gaul.

The idea of confiscating the land of the Senones and settling Roman
citizens on it was introduced by a plebeian politician named Gaius
Flaminius. His plan was to give the Roman proletariat a stake in the
land. The idea of giving land to commoners was strongly opposed
by the patrician Senate, whose members had usually profited by
Roman conquest and confiscation of land. Flaminius had been able
to carry his proposals in the popular assembly. For the Roman plebeians, of course, it was looked upon as an assertion of 'democratic
rights'. To Polybius, favouring the patricians, it 'may be said to have
marked the first step in the demoralisation of the Roman people'.
What this 'ethnic cleansing' did, in fact, was precipitate the inevitable
war with the Cisalpine Celts. Even Polybius admits, 'The truth is
that many of the Celts and especially the Boii, whose territory bordered that of the Romans, became convinced that the Romans were
no longer fighting to establish their sovereignty over the Celts, but
to expel them and finally to exterminate them altogether.'

This, indeed, was Roman policy.

The Boii and their neighbours, the Insubres, north of the Po,
formed an alliance and sent envoys to the Celts of Transalpine Gaul.
They recruited mercenaries whom Polybius and other Roman com-
mentators thought were a tribe called the Gaesatae 'because they
were mercenaries'. In fact, the name meant 'spearmen'. It becomes
obvious that the Gaesatae were a band of élite warriors. Such bands
have often appeared among the Celts.

The stories of some of the most famous bands of the Celtic warrior
élite have been preserved for us in Irish tradition. The Fianna were

said to be the bodyguard of the High Kings and insular records tell us that they were founded in 300 BC by the High King Fiachadh and consisted of twenty-five battalions or units. They were usually recruited from two clans, the Clan Bascna and the Clan Morna. Provincial kings also had their warrior élites. Just as famous as the Fianna in Irish myth were the warriors of the Red Branch of Ulster. 'Craobh *Ruadh*' (red) has been argued by some scholars to be a misreading of 'Craobh *Rígh*' meaning 'kingship'. So instead of the 'Red Branch' warriors, they were originally the 'Royal Branch' warriors. The Connacht kings had their military élite known as the Gamhanrhide, which simply means 'warrior band'. In Munster there were two élites: the Degad, 'the seekers', and, more famously, the Nasc Niadh, 'warriors of the golden collar', who later existed as a nobiliary order which could be awarded by the kings of Munster and later still by The MacCarthy Mór, the heir to the kings and princes of Munster and Desmond (south Munster). Donal IX Mac-Carthy Mór was the last regnant king of Desmond and the Two Munsters, 1558–1596. However, the Nasc Niadh became the Niadh Nask during the exile of The MacCarthy Mór in France from 1690 to 1927. In 1996, the Rt. Hon. The Lord Borthwich, then president of the International Commission for Orders of Chivalry, wrote: 'The Niadh Nask is without doubt one of the most ancient nobiliary honours in the world, if not the most ancient! Its origins are shrouded in the mists of time. According to Gaelic historians, writing in the fifteenth century, it was founded almost a thousand years before the birth of Christ! Whether this is true or not we cannot say, but it is evident that the Order is at least pre-Chivalric in origin if not pre-Christian.'

The legends of Arthur, the British Celtic warlord, for early records never describe him as a king, and his warrior élite, his Knights of the Round Table, have their origin in the concept of Celtic warrior élites. So the Gaesatae were not an isolated example of such warrior groups. But they are, in fact, the first named Celtic warrior élite that we know of.

The Romans, according to Polybius, had received news of the Celtic preparations and, in their turn, were recruiting new legions and laying in stocks of corn and other stores ready for the campaign. It is at this stage that Polybius makes the observation that it was largely because of Rome's preoccupation with the Celts that the

Carthaginians were allowed to develop their empire in Spain without interference. 'The Romans, as I have mentioned above, regarded the threat from the north as by far the most pressing of their problems because it endangered their flank, and so they were compelled to ignore what was happening in Spain, and to devote their attention to dealing with the Celts.'

A Celtic army, including the professional warriors, the Gaesatae, crossed the Alps in 225 BC and joined the Boii, Insubres and Taurini, the last also emerging for the first time in arms against Rome. Again we learn the names of the Celtic leaders, Aneroestes and Concolitanus. A picture seems to be emerging of the Celtic armies being always under joint command, almost a parallel to Rome's system of having two consuls. But no further details are given as to who these kings were or from what tribes they came. We are told that Rome sent envoys to the Veneti and Celtic Cenomani and managed to bribe or otherwise persuade them not to join forces with the Celtic army. According to Dio Cassius, the Celts swore an oath not to take off their swords, belts or breast plates until they had entered the Roman Capitol. The oath was fulfilled with irony when the Celtic prisoners were marched in triumph to the Capitol still wearing their military accoutrements.

Polybius gives the Celtic strength as 50,000 infantry and 20,000 cavalry. Having detached warriors to secure their flank against any surprises coming from Veneti and Cenomani territory, they marched across the Apennines and into Etruria. Rome acted quickly, sending a praetor with an army into Etruria while one of the consuls, Lucius Aemilius Paullus, was sent to Ariminum with his army. He had two legions, each consisting of 5200 infantry and 300 cavalry. A similar number of soldiers had been dispatched with the other consul, Gaius Atilius, to Sardinia to ward off an expected Carthaginian attack. The two consular armies could call on an allied force of 30,000 infantry and 2000 cavalry. But as the Celts marched into Etruria, the Romans were able to raise an additional force from the erstwhile allies of the Celts; some 4000 Etrurian and Sabine cavalry with 50,000 infantry. The Umbrians and Sarsinati hill tribes of the Apennines raised a further 20,000 men. It was claimed that the Veneti and Cenomani had promised to send 20,000 but they certainly never appeared. Even so, the Celts were well outnumbered.

Indeed, Polybius proceeds to give a list of Roman reserve forces.

In Rome itself there were 20,000 infantry and 1500 cavalry, plus 30,000 infantry and 2000 cavalry from allied contingents. The number of Romans and their allies listed as being ready to bear arms totalled more than 700,000 infantry and 70,000 cavalry. In spite of such overwhelming odds in their favour, we are told that Rome was in dread of the Celts. The old fear of the Celts had not gone away in spite of Rome's continued denigration of them. Polybius explains:

> Meanwhile in Rome itself the people were filled with dread; the danger that threatened them was, they believed, both great and imminent, and these feelings were natural enough, since the age-old terror inspired by the Celts had never been altogether dispelled. Their thoughts always returned to this possibility and the authorities were continuously occupied with calling up and enrolling legions and summoning those of the allies who were liable to service to hold themselves ready. All Roman subjects in general were required to provide lists of men of military age, since the authorities were anxious to know the total strength that was available to them, and meanwhile stocks of corn, of missiles and of other warlike stores had been collected on a scale which exceeded any such preparations within living memory.

In spite of the overwhelming number of Romans and their allies, we are told by Polybius that the Celtic army not only descended on Etruria but 'overran the whole region, plundering the country as they chose, and as they met no opposition, they advanced upon Rome itself.' It seems, reading between the lines, that the Roman commanders were reluctant to meet the Celts in battle. Why would they be so hesitant, why would the Roman people be 'filled with dread'? After all, Roman historians had recited a litany of 'devastating' victories over the Celts during the last century and a half. The only reason is that the catalogue of victories were not as devastating as they claimed.

The Celts reached Clusium and here they learnt that a Roman army, commanded by a praetor, was marching on their rear. 'They turned to meet it, full of ardour to engage the enemy. At sunset the two armies were almost in contact, and they encamped the night with only a short distance separating them.'

Here Aneroestes and Concolitanus showed astute generalship.

They ordered campfires to be lit, so the Romans thought they were encamped for the night. But the infantry was then withdrawn towards Faesulae (Fiesoli). Faesulae lay some 80 miles from Clusium so we must assume that the Celts only marched in that direction and not to the town itself. Aneroestes and Concolitanus had ordered their cavalry to remain in the camp and then, as soon as it was daylight, in view of the Romans, they were to apparently withdraw towards the Celtic infantry who had, under cover of darkness, taken up defensive positions.

The subterfuge worked. At dawn, the Roman praetor saw that the infantry had apparently fled and the cavalry, unsupported, was withdrawing. The praetor gave the order to pursue the Celts in what he thought was their retreat. These manoeuvres of the Celtic army give lie to the Roman claims that the Celts had no sophistication in battle, no discipline and no knowledge of military art.

As the Roman legions approached, the main body of the Celts sprang forward from their positions and charged them. A fierce battle followed, which was stubbornly contested on both sides, but in the end the courage and superior numbers of the Celts prevailed.

Polybius tells us that 6000 Romans were slain in the battle and the survivors were put to flight, retreating to a hill where they barricaded themselves into fortified positions. The Celtic leaders now left only a detachment of cavalry to prevent the Romans from breaking out and set up camp to recuperate after the engagement.

The consul Lucius Aemilius Paullus had marched his army from Ariminum into Etruria and reached the area within days of the Celtic victory at Clusium. Paullus decided to give battle after resting for the night. He would personally lead his cavalry to the hill where the survivors of the praetor's army were sheltering and relieve them while his infantry, at dawn, moved into battle positions.

The Celtic leaders, watching the arrival of the consular army, had, according to Polybius, held a council. Aneroestes argued against giving battle and favoured a withdrawal, with their booty, back across the Apennines. The council of chieftains decided to follow his advice. During the night they quietly broke camp and marched north.

Paullus had rescued the survivors of the praetor's army and, finding the Celtic army moving north, decided against joining battle with them. We are not told why; perhaps he thought it was another ruse the like of which had brought about the annihilation of the praetor's army. However, he decided to follow at a respectable distance in the rear as Aneroestes and Concolitanus moved their forces towards the Apennines.

Now the Romans had a piece of luck. The second consul, Gaius Regulus Atilius, the son of the consular hero of the war against Carthage, realising there was no Carthaginian threat, had decided to return his army from Sardinia to the Italian mainland, had landed at Pisae (Pisa) and was marching south to Rome along the very road on which the Celtic army was heading north. The Celtic army, unknowingly, was placed between Atilius in the north and Paullus in the south.

Some Celtic advance scouts were captured by members of Atilius' vanguard as they reached the vicinity of Telamon, a town in Etruria named after the Argonaut who was the father of Ajax. The hapless Celtic prisoners were vigorously interrogated by Atilius and from them the consul learned not only of the approach of the main Celtic army but of the approach of his fellow consul Paullus in the rear of them. The consul was astonished and delighted as he now realised that the Celtic army was trapped between the two consular armies. He ordered his military tribunes to form the legions into battle lines and advance at marching pace until they came to some high ground which dominated the road along which the Celts were marching. He galloped his cavalry up, anxious to occupy it before the Celts arrived. The taking of the high ground ensured that he was able to have a dominant position in the forthcoming battle.

Aneroestes, Concolitanus and their fellow chieftains initially supposed that Paullus' cavalry had outflanked their column. A detachment of Celtic cavalry and lightly armed troops was sent forward to capture the hill. But when some Roman prisoners were brought in, the Celts learnt of the arrival of the second Roman army. The Celtic leaders did the only logical thing they could and deployed their infantry so that the Celtic army faced in both directions, front and rear. The Gaesatae were posted to face Paullus, with the warriors of the Insubres in support. Facing Atilius were the Taurini and the Boii. The cavalry and the chariots had been placed at the end of either wing. The baggage had been sent to a neighbouring hill under guard. Even Polybius had to admit: 'This Celtic order of battle which faced both ways was not only awe-inspiring to see but was also well suited to the needs of the situation.' It was a new tactic and the fact that the Romans were amazed by it is another indication of how illusory were their claims that the Celts knew little of the art of war.

The consul Paullus had also learnt of Atilius' arrival and had sent his cavalry, in a flanking movement, to reinforce Atilius while he marched his legions into battle lines.

Polybius gives an exciting account of what was to be the fateful battle of Telamon.

The Insubres and the Boii wore their trousers and light cloaks, but the Gaesatae had been moved by their thirst for glory and their defiant spirit to throw away these garments and so they took up their positions in front of the whole army naked and wearing nothing but their arms. They believed that they would be better equipped for action in this state, as the ground was in places overgrown with brambles and these might catch in their clothes and hamper them in the use of their weapons.

In this Polybius was entirely wrong. As has already been pointed out, the Gaesatae were professional warriors who fought naked in the belief that nakedness, the contact with Mother Earth, added to their spiritual aura, ensuring rebirth in the Otherworld if they perished in this one.

The battle opened with a cavalry engagement and in this action there came an immediate setback for the Romans. The consul, Gaius Atilius, was killed. He had demonstrated particular individual bravery and so his head was taken and brought to Aneroestes as a token of respect for the Roman commander. In spite of the loss of the consul, the Romans fought on stubbornly and were able to eventually command the heights. Unfortunately, we are not told who took over command of Atilius' army. Polybius says: 'The battlefield provided a strange and marvellous spectacle, not only to those who were actually present but to all those who could afterwards picture it in their imagination from the reports.'

The Romans were, he says,

157

. . . dismayed by the splendid array of the Celtic host and the ear-splitting din which they created. There were countless horns and trumpets being blown simultaneously in their ranks, and as the whole army was also shouting its war-cries, there arose such a babble of sound that it seemed to come not only from the trumpets and the soldiers but from the whole surrounding country-side at once. Besides this, the aspect and the movements of the naked warriors in the front ranks made a terrifying spectacle. They were all men of splendid physique and in the prime of life, and those in the leading companies were richly adorned with gold necklaces and bracelets. The mere sight of them was enough to arouse fear among the Romans but at the same time the prospect of gaining so much plunder made them twice as eager to fight.

The Gaesatae were warriors who were imbued with the concept of single combat and hand-to-hand fighting. They were armed with sword and shield. Therefore when the Roman commanders advanced their javelin throwers (*velites*), who moved ahead of the infantry and discharged their missiles, the Gaesatae were soon in difficulties. 'The shield used by the Celts does not cover the whole body, and so the tall stature of these naked warriors made the missiles all the more likely to find their mark.' Yet if the Gaesatae were carrying the usual Celtic oval shield, they were surely well protected?

The Gaesatae found themselves subject to a murderous barrage of javelins while being unable to close with their adversaries. Some of them broke ranks, and rushed forward to engage the enemy, throwing away their lives as they ran forward and thus made themselves a more vulnerable target. The others were pushed back on the Insubres, who were behind their ranks. They were thrown into disorder. Unable to get near the Roman ranks for hand-to-hand combat, cut to pieces by the rain of missiles, the Gaesatae were finally broken.

Once the Gaesatae were broken, the Roman commanders ordered a head-on charge. Insubres, Boii and Taurini held their ground and hand-to-hand fighting ensued. It was bloody. Even Polybius admits that the Celts stood firm at first and were the equal to the Romans in courage. However, he believed that the Roman shields were better designed for defence and the Roman swords superior for attack. The Celtic sword, he observes, could only be used for cutting and not for thrusting.

The end finally came, however, when the Roman cavalry charged against the flank. The Celtic cavalry tried to counter the measure but were too late. They were pushed aside and the Celtic infantry were cut down where they stood. Polybius gives a figure of the Celtic dead at 40,000 with 10,000 taken prisoner. Among the prisoners was Concolitanus. Aneroestes fled the battlefield with his retinue but, finding themselves cut off and surrounded, they committed suicide rather than fall into the hands of the Romans.

The surviving consul Paullus ordered the spoils and trophies from the Celts to be gathered and sent them under escort, with his prisoners, to Rome. Taking command of the legions, he rested them awhile before marching along the frontier of Liguria and invading the territory of the Boii, pursuing the scattered remnants of the Celtic army. He allowed his troops a free hand at raiding, burning farmsteads and villages and plundering the countryside. As summer ended, he pulled his troops back and returned to Rome. Paullus' army was the first Roman army to cross into the Po Valley and ravage the country of the Celts.

In Rome, a triumph was ordered. The Celtic standards and the gold torques of the warriors were sent to decorate the Capitol. The rest of the spoils and the prisoners were used to adorn Paullus' triumphant entry into the city.

'This was how the most formidable of the Celtic invasions, which had placed all the Italians and, above all, the Romans in mortal danger, was finally destroyed,' observed Polybius.

Among the prisoners paraded in Rome was a young Insubrean warrior from Mediolanum. He was taken as a slave into the family of Caecilius, a celebrated plebeian *gens*. His first name was Caius. What his work was we do not know, but it is likely that he was a house slave – it might be that he was frequently being told to stand still (*statio!*), for he took the Latin name Caecilius, from his master, and the *cognomen* or nickname, Statius. He was, apparently, highly intelligent and learnt the language of his masters fluently. So well did he develop his ability that he was, some twenty years later, made a freedman and subsequently became the chief comic dramatist of Rome of his day. Some forty-two titles of his plays are known but, alas, no complete texts survive, only fragments in quotations. Caecilius was still alive in 166 BC when he passed judgement on the play *Andria* by Publius Terentius Afer (193–159 BC), a friend of his.

Terence had also been a slave in Rome, taken from Carthage. Another friend of the Celtic dramatist was Quintus Ennius who recorded the tradition that the Celts actually did capture the Capitol. Perhaps, as has already been pointed out, he picked this up from Caecilius Statius. It is impossible not to indulge in one historical 'if only' here. If only this young Insubrean warrior turned playwright had recorded his experience at Telamon as seen from the Celtic viewpoint – or, if he did do so, if only his text had survived . . .

Caius Caecilius Statius is the first in a long tradition of Celts winning fame as writers in the language of their conquerors, a tradition which has lasted until the present day.

Polybius says of Telamon: 'The victory encouraged the Romans to hope that they could clear the Celts from the entire valley of the Po.' Indeed, this now became Rome's firm policy and in 224 BC, the year after Telamon, both consuls Quintus Fulvius and Titus Manlius, with two full-strength armies, marched north with orders to invade the territory of the Boii. We are told that the invasion took the Boii by surprise and caused them to submit to Rome. But the campaign, in fact, produced no practical results and the onset of heavy rains and the outbreak of an epidemic among the Roman ranks caused the armies to withdraw.

Undaunted, in 223 BC, the consuls Gaius Flaminius and Publius Furius invaded the Celtic territory for the second time. Polybius says that they entered through the country of the 'Anares, who live not far from Massilia'. However, Polybius was in error and the Anares' territory he referred to was just to the south-east of what became Placentia, modern Piacenza. The Romans seem to have decided to bypass the territory of the Boii, to establish friendly relations with the Anares, perhaps a Ligurian tribe, and then to march into the territory of the Insubres, north of the Po. They did so by crossing the Po at the junction with the River Adda, west of Placentia. The Romans suffered many losses during their crossing and while they were setting up a fortified encampment.

The Roman historians are unwilling to go into much detail but they say: 'The Romans occupied this encampment for a time but later concluded a truce by the terms of which they agreed to leave Insubrean territory.' This undoubtedly means that the Insubres were able to defeat the Roman army and force it to withdraw from their lands under the terms of this truce.

Marching in a north-easterly direction, the Romans crossed the River Clusius and entered the territory of the Cenomani with whom they had already concluded a treaty prior to Telamon. The Cenomani were persuaded to join the Romans in a new invasion of the Insubrean territory. This event underscores the fact that the 'treaty' by which they had left Insubrean territory had been rather one-sided and not in favour of Rome. The Cenomani and Romans ravaged the countryside and burnt many of the Insubrean settlements. It is difficult to understand the short-sighted policy of the Cenomani leadership in trying to 'sup with the devil'. It was surely obvious that the Romans were applying their time-honoured policy of *divide et impera* (divide and rule). Once they had used the Cenomani to deal with their fellow Celts, then the Romans would eventually deal with the Cenomani.

The leaders of the Insubres, angered by the piecemeal attacks on undefended settlements in their territory, decided to bring the Romans and Cenomani into a decisive battle. Polybius said that the Insubres 'took down the golden standards which are known as the "Immovables" from the temple of Minerva, and made all other necessary preparations for war'. The standards were probably in a Celtic sanctuary sacred to their equivalent of the goddess Minerva. In Britain the goddess Sulis was equated with the Roman Minerva and a triune goddess, the Suleviae, has been found on the Continent. The sanctuary from where these standards were taken might well have been at the Insubrean capital of Mediolanum, the central sanctuary.

The Roman historians put the Insubrean army at a total force of 50,000 men. Thus the Romans could be seen, as usual, as being greatly outnumbered by their enemies. Polybius says they had to rely on the Cenomani to help them.

But at the same time they remembered the habitual treachery of the Celts and the fact that their allies were the fellow nationals of their opponents, and so they hesitated to call upon men of such unpredictable loyalties to fight beside them in a battle where so much was at stake. In the end, they overcame their misgivings. They themselves remained on the right bank of the river, placing their Celtic allies on the other side and destroyed the bridges. They did this partly as a precaution against their allies, and partly so as to leave themselves no prospect of safety except through victory, since the river, which was now impassable, lay to their rear. After making these dispositions they were ready for action.

The Romans, say their historians, had learnt from previous battles that the Celts were most dangerous in the initial attack and while their ardour was still fresh. It is at this point that Polybius informs us that Celtic swords were poorly made, that after the first encounter the edges were blunted, that they could be bent both lengthwise and sideways, and that Celtic warriors had to straighten them with the foot against the ground. The same details about the Celtic swords are found in Plutarch's account of Camillus' victory over the Celts in 377 BC. This criticism, as we have seen, does not accord with surviving examples of Celtic sword craftsmanship.

The Romans attacked the Insubreans first. The front ranks carried the thrusting spears which were normally carried by the third ranks, the *triarii*. This was apparently so that the Celtic warriors could not get near enough to cause any casualties with their swords. The Romans then closed with the Celts, leaving them no room to raise their sword arms to slash in 'the stroke which is peculiar to the Celts and the only one they can make, as their swords have no points'.

The Romans moved forward thrusting with their swords and thus inflicted heavy casualties. Even though it is claimed that the Romans had achieved a 'brilliant victory', Polybius severely criticised the consul Flaminius. He considered the consul had made a serious error in deploying his troops with their backs to a river without room to fall back and reform if the need arose. As it was, there was no need to fall back and the Romans returned home victorious from the campaign of 223 BC.

Certainly, it seems that the campaign had been a successful one so far as Rome was concerned, and before the start of the campaigning season in 222 BC the Celtic tribes of the Po Valley sent an embassy to Rome to sue for peace before a new invasion could be mounted. The envoys from the Celtic tribes were not bound by conditions and were open to any proposals. However, Marcus Claudius Marcellus and Gnaeus Cornelius Scipio were the new consuls and, feeling that Rome now had the upper hand over the Celts of northern Italy, they refused to discuss peace terms. Rome declared a war of extermination on the Celts of the Po Valley.

The Celtic envoys returned with the news and once more the chieftains decided that their only hope lay in sending for outside aid. We know that the Celts of the Po Valley were a settled agricultural community. It could be that, unlike the Senones, they were not a warlike people. They persuaded, or hired, an army of 30,000 Gaesatae from Transalpine Gaul to join them.

The consuls marched their armies once again for the territory of the Insubres and laid siege to a town named Acerrae, which lay between the Po and the Alps. It was impossible for the Insubres to raise the siege by attacking the Roman positions. There now appears a Celtic chieftain called Viridomarus. This name is a compound of *virido* and *marus*, the second element being the Celtic for 'great', while the first is derived from the word either for 'man' or for 'true'. Interestingly, Viridomarus called himself 'a son of the Rhenos'. Did this mean 'son of the Rhine', as most have interpreted it, seeing in it proof that he was a Transalpine mercenary? Or did it mean 'son of the Reno' in the Po Valley itself? Whichever, to the Celts both rivers were sacred and represented by gods and goddesses who were the ancestors of the people.

Viridomarus marched an Insubrean force to Clastidium (Casteggio) and laid siege to the Roman garrison there. The reason behind this tactic was to draw off the Roman army from their siege of the Insubrean town. It partially worked. Marcus Claudius Marcellus was forced to take a body of horse and infantry and set off to rescue the garrison. As soon as Viridomarus learnt of his approach, he raised the siege and deployed his Insubres to meet the Romans in battle order.

The Romans began the battle with a furious cavalry charge. The Celts stood their ground but were eventually surrounded. At this point we find a surprising development. Viridomarus offered a challenge to single combat in traditional Celtic fashion to settle the affair. Propertius describes the Celtic chieftain as tall in stature, dressed in striped trousers and hurling his javelins from his chariot. The surprise is that the consul Claudius Marcellus accepted the challenge in spite of the law forbidding single combat by Roman officers. He succeeded in slaying Viridomarus and the Celtic army crumbled before a renewed Roman attack. Some Celts managed to escape the encirclement; some plunged into the nearby river and were swept away by the strong current; others were cut down where they stood. The battle of Clastidium was as fateful for the Insubres as that of Telamon.

Clastidium is also noteworthy as the occasion when the Germanic peoples, the ancestors of the English, Franks (who gave their name eventually to France), Germans and others, first emerged into recorded history. The Roman *Acta Triumphalia* says that Marcus Claudius Marcellus gained the *spolia opima*, spoils of honour, for triumph 'over the Insubrean Celts and the Germans (*Germani*)'. It has been suggested that because the Romans often confused Celts and Germans, there is no proof that there were indeed Germans at Clastidium and that these were probably Belgae Celts, part of the Gaesatae contingent. But if we do accept that there were Germans at Clastidium, then they were not there as invaders nor were they fighting for their own lands. They were fighting under a Celtic commander in a Celtic army. Professor Eoin Mac Néill claimed that we are faced with the conclusion that the first mention of the Germanic peoples in history is as fighting for the Celts of the Po Valley against Rome, either as hired troops or as a force levied on a subject territory. Professor Mac Néill regards the presence of the German troops at Clastidium as indicating that they, or some portion of them, were then under Celtic political dominance.

He goes on to point out that this interpretation is supported by philological evidence and that a number of words of Celtic origin are found spread through the whole group of Germanic languages. Most of these words are connected with political organisations, says Mac Néill, which is indicative of Celtic political dominance at the time of their adoption into Germanic speech. Mac Néill was, of course, not the first to notice this. H. d'Arbois de Jubainville, in his *Eléments de Grammaire Celtique* (Paris, 1903) had already commented on the fact that all the Celtic loan words he had observed in the Germanic language were connected with law, government and politics. For example, the German *reich* meaning 'state', originally 'realm' or 'royal dominion', is traced to the Celtic *rigion*. From the Celtic word *ambactus*, used by Caesar in the sense of 'client' or 'dependant', and indicating one of the retainers of a Celtic chieftain who acted as an envoy, comes the German word *amt* meaning 'office', 'charge' or 'employment'. *Ambactus* provides the Romance languages, and English via Norman French, with the word 'ambassador'. The Celtic word *dunon*, a fortified place, found in the *dun* group of place-names, made its way through the German languages and arrived in English as the word 'town'.

The battle of Clastidium provides an all too brief glimpse of the *Germani*, who were not to enter historical record again for another century or so.

While the battle of Clastidium was being fought, the second consul, Gnaeus Cornelius Scipio, continued his siege of Acerrae and eventually captured it, with its large stocks of corn. The Insubres fell back on their capital city, Mediolanum. Cornelius appeared before the city but decided not to invest it, turning back towards Accerae. At this, the Insubres launched a bold attack on his rear, killed many of the Roman soldiers and routed the rest. Realising his mistake, Cornelius managed to regroup and turn his legions to meet the Celtic attack. A counter-attack was met by a stubborn resistance by the Insubres who held their ground. Cornelius' reserves arrived and the attack was renewed. The Insubres' lines were broken and their army scattered. Cornelius pursued and harried them, ravaging the countryside before capturing Mediolanum by a storming attack.

With the capture of their chief city, the Insubrean leaders met and offered their submission to Rome. During the course of this campaign there is no word of how the Gaesatae were engaged nor of any action from the Boii, the Taurini or the Cenomani. By 220 BC, however, it is recorded that the Roman legions had received the submission of all the Celtic tribes in Cisalpine Gaul with the exception of a few tribes in the Alpine foothills and the Taurini of Piedmont.

Polybius says of the campaign of 222 BC:

So ended the war against the Celts. If we consider it in terms of the audacity and the desperate courage displayed by those taking part and of the numbers who fought and died in the battles, this conflict is unsurpassed by any war in history; but from the point of view of the planning of the various offensives or of the judgment shown in executing them, the standard of generalship was beneath contempt.

Curiously, Polybius claims that 'not long afterwards I was to see these tribes completely expelled from the valley of the Po, except for a few districts at the foot of the Alps . . .'

Polybius died *c.*118 BC, and certainly saw the Po Valley being settled by Roman colonists with the Celtic tribes gradually submerged into what became known as Gallia Togata, the Celts who wear the toga – meaning Romanised Celts – but this was not as the result of the campaigns of 225–222 BC. What territory the Romans had managed to seize in this period was regained by the Celts and their hold was consolidated after Hannibal's invasion of 218 BC.

Meanwhile, the Romans were able to achieve the submission of the Po Valley after 222 BC by extending their lines of communication from Ariminum and, in 217 BC, building two more military colonies at Placentia and Cremona. These colonies had populations of 6000 people each and their role, once looked at in geographic terms, becomes obvious. Tacitus was later to remark of Cremona: 'The design was to have a frontier town, to bridle the Celts inhabiting beyond the Po, or any power on the other side of the Alps.' Certainly the new colonies formed defensive points along the valley. Tenney Frank, in the *Journal of the Royal Society*, IX, 1919, p. 202, argued that the first Roman colony of Placentia was probably built some 15 miles to the west of its later site because only with it sited here do Livy's and Polybius' descriptions of the subsequent battle of Trebbia make sense. Cremona, on the other hand, was placed to form a bridgehead for forthcoming Roman offensives over the Po river.

These military outposts of the Roman empire were placed beside an ancient road which ran down to Ariminum, a road which the Romans later rebuilt for military purposes. Along this line, all along the foothills of the Apennines, were several Etruscan and Celtic towns. Dr Ursula Ewins has argued that the Romans had also established a military garrison at Mutina (Modena), formerly an Etruscan town. They had established friendly relationships with the Veneti and felt they were able to check any Celtic uprising by means of these strategically placed military garrisons. Also the Placentia and Cremona garrisons, together with the military garrison of Clastidium, south of the Apennines, had the strategic importance of standing as a gateway to Liguria.

Importantly, the former consul Gaius Flaminius was given charge of the construction of Rome's 'Great North Road', the Via Flaminia, which would stretch to Ariminum while a parallel road, the Via Aurelia, would be built along the coast of Etruria to Pisae. Roman naval stations were built at Luna (Spexia) and Genua, modern Genoa. For a brief period Rome was able to boast that the conquest of the Celts of Cisalpine Gaul had been achieved . . . but only for a brief period.

[11]

Hannibal and the Celts

THE catalyst which caused the reassertion for independence by the Celtic tribes in the Po Valley was Carthage. Still smarting from the unjust and inequitable peace treaty with Rome, Carthage had turned to the Iberian peninsula to recoup her wealth and manpower. In 237 BC Hamilcar Barca, Rome's old antagonist, had established the city colony of Carthago Nova or New Carthage, now Cartagena, on the east coast of the Iberian peninsula. Between 237 and 219 BC Hamilcar, his son-in-law Hasdrubal and his young son Hannibal began to expand in the region south of the River Ebro, which Rome had set as the limit of their northern expansion. They overran the Greek colonies and the neighbouring Celtic tribes of the area. During this period of battles and sieges, the young Hannibal grew to manhood. In 228 BC Hamilcar was drowned while conducting a siege. Hasdrubal became Carthaginian commander and decided to move the borders of the empire up to the very banks of the River Ebro. In 221 BC, however, he was assassinated by an unnamed Celt. At the age of twenty-nine Hannibal was elected commander of the Carthaginian forces.

For two years Hannibal continued to expand Carthage's empire in Spain and then, in 219 BC, he laid siege to Saguntum, modern Sagunto, a colony 19 miles (30 kilometres) north of Valencia but south of the Ebro river. The Romans declared that Saguntum was a neutral city in alliance with Rome and an exception to the agreement that Carthage had a free hand south of the Ebro. Whether Saguntum's treaty with Rome was negotiated after the treaty with Carthage became a matter of dispute. Whatever the reality, Hannibal's siege of Saguntum took eight months.

Rome sent an embassy to Carthage led by Quintus Fabius. They were given an audience before the Carthaginian Suffete or Senate. The Roman Senate had instructed its envoys to ask whether

Hannibal's attack on Saguntum was in accordance with Carthaginian government policies. If so, Rome would declare war unless reparation was immediately made and Hannibal was handed over to Roman justice – that is, for execution. The Carthaginians accepted that the treaty had agreed that neither side was to interfere with the allies of the other, but insisted that at the time Saguntum was not in alliance with Rome. Quintus Fabius objected at the semantics of the reply and asked if Carthage wanted war or peace. The Suffete replied that it was indifferent to what Rome decided. Fabius then declared war on Carthage.

It must have been clear that an attack on Rome would emanate from Iberia and by a land route. A Carthaginian army would have to cross the Pyrenees through southern Gaul and then cross the Alps into northern Italy.

Following Fabius' declaration of war, the same envoys went to Iberia and attempted to persuade both the Iberians and Celtiberians to make alliances with Rome instead of with Carthage. They were given short shrift and so crossed into southern Gaul where they were faced with 'the strange and alarming spectacle' of the Celtic tribal assemblies being attended by men clad in battle armour. The Roman envoy was invited to speak at one assembly and began by extolling the virtues of Rome and the extent of her dominions. The envoy went on to ask the Celts not to allow a Carthaginian army to pass through their territory if it was attempting to invade Italy.

This request was met by a roar of anger and shouts of laughter from the young warriors present so that the chieftains had difficulty in restoring quiet. The Romans were told that it was impudent and ridiculous to suppose that the Celts would save Rome from invasion especially when it would be their own country which would be ravaged by a foreign army, their corn and crops which would be destroyed. The chieftains told the envoys that Rome had never helped the Celtic peoples, nor had Carthage ever injured them as Rome had. These words were recorded by the Romans but we do hear later that the Celtic tribes were well aware that the Carthaginians had been in conflict with the Celtiberians. However, the Roman ambassadors were informed that there was no good reason for Rome to expect that the Celts would help Rome maintain her empire. Furthermore, the Celts of southern Gaul had heard that their compatriots of

Cisalpine Gaul were being expelled from their territories or forced to pay tribute to Rome.

This answer makes apparent some very important facts. We see just how close-knit the Celtic world was. The injuries done to the Cisalpine Gauls were known among the Celts of the Pyrenean foot-hills. A few decades later, in 197/196 BC, the people of Lampsacos, a Phocian colony, contacted their kinsmen in Massilia, asking them to request their Celtic neighbours to mediate with the Celts of Galatia, on the central plain of what is now Turkey, specifically with the Tolistoboii, to persuade them to enact policies more helpful to them. The people of Lampsacos must have known how closely the diverse Celtic world kept in communication. These are early examples of the solidarity that existed between all the Celtic peoples even when of different tribes living at great distances from each other.

Livy says that at every tribal assembly the Roman envoys attended in southern Gaul, the reply was the same. They had no friendly reception until they reached Massilia where the Greek city made friendly overtures to them. 'They learned that Hannibal had already successfully worked upon the Celtic tribes and determined their atti-tude. It was added, however, that not even to Hannibal would the Celtic peoples, with their warlike and independent spirit, prove very tractable friends unless he mollified their chiefs from time to time with presents of gold – which all Celts coveted.' Is this a piece of Roman 'face-saving'? If the alliance of the Celts depended on bribery then surely Rome could have matched any sums that Carthage might put forward? No; it is obvious that the reason for the Celtic support of Hannibal was one of 'national' feeling, of kinship with the Celts of Italy.

The tour of the Roman envoys was not successful and they eventu-ally returned to Rome. It seemed that Livy was partially right in that the Carthaginians had also sent envoys to the Celtic tribes of Transalpine Gaul not only to reconnoitre the Alpine passes into Italy but to form alliances with the tribes in whose territory lay the best routes. While the Celts of the territory between the Pyrenees and Liguria had rejected the Roman overtures, they also knew that the Carthaginians in Iberia had subjugated many Celtic tribes there, and some of the Celtic chieftains had doubts whether the Carthaginians meant to deal fairly with them. Some of the tribes took to arms and gathered at the town of Ruscino, now Tour de Rousillon, on the coast north of the Pyrenees. The Carthaginian commander sent envoys to these Celtic chieftains and invited them to a conference with him either at Ruscino or at neighbouring Iliberris, now Elvira. The Celtic chieftains decided to meet Hannibal at Iliberris. Hannibal told them that 'he had entered Gaul not as an enemy but as a friend and had no intention, unless they compelled him, of drawing the sword before he was in Italy'. The conference agreed a treaty whereby the Carthaginian army was able to pass through Celtic territories without molestation. But Hannibal knew that he had to have not only the goodwill of the Celts of southern Gaul but the alliance and participation of the Celts of the Po Valley. As Polybius says:

> He knew that the only means of carrying the war against the Romans into Italy was, after surmounting, if possible, the difficulties of the route, to reach the above country [Cisalpine Gaul] and to employ the Celts as cooperators and confederates in his enterprise.

Hannibal had placed one of his brothers, another Hasdrubal, in command of the garrisons in Iberia. He had two other brothers, Hanno and Mago, who were also in positions of command in his army which he gathered at New Carthage. The army numbered over 100,000 men, 90,000 foot and 12,000 cavalry, plus a siege train and about fifty war elephants. He had his Carthaginian troops and cavalry from Numidia but the bulk of the army consisted of Celtiberians and Iberians, many of them warriors who had recently been fighting the Carthaginians. Why this abrupt switch of alliance? These Iberian Celts, I would suggest, had been persuaded into the alliance to go to the aid of the Celts of the Po Valley.

In May 218 BC, Hannibal's army began to march north to the Pyrenees. It has been estimated that even marching ten abreast, with horsemen on either side, it would have constituted a column 5–7 miles long. It was a journey of 600 miles through Iberia into southern Gaul. Sometimes the army had to march through unfriendly territory whose tribes had not been subdued nor accepted an alliance or treaty. Before crossing the Alps, Hannibal placed his brother Hanno in charge of the area with 10,000 foot and 1000 cavalry, to protect his lines of supply or retreat.

Obviously word of the Carthaginian objective had reached the tribes of the Po Valley and given them new hope in their struggle for independence. Hannibal had sent envoys to them and a treaty had been made. The Boii and Insubres once more joined forces. We later hear the name of a prominent Boii chieftain, Magalus. Without waiting for Hannibal to arrive, the Celts moved against the new Roman garrison settlements of Placentia and Cremona. The Roman colonists fled with three Roman officials whose job had been to superintend the confiscation of Boii lands and their allocation to the Roman settlers. These officials were named as Gaius Lutatis, Gaius Servilius and Titus Annius, although other records give the last two names as Quintus Aucilius and Gaius Herennius or Publius Cornelius Asina and Gaius Papirius Maso. Only the name of Gaius Lutatis appears constant in all the accounts. Fearing that the newly constructed garrison towns of Placentia and Cremona would not have sufficient protection, the Roman settlers withdrew to Mutina.

Livy says that the Celts 'were no great hands at military tactics and without any experience in siege warfare'. They made no effort to storm Mutina. However, he does say that the Celtic chieftains invited the Roman envoys to talks about peace. When the Roman envoys went to speak with the Celtic chieftains, they were seized and imprisoned by them: 'an action which violated not only the accepted conventions of international procedure but also the specific guarantees given on the occasion', condemns Livy. There is an irony here for Livy has forgotten the fact that Roman envoys at Clusium had first demonstrated to the Celts that sometimes the conventions of international procedures did not count for much. The Celts seemed merely to be following a Roman precedent. However, as with most things, there was a reason why the Celts seized the Roman envoys. The reason is hidden in Livy's text when he says that 'the Celts refused to release them unless their own hostages were restored'.

The Romans' seizure of prominent Celts among the Po Valley tribes to use as hostages was now being countered and their release demanded. The news of the Celtic uprising and attack on Mutina caused the praetor Lucius Manlius to set out with a relief column. Again Livy excuses the poor generalship of the Roman commander: 'Indignation prevented proper precautions being taken.' Probably it was an underestimation of his opponents that led to his rashness. As Lucius Manlius hurried his relief force through uncultivated lands and woodlands, without putting out scouting parties or flanking protection, the Celts ambushed his column. Heavy casualties were suffered.

Lucius Manlius and the survivors managed to raise a fortified encampment. The Celts then seemed to fade into the surrounding forests and vanish. Celtic tactics appear obvious. When the Romans, thinking the Celts had moved off, finally ventured out of their encampment and began to march forward again, the Celts reappeared and attacked the rear of the column. 'Discipline went to pieces and panic spread,' says Livy. Some 500 Roman soldiers had been killed in the first attack. In the second, Livy reckons a further 700 men were killed and six Roman standards were captured. Lucius Manlius and the survivors, fighting determinedly for every hundred yards gained, managed to reach a village near the Po called Tannetum, which they then fortified. Livy says that the Celts of Brixia (Brescia) sold the Romans some provisions, which were brought downriver at night. As all Cisalpine Gaul was in arms against Rome, this seems an odd thing for the Brixians to do, unless Livy is trying to reinforce the Roman prejudice that the Celts were always quarrelling amongst themselves. Or, indeed, perhaps a few renegade merchants did see a way of making a quick profit from the Romans.

The Roman Senate realised that they had a new war with the Celts of the Po Valley on their hands. They had been too busy considering the threat from Carthage to notice the build-up of discontent. Fresh troops were raised and placed under the command of a new praetor, Gaius Atilius, who immediately set off northwards to attempt a rescue of Lucius Manlius and his men. The new force consisted of one Roman legion, 5200 men, plus 5000 allied troops. At this time, one of the consuls, Publius Cornelius Scipio, had sailed from Rome with sixty warships. He was intending to go to Iberia and attack the Carthaginians there. However, news reached him that Hannibal was already across the Pyrenees. He made his way along the Etrurian coastline and around the Ligurian shore to Massilia, which was in alliance with Rome.

Scipio took up a position on the east bank of the mouth of the Rhône to watch for the approach of the Carthaginian army. Most of the Roman soldiers were incapacitated by seasickness and fever. Scipio sent out some Massiliot guides and local Celtic mercenaries to scout the countryside. To their astonishment, for Scipio had not really believed that Hannibal had actually crossed the Pyrenees, they found the Carthaginian army crossing the Rhône about four days' march north of Massilia. In spite of the earlier failure of the Roman envoys, Scipio had, surprisingly, been able to persuade a Celtic tribe, the Volcae Tectosages, to ally themselves with Rome. The Massiliots were probably the cause of this volte-face and they persuaded the Tectosages to take up an alliance. The Massiliots and Tectosages had always enjoyed good relations and perhaps they did not want to lose the Massilia trading concessions. Scipio, via the Massiliots, demanded that the Tectosages should dispute Hannibal's crossing of the Rhône until Scipio's own Roman troops recovered sufficiently from seasickness to join the fight. The Tectosages took up positions on the eastern bank of the river.

Polybius gives a vivid description, perhaps having copied it from an eyewitness, one of the lost books of Sosilos, a Greek historian who accompanied the Carthaginian army. He says that on coming to the river bank, Hannibal attempted to make friends among the local peoples while hiring and requisitioning as many boats and canoes as he could, even cutting down trees for the making of rafts.

According to Livy: 'The Celtic warriors came surging to the river bank, howling and singing as their custom was, shaking their shields above their heads and brandishing their spears...' But Hannibal had outflanked them, sending Hanno, with the Numidian cavalry, to forge upstream and come round behind them. If this was his brother, Hanno, then presumably he had delegated his command at the Pyrenees to someone else. But this might be another Hanno. Certainly, like Roman names, Carthaginian names are repetitive. The Tectosages dispersed in confusion. Hannibal then sent a detachment of 500 Numidian cavalry to apprise him of where Scipio's legions were while his army continued their crossing. They were still on the coast.

Magalus, chieftain of the Boii, and envoys from the Celts of the Po Valley, arrived at Hannibal's encampment at this point. It is obvious that they had arrived in accordance with a previously arranged plan to guide Hannibal's army through the Alpine passes. It seems that many of the Carthaginian troops viewed the towering Alps with a degree of awe. Hannibal had to call his men together and address them.

'What do you think the Alps are? Are they anything worse than high mountains? Say, if you will, they are higher than the Pyrenees, but what of it? No part of the earth reaches the sky; no height is insuperable to men. Moreover, the Alps are not desert; men live there, they till the ground; there are animals there – living creatures. If a small party can cross them, surely armies can?

'These very ambassadors whom you see before you have crossed the Alps. They didn't fly over them on wings . . . Are you going to let it be said that the Celts gained possession of a country which the Carthaginians were afraid to even approach? Why, even the Celts once captured Rome – and you despair of being able even to get near it. Take your choice. Either submit that the Celts are better men than you, or else follow me; and look forward at the end of your journey to that rich plain which spreads between the Tiber and the walls of Rome.'

Nothing seems to work better in galvanising men into action than hinting that they are not equal to the task or that others are better than they. Within a couple of days, the Carthaginian army, guided by Magalus and his Boii, were heading through the mountain passes.

Publius Cornelius Scipio, having failed to intercept Hannibal, sent a frantic message to Rome. According to Polybius:

> . . . finding the enemy gone, he was in the highest degree astonished, as he had been convinced that they would never venture to march on Italy by this route owing to the number and unruly character of the native inhabitants. On seeing that they had gone, he returned with all speed to his ships and began to embark his forces. Sending his brother to conduct the campaign in Iberia, he himself turned back and made sail for Italy with the design of marching through Etruria and reaching the foot of the pass over the Alps before the enemy.

Publius Cornelius Scipio's brother, Gnaeus Cornelius Scipio Calvus, was serving as his second-in-command. He had been consul in 222 BC. He was now dispatched with the main body of the army to continue to Iberia and carry the fight to Carthage there. Scipio took part of the force to the Po Valley.

The Roman Senate had already instructed Gaius Atilius to attempt to check the Carthaginian descent into Italy through the Alpine passes but the praetor's army was bogged down in skirmishes with the Boii and the Insubres. Scipio had landed at Pisae and began to advance towards the Po Valley. The Senate anxiously ordered the second consul Tiberius Sempronius Longus, then in Sicily, to leave the defence of Sicily to his second-in-command, Marcus Pomponius Matho, and set out with his remaining legions, numbering 40,000 men, to Ariminum in order to support Scipio's army. Hannibal's descent into the Po Valley was to be stopped at all costs.

Meanwhile, the Carthaginian army had turned northward, along the Rhône beyond Avignon, into the country of the Cavari, then north of the River Aygues into the country of the Tricastini and Vocontii, turning away from the Rhône, where the tributary of the Druentia (Drôme) enters it, and marching upriver through Col de Grimone. Druentia means 'the oak-lined river' but it had dangerous, sudden currents especially when swollen by autumnal rains. There were many changing channels and deep potholes.

The Carthaginians were now passing along the southern borders of the Allobroges, which Celtic name seems to indicate 'foreigners'. Livy says that they were 'a Celtic people even in those days inferior to none in Gaul for power and fame'. The Allobroges, at the time of Hannibal's arrival, had been seized by discord. Two brothers were disputing the kingship. Brancus, the elder brother, was king, but his younger brother was claiming that he should be king under the Celtic system of election by three generations of his family meeting in council. Hannibal was asked to arbitrate between them and supported Brancus who was the popular choice. In return Brancus and his Allobroges agreed to provision the Carthaginians, especially with clothing more suitable to the autumn weather. Brancus even supplied an armed contingent to act as a rearguard for his army.

There now comes a confusing account. Polybius says that once Brancus' contingent left Hannibal's army, the Allobrogian chieftains decided to attack the Carthaginians.

As soon as the latter had set off for home and Hannibal's troops began to advance into difficult country, the Allobrogian chiefs gathered a large force and took up commanding positions alongside the road by which the Carthaginians would have to climb.

It seems unlikely that Brancus had suddenly revoked his treaty with Hannibal. The obvious answer is that these Allobroges were those who supported Brancus' brother in his attempt to gain the chieftainship. No historian seems to have offered this explanation, all preferring to believe the Roman view that the Celts were just generally untrustworthy. Polybius says:

> If they had only kept their plans secret they would have completely destroyed the Carthaginian army. But in the event, their scheme became known, and though the Celts inflicted heavy casualties on Hannibal's troops, they suffered at least as many themselves. Hannibal received intelligence that the Celts had seized these points of vantage and he pitched camp at the foot of the pass; there he halted while he sent forward some of his Celtic guides to reconnoitre the ground and report on the enemy's dispositions and general situation.

Indeed, it was the Boii guides who alerted Hannibal that the Allobrogian rebels were planning an ambush in a narrow pass known as the Gorge des Gas. Hannibal selected a small force of men, carrying only light arms, outflanked the rebel tribesmen and scattered them.

It took the Carthaginians fifteen days to cross through the Alps. Of the 102,000 troops he had set out with, only 60,000 made it to the Rhône and those who started the final movement through the Alps numbered about 40,000. Garrison troops had been left along the way but many thousands had either deserted, been taken captive or been killed. Lucius Cincius Alimentus, who was taken prisoner by Hannibal, recorded that he had 80,000 infantry and 10,000 cavalry with him. Other historians vary the figures from 100,000 infantry and 20,000 cavalry to 20,000 infantry and 6000 cavalry. A fair estimate of the Carthaginian army as it finally emerged into the Po Valley would be 23,000. Of the war elephants, variously given as between thirty-seven and fifty when Hannibal started out, only a few remained.

The use of elephants in battle was unusual but not new to Rome: we have seen that Pyrrhos had used Indian elephants in his campaigns. It has been argued that Hannibal used both African and Indian elephants. Representations of African elephants appear on

Carthaginian coins at this time while an Etruscan coin has an Indian elephant. Hannibal's personal elephant was called Surus, the Syrian. Many of these elephants perished in the Alps, being used to eating vegetation and roots not found in the snowy, wintry conditions of the crossing.

Hannibal's Celtic guides had led him through the land of the Tricorii, south of Mont Genève between Col de la Traversette in the north and Château Queyras to the south, before swinging north to the capital of the Taurini at Turin. Magalus and his Celtic guides had done a splendid job. Without the support of the Celts, Hannibal's famous passage through the Alps could not have been accomplished, yet, as we have already discussed, it is Hannibal who gets the praise for his 'genius'.

Hannibal was able to give a 'pep talk' to his men as they prepared to move down into the Po Valley.

'Soldiers . . . ! You are entering friendly country, inhabited by people who hate the Romans as much as we do. The rest of your journey will be smooth and downhill, and after one, or, at most, a second battle you will have the citadel and capital of Rome in your power and possession.'

Hannibal was wrong. The journey into the Po Valley was not at all smooth. Marching down the mountain road, the army found the track, passing between a steep mountain wall on one side and a 1000-foot precipice on the other, was blocked by large boulders. There had obviously been a landslide that autumn. Lightly armed troops could climb across but the horses, elephants, siege train and baggage could not. Having seen the Po Valley below, Hannibal was not prepared to give up now. Science came to his aid. His engineers built fires around the rock, piling wood on the fires. Vinegar, probably just bad wine, was ordered to be brought forward. Such wine vinegar has a low alcoholic content and contains between three and nine per cent of acetic acid. At the right moment the vinegar was thrown on to the heated boulder, while more men with iron hammers and picks stood ready to rush in and pound it. The boulder split and crumbled and was dragged out of the path.

According to Livy:

Four days were spent about this rock, the beasts nearly perishing through hunger; for the summits of the mountains are for the most part bare, and if there is any pasture the snows bury it.

It was October 218 BC when the survivors of the Carthaginian army approached the capital of the Taurini. But at Turin there were more problems. The Celtic Taurini were in disagreement with the Insubres over some unexplained matter. Because the Insubres had allied themselves with Hannibal, the Taurini now refused to do so. Hannibal found that he had to take Turin by storm. To do this took time and the winter had already set in. This gave Cornelius Scipio and his legions time to reach the remnants of the Roman garrison at Placentia and take over command from Gaius Atilius and Lucius Manlius.

In December, hearing that Cornelius Scipio was near, Hannibal hurried his army along the northern bank of the Po and came to the Ticinus. This river was a tributary of the Po, on whose banks, a couple of centuries before, the Celts had inflicted their first major defeat on the Etruscans and marked the beginning of the decline of the Etruscan empire. Hannibal hoped to meet Scipio here and issued special instructions to his troops not to devastate Celtic property or lands. He urged all Celtic tribes to rise against Romans.

The two armies seemed to have encountered one another on a dark, wintry, rainswept day, simply by accident. Hannibal's Numidian cavalry fell on the rear of the Roman column and inflicted heavy casualties. The Celtic cavalry, at the same time, attacked their vanguard. The consul himself was severely wounded in this disastrous defeat for Rome. It is reported that the consul's life was saved by the bravery of his young son who was eventually to win fame as Scipio Africanus, Rome's greatest general. The remnants of Cornelius Scipio's army fled across the Ticinus, destroying the bridge after them, and took refuge behind the walls of Placentia.

The news of Hannibal's victory spread quickly through the Po Valley. Within days, Celts from the various Po Valley tribes flocked to join the Carthaginians and the Celts who had already taken up the sword against Rome. Hannibal had encamped his army 6 miles from Placentia where the Trebbia rose in the hills to the south-west. The second consul, Tiberius Sempronius Longus, who had arrived with his army from Sicily at Ariminum, had been waiting for Scipio to join him. Messengers brought him news of the disaster. He was not a cautious general and, without waiting further, he made a forced march from Ariminum through hostile territory to relieve the besieged survivors of Scipio's army. The combined Roman army was now 40,000 strong and determined to avenge themselves.

Some of the Celtic sub-tribes, between the Trebbia and the Po, had been unwilling to support Hannibal. Livy suggested 'they were unwilling to declare their allegiance outright, and looked for the favour of the winning side'. In other words, they would support whichever side won. However, Hannibal needed provisions and he sent some of his Celtic allies with Numidian cavalry, a force of 3000 men, to raid their territories. This caused these Celts to send a delegation to Scipio at Placentia asking for assistance. 'Scipio, however, found the request untimely and disliked the manner of it; he had no reason to trust the Celts, remembering, as he did, their many acts of treachery, not to mention others which time might have obliterated, and the recent perfidy of the Boii.'

The Celts in this area were septs of the Boii and it does seem curious that they, above all the tribes, should seek Roman aid when one of their own kings, Magalus, had made an alliance with Hannibal and, with other Boii, had guided him through the Alps. It might be more likely that these were Ligurian or Celto-Ligurian tribes to the west of the Trebbia. Notwithstanding Scipio's reservations, Sempronius Longus suggested that to offer assistance to the tribes might be a way of retaining their loyalty to Rome. He dispatched troops to the area on the west side of the Trebbia and was able to drive out the raiders. This filled Sempronius with enthusiasm and he determined, in spite of the cautions from the wounded Scipio, to make a surprise attack on the main Carthaginian army.

Hannibal had been warned of the Roman approach by the local Celtic population and prepared a trap. On the evening before the battle, Hannibal, in the words of Leonard Cottrell, one of the historians of his campaign, showed 'an almost diabolical understanding of primitive human psychology'. He had brought along some prisoners, young Celts who had been taken in the skirmishes with the Volcae and the Allobrogian rebels. He had these prisoners brought into a circle of his soldiers and offered them armour and weapons 'such as Celtic kings are wont to wear when engaged in single combat', observes Livy. He also showed them rich military cloaks and fine horses. He gave them the choice to remain as his slaves, wretched and ill-treated, or to fight one another to the death in single combat. Death would release them from their suffering; on the other hand, the winners would get the horses, cloaks and armour and be allowed to join his army. Polybius says that 'the young men, the moment they heard this, lifted up their hands and prayed to the gods, each eager to be himself one of the chosen'.

During the night before the battle, Mago, one of Hannibal's younger brothers, had taken 2000 cavalry and hidden in ambush positions. Then Hannibal sent other troops in a feint against the Roman camp to lure them out. Sempronius, impetuous as usual, fell into the trap. The feint drew the Romans out and Mago fell on them in the rear. Sempronius Longus' legionaries fought desperately as they found themselves surrounded. By the end of the day only half of their original force survived and managed to fight their way back to Placentia. The rest were fugitives, captured or dead in the drifting snow or icy river, which they had tried to recross.

The news of the defeat of both consular armies caused panic in Rome. New consuls were elected. These were Gnaeus Servilius Geminus and Gaius Flaminius. Flaminius was now consul for the second time in his career and he was a veteran of the previous war with the Celts of the Po Valley. Polybius dismisses Flaminius as a 'mob courtier' and a 'demagogue' who had a short temper and, when roused to anger, was prone to make mistakes. Flaminius had left an unsavoury reputation among the Insubres of his indiscriminate burning and pillaging of their towns and farms. Publius Cornelius Scipio was ordered, once he had recovered from his wound, to join his brother Gnaeus Cornelius Scipio Calvus in Iberia.

The Carthaginian victories had put heart into the Celts of the Po Valley. Thousands of Celts now poured into the Carthaginian encampment to enlist in Hannibal's service. Even during the winter, while Hannibal's main forces rested at Bononia, being fed and supplied by the Boii, his troops continually raided the Roman winter quarters. While the Celts of the Po Valley were allies of Hannibal, nevertheless Hannibal's army had to live off their land, consuming their food and imposing a great strain on their agricultural and pastoral resources and economy. For Hannibal it was essential to remove that strain on his allies as soon as possible. Still in the height of the winter Hannibal decided to make an attempt to lead part of his army into Etruria. It was a bold move for the campaigning season usually came to an end with winter and Rome would not expect any such moves. Presumably, though it is not reported, Celtic guides conducted Hannibal through the Apennine passes just as they had through the Alpine routes. Hannibal, however, was driven back by the foul weather conditions in the mountains. During the withdrawal, he encountered Sempronius Longus and the remnants of his legions foraging for winter stores near Placentia and another battle took place with the Romans losing five senior commanders. Their foreign levies also lost three senior commanders. Sempronius retreated to Luca, modern Lucca, where the Ligurian tribes attacked them and captured two quaestors, paymasters-general, Gaius Fulvius and Lucius Lucretius, plus two other general officers and five sons of Roman senators. The Ligurians handed these prisoners to Hannibal.

The new consul Flaminius had arrived at Ariminum during early spring. The second consul, Servilius, had managed to reach Placentia and taken command of Scipio's decimated legions. Sempronius, however, was ordered to march his men to Ariminum to join Flaminius by the Ides of March (15 March). Flaminius was to take over command of the remnants of Sempronius' army. He had brought reinforcements to fill the depleted ranks together with two other legions under the praetor Atilius. Sempronius does not appear to have been dishonoured nor dismissed on account of his two major defeats at the hands of Hannibal.

[12]

Litana: A Forgotten Celtic Victory

WITH the weather changing for the better that spring of 217 BC, Hannibal began to march south again into Etruria. Livy maintains that the Celtic chieftains continually plotted against Hannibal's life 'but it was their own mutual treachery that saved him; for they would inform against each other as frivolously as they would themselves conspire'. This seems a curious notion for without Celtic co-operation and alliance, Hannibal would have been in no position to conduct the war in Italy. The backbone, indeed the major part of his army was now made up of Celts from Iberia and Celts from the Po Valley. Once more we are seeing the typical Roman prejudice towards the Celts.

Hannibal, learning that Flaminius was at Ariminum, decided not to march towards his army but to head immediately south towards Rome. This caused a surprised Flaminius to rush with his army to Arretium (Arrezo). However, the Roman historians, as usual, prepared their readers for what was about to happen by claiming that Flaminius had not made the correct sacrifices and thus his consulship began with portents of disaster.

Hannibal moved to Faesulae, modern Fiesole. The campaign had not started well for he had contracted an eye infection crossing the marshes and this led to the loss of the sight of one eye. Flaminius, hearing of Hannibal's movement, sent word to Servilius Geminus ordering the second consular army to attempt to place itself in front of Hannibal. The idea was to trap him between the two Roman armies as had been done at Telamon. Hannibal moved near to Flaminius' positions at Arretium. Once more we hear disparaging remarks about Hannibal's Celtic allies from Livy. He claims they were unused to the hardship and fatigue of campaigning.

They could neither support themselves when fallen, nor raise themselves from the eddies [of the mud flats of the lower Arnus]; when
the water covering every place, not a dry spot could be found
where they might stretch their weary bodies, they laid themselves
down upon their baggage, thrown in heaps into the water.

The Arnus was the chief river of Etruria, now the Arno.

Hannibal had set a bait. Flaminius, observing the proximity of the
Carthaginian army, moved his troops out to do battle, refusing the
advice of his junior officers that he should wait until Servilius and
his consular army drew nearer. Hannibal had set his trap. He took
up positions in the woods overlooking the waters of Lake Trasimene
(Trasimeno). Livy observes:

The place was formed by nature for an ambush, where the Trasimene comes nearest to the mountains of Cortona. A very narrow
passage only intervenes, as though room enough just for that
purpose had been left designedly; after that a somewhat wider
plain opens itself, and then some hills rise up.

Flaminius and his legions were hurrying rapidly along this road.
According to Polybius:

The road led through a narrow strip of level ground with a range
of high hills on each side of it lengthwise. This defile was overlooked in front crosswise by a steep hill, difficult to climb, and
behind it lay the lake, between which and the hillside the passage
giving access to the defile was quite narrow. Hannibal marched
by the shores of the lake and passed through the defile to occupy
the hill in front, encamping on it with his Iberians and Numidians;
his slingers and pikemen he brought round to the front by a detour
and stationed them in an extended line under the hills to the right
of the defile, and similarly taking his cavalry and the Celts round
the hills on the left, he placed them in a continuous line under
these hills, so that the last of them were just at the entrance to
the defile, lying between the hillside and the lake.

On the mist-shrouded morning of 21 June, the unsuspecting Flaminius was urging his legions to hurry, believing he was chasing an

army in retreat, and not realising that Hannibal was waiting in ambush positions for him. Suddenly he found himself caught in the Carthaginian trap. His 40,000 legionaries were assaulted by 35,000 Celts, Celtiberians, Carthaginians and Numidians while his troops were strung out in marching formation. It was one of the bloodiest ambushes of history. The entire Roman army was destroyed, its soldiers killed or taken captive. Among the dead was Flaminius himself. There were 15,000 Roman dead, a similar number of allied levies and 10,000 more scattered in flight. On Hannibal's side there were only 2500 casualties, mostly Celts. The large number of Celtic dead demonstrated the leading part they had played in the attack.

Indeed, we are told that an Insubrean Celt, a chieftain leading a cavalry band, named Ducarius, personally killed the consul Flaminius. Ducarius recognised Flaminius from the campaign in the Insubrean territory. The Insubrean warrior cried out to his fellow Celts: 'There is the Roman, Flaminius, who destroyed our warriors and laid our towns and our fields in ruin! I will offer him as a sacrifice to the ghosts of our people who he has foully slain!' Spurring his horse into the Roman lines, he cut down a legionary who tried to defend the consul, and drove his lance through Flaminius' body. Livy, in recounting this story, based his account on one given by Quintus Fabius Pictor.

The death of Flaminius marked the beginning of the end for the Roman army. The surviving consul, Sevilius Geminius, had dispatched some 4000 cavalry, commanded by the pro-praetor, his second-in-command, Gaius Centenius, to relieve Flaminius, before he heard the full news of the defeat. Before he could recall Gaius Centenius, the pro-praetor's troops had also been annihilated.

The news now reaching Rome caused shock and dismay. Quintus Fabius Maximus Verrucosis (c.275–203 BC) was voted acting dictator. It was the second time he had filled this role for he had been dictator and consul in 221 BC. He appointed Marcus Minucius Rufus as his master of horse. Hannibal had, curiously, turned aside from Rome and made for Picenum to take advantage of the rich agricultural lands to replenish his supplies depleted by winter. Servilius found himself bogged down with skirmishes with Celtic war bands, acting independently of Hannibal's main army. These made lightning strikes on Roman positions, attacking mainly as irregular cavalry and moving off before the Romans knew what had hit them. Servilius finally arrived in Rome and was removed from command of the second consular army. Instead, he was given a fleet of 120 ships and ordered to protect the Italian coast along the western shore in case the Carthaginians attempted to land reinforcements from the sea.

Mistakes were made on both sides, however, because had Hannibal marched on Rome immediately after Trasimeno, the city would undoubtedly have fallen to him. But Hannibal had not realised that there were no veteran troops left to defend the city. He could not believe that his victories were so easy and thought that Rome was holding back its best troops.

Quintus Fabius Maximus had begun to organise a new army. It is recorded that even freedmen were allowed to join up and the military age was extended to anyone under thirty-five years. While Hannibal delayed in Picenum, the Romans eventually raised an army of 150,000 men, a force several times the size of Hannibal's army, but one that was barely trained and untried in battle. Fabius Maximus found himself unpopular in Rome for he constantly refused to meet Hannibal in a set battle. He was now being nicknamed Cunctator or 'the delayer'. This could be explained by his desire not to engage Hannibal until he had trained his new army to his satisfaction. However, mutiny began to brew and Marcus Minucius Rufus was a leading figure in criticising his commander. He told his men that Rome would have been a Celtic town had Camillus contented himself to defend it by simply marching around without coming to grips with the invaders.

Fabius, finally bowing to pressure, sent Lucius Hostilius Mancinus with a force of cavalry to reconnoitre the advance guard of Hannibal's army. Hostilius Mancinus' troops were surrounded and most of them slaughtered, though a few, including their commander, managed to fight their way back to the main Roman positions. More skirmishes took place. Fabius was recalled to Rome to be questioned by the Senate as well as to perform a religious function of his office, and command, in his absence, was given to Minucius Rufus. Fabius instructed him, in spite of Minucius' criticisms, to continue not to hazard all in a set battle. He still regarded his troops as inadequately trained to meet Hannibal.

Skirmishes with Celtic cavalry forces continued. Irritated by this inactivity, Minucius Rufus decided to ignore Fabius' instructions. Taking command of the I Legion and IV Legion with auxiliary cavalry, he marched out towards Hannibal's army to give battle. The result was, as Fabius had predicted, a total rout of the Romans. Fabius, returning from Rome, was in time to see the end of the battle; without pause for rest, he took the II Legion and III Legion to the aid of Minucius' retreating troops and was able to prevent a complete disaster. Minucius, who survived, thereafter stopped his criticism of Fabius' tactics.

Fabius' period of six months as dictator was now up and the time came for the election of new consuls. One of the consuls was a veteran of the war against the Cisalpine Celts, Lucius Aemilius Paullus. The other was Gaius Terentius Varro. Varro was of humble origin, the son of a butcher who had employed him in the trade of retailing meat. Varro's election to office was seen as a deliberate plebeian insult to Fabius by the Roman aristocrats.

In 216 BC Gaius Terentius Varro was given full command of the army. He set off immediately to engage Hannibal, not having learnt the lessons Fabius had demonstrated. He arrived in Apulia in June. After further minor skirmishes, the Roman army finally faced Hannibal near the city of Cannae (Cannosa) near modern Barletta, overlooking the low flat lands beside the River Aufidus (Pfanto).

Varro had placed in the field the largest Roman army ever assembled: some 80,000 infantry and 6000 horse. He drew up his forces in the traditional manner with infantry in the centre and cavalry on either wing, his lightly armed troops placed in front of the more heavily armed legions. Hannibal positioned his Celts and Celtiberian troops in the front ranks of his centre, under his personal command with his brother Mago. Whatever Livy's views as to the treachery and unworthiness of the Celts, Hannibal obviously regarded them as his mainstay and always placed them in his centre front ranks. Behind them were Carthaginians. On the left flank were placed Celtic cavalry under Hasdrubal and on the right Numidian cavalry under Hanno, according to Polybius, or Maharbal, according to Livy. Hannibal's troops numbered 40,000 infantry and 10,000 horse. The Roman sources admit that over half of Hannibal's army were Celts. Livy says:

> The Celts and Celtiberian contingents carried shields of similar shape, but their swords were of different pattern, those of the Celts being very long and not pointed, those of the Celtiberians,

who were accustomed to use them for piercing rather than cutting, being handily short and sharply pointed. One must admit too, that the rest of the turn-out of these peoples, combined with their general appearance and great stature, made an awesome spectacle; the Celts naked from the navel upwards, the Celtiberians ranged in line in their dazzling white linen tunics bordered with purple.

The Roman army must have looked overwhelming to the multi-national force under Hannibal. They were outnumbered at least two to one. Plutarch relates an anecdote which demonstrates the cama-raderie of the Carthaginian officers. As they examined the deploying Roman army, one of Hannibal's best commanders, Gisgo, expressed his trepidation at the overwhelming numbers of the enemy. Hannibal turned to him with a serious glance.

'You are right, Gisgo. But there is one thing you have apparently not noticed.'

'What is that, general?' demanded the puzzled commander.

'Just this; in all that great number of men opposite there isn't a single one called Gisgo.'

Gisgo's mournful expression broke into a grin. He joined in Hanni-bal's laughter and Plutarch tells us that the men of his army, seeing their officers in good humour, began to feel more confident.

On 3 August 216 BC, as the sun began to rise across the plain, the Romans opened the battle with an attack on the Celts and Celtiberian centre ranks. In a prearranged plan, they moved out to meet the attack and then, still acting under orders, began to fall back as if being forced by the weight of the Roman troops. Varro, believing the centre of Hannibal's army was weakening, ordered his troops to push forward into the bulge. As soon as this movement began, Hanni-bal sounded another prearranged signal. On either side of the Romans pushing on towards the apparently retreating centre, the infantry wings now swung round to attack on the flanks. The Roman infantry was caught in a vice.

The consul, Aemilius, wounded in the opening moments of the battle, still managed to ride his horse to the besieged infantry urging them on. But now the Numidian cavalry and the Celtic cavalry were swinging round into position, like the pincers of a giant crab. Another commander named Hanno, son of Bomilcar, a nephew of Hannibal, took the Celtic cavalry around the right flank of the Roman lines, while either Hasdrubal or Maharbal led the Numidian cavalry from the left flank. The Roman cavalry was routed and the encirclement of the Roman army was complete. Hannibal pressed mercilessly on the Roman infantry. They were assailed on all sides and cut to pieces.

Livy recounts how a tribune named Gnaeus Lentulus was riding off the battlefield when he saw the consul Lucius Aemilius Paullus sitting on a stone and bleeding profusely. He offered the consul his horse to escape. 'Lucius Aemilius! Take this horse while you have strength, and I am with you to strengthen and protect you. This battle has been calamitous enough without the death of a consul.' Aemilius Paullus refused and told the young officer to escape himself.

> 'God bless your courage, but you have little time to escape; do not waste it in useless pity – get you gone, and tell the Senate to look to Rome and fortify it with strong defences before the victorious enemy can come . . . Tell Quintus Fabius Maximus that Lucius Aemilius lived, and now dies, mindful of his injunctions. For myself, I would rather die among my slaughtered troops than be accused for a second time after my consulate, or stand forth as the accuser of my colleague [Varro] in order to defend my own innocence by incriminating another.'

Soon after, Aemilius Paullus was cut down by Numidian cavalry but Lentulus was able to escape. So, too, did Varro and his aides, some seventy horsemen, who reached the protection of Venusia (Venosa), an old Samnite town. Among the dead, as well as Aemilius Paullus, were the former consuls, Gnaeus Servilius Geminus, Lucius Atilius, serving as a quaestor, and Marcus Minucius, who had also been master of horse under Fabius Maximus. Another quaestor, Lucius Furius Bibaculus, was killed. Some twenty-nine military tribunes were killed out of the total of thirty-three; eighty Roman senators or those of the rank of praetor or aedile were also slain.

Roman deaths at Cannae are given by Livy, Appian and Plutarch at some 50,000 with 4500 taken captive. Quintilian puts the deaths at 60,000 and Polybius gives an even higher estimate of 70,000. Hannibal's losses were given as 5700 of which 4000 were Celts and 1500 Celtiberians and Numidians. To put this in some sort of context, more men were killed in these few hours of fighting that the total number of Royal Flying Corps and Royal Air Force personnel throughout World War One and World War Two put together.

Livy compared the defeat at Cannae to that of the defeat of Rome on the Allia by Brennus and his Celts. According to Leonard Cottrell: 'Cannae is one of those names – like Blenheim, Austerlitz, Gettysburg, Ypres, Alamein – which have a permanent place in the history of warfare. It appears in modern military text books and will probably go on appearing as long as men, and not missiles, fight battles.'

The victorious Carthaginian general now made yet another mistake. Having destroyed all Rome's fighting forces in one great battle, he once more refused to march on Rome itself in spite of the urging of Maharbal, the Numidian cavalry general, who suggested he take the cavalry and ride directly to Rome. Hannibal gave Rome valuable time to rebuild her defences once again, claiming he did not have the necessary siege equipment to march on Rome.

In Rome, the Senate called back Fabius Maximus, the former dictator. Carthalo, one of Hannibal's cavalry commanders, was sent to demand Rome's surrender but the Senate refused. Hannibal was content to make Capua, in Campania, his headquarters and accept alliances and support from the Greek cities of southern Italy. These cities seemed happy to be liberated from Roman control once again. Capua became capital of a powerful alliance supporting Carthage. The fortunes of the Celts of the Po Valley were also in the ascendant. In Rome, Lucius Caecilius Metellus and several other patricians announced that Romans should abandon Italy and seek their fortunes abroad in some foreign land. It was a measure of how low the Romans felt their fortunes had sunk.

The Roman Senate refused to submit. The disaster sent them scurrying back to religion as a refuge and events seen as evil omens were countered by a ruthlessness of the kind that Romans were later fond of accusing the 'barbaric' Celts of practising. Two of the Vestal Virgins, Opimia and Floronia, were found guilty of a sexual liaison and were buried alive at the Colline Gate, which Livy says was a traditional punishment. Lucius Cantilius, a secretary to the Pontiffs, was publicly whipped to death in the presence of the Pontifex Maximus when it was claimed he was Floronia's lover. It was at this point also that the Senate, on the advice of the priests, had two Celtic prisoners and two Greeks buried alive in the Forum Boarium, or cattle market, as mentioned in the discussion of human sacrifice in Chapter 3.

However, some Romans committed heroic acts during this time of peril. A young officer named Publius Sempronius Tuditanus with 600 men – Livy claims 7000 men – managed to escape from behind the Carthaginian lines. They became heroes of the day at a time when Rome needed heroes. Sempronius, who later became consul in 202 BC, wrote an account of the rise of Rome in which he maintained that the Etruscans themselves were a Celtic people; this gave birth to a myth which has existed to this day about Etruscan identity and with which I have dealt in *The Celtic Empire*. The historian Quintus Fabius Pictor was dispatched from Rome to consult the Oracle at Delphi and returned with advice telling the Romans to make gifts to the Pythian Apollo and their burden would get better. The victor over the Celts at Clastidium, Marcus Claudius Marcellus, was now given charge of raising and training yet another Roman army.

A few thousand survivors of Varro's army had sought refuge at Canusium. Among them were the four surviving military tribunes. They were Quintus Fabius Maximus, son of the dictator, who had served with the I Legion, Lucius Publicius Bibulus and Publius Cornelius Scipio of the II Legion, son of the consul defeated by Hannibal in the first clash with the Carthaginians in Cisalpine Gaul, and Appius Claudius Pulcher of the III Legion. By universal consent, the command of the surviving soldiers was offered to Appius Claudius and Cornelius Scipio who was then only nineteen years old. When Varro, and the other survivors who had fled the battlefield with him, left Venusia and managed to reach Canusium, he was not welcomed with enthusiasm. However, he remained at Canusium until Marcus Claudius Marcellus arrived to take over command of the remnants and merge them with his new troops. Varro then returned to Rome to face the wrath of the Senate. Here was the man who by his inefficiency was responsible for the annihilation of the most considerable Roman army ever put into the field. He had not even perished with his troops. Was there irony when the Senate actually voted him its thanks 'because he had not despaired of the commonwealth'?

Hannibal meanwhile had marched to Naples in an attempt to secure a seaport through which he could bring reinforcements from Carthage. He sent his brother Mago to tell the Carthaginian Suffete of his successes. However, at Nola, 16 miles north-east of Naples, the new Roman commander Marcellus had established a strong defensive position. Hannibal was forced to attack it and, for the first time in his campaign, was repulsed. Young Fabius Maximus had begun to raid the countryside around Capua. The success at Nola put new heart into the Romans but another disaster was about to overwhelm them.

Lucius Postumius Albinus, who had been consul in 234 BC and again in 229 BC, had once more been elected consul and been given two legions with allied contingents amounting to an army of 25,000 men. Rome had realised that the Celts of the Po Valley had opened the doorway into Italy for Carthage. She was determined to punish them and stop any resupplying of Hannibal's army from that quarter. During the summer of 215 BC Postumius Albinus marched his army into Boii territory, through a desolate stretch of forest, known to the Boii as Litana.

We are definitely into Celtic territory here for it bears a Celtic place-name as does the hill nearby, Litanbriga. The same word existed in Old Welsh, *litan*, with its modern descendant *llydan*, and the modern Breton and Cornish cognate *ledan*, meaning 'wide' or 'broad'. So this was the wide or broad forest with its nearby wide or broad hill. The Celts obviously knew the route well and had organised a rather spectacular ambush for the Roman consul and his legions.

The Celts had cut through the tall trees along either edge of the forest road, cutting nearly through the base so that each tree remained precariously upright. Then, as the Romans marched along the forest road, the Celtic warriors pushed over the trees at one end. 'Down they all came,' says Livy, 'each tree bringing to earth its tottering neighbour, and all overwhelming, from both sides of the track at once, arms, horses, and men beneath. Scarcely ten escaped alive.'

While Livy is inclined to believe that the greater number of Roman troops were killed by falling trunks and broken branches, the idea of 25,000 casualties being caused in this manner is pretty fantastic. The number of trees which would have had to be cut would have been colossal. The sound of the sawing would have alerted people for miles, for the ambush would have had to have been prepared not long before the Romans approached the forest. However, we may assume that the Celts followed up their handiwork by attacking the marching column after they had been thrown into disarray by the falling trees. Some Romans were taken prisoner when they tried to escape over a river bridge. The consul Postumius was reportedly with this group but fought to avoid capture and was killed.

Livy says the Boii warrior cut off Postumius' head.

The Boii stripped his body, cut off the head, and carried their spoils in triumph to the most hallowed of their temples. There they cleaned out the head, as their custom is, and gilded the skull, which thereafter served them as a holy vessel to pour libations from and as a drinking cup for the priest and the temple attendants.

Of course, this was very unusual; the Celts normally kept the heads of those they respected in the sanctuary, usually preserving them in cedar oil.

The destruction of the Roman consular army of Postumius by the Boii was a great triumph for the Celts, demonstrating they could still win victories against Rome on their own account with Carthaginian generalship. The spoils from the fallen Roman legionaries consisted of valuable military equipment, swords, shields, javelins and armour, as well as the baggage train.

The defeat of a consular army, indeed, its complete annihilation, including the death of the consul, is curiously down-played by Roman historians. Had this been a defeat attributed to Hannibal, then we would have learnt the names of the Carthaginian commanders, details of deployment and other particulars. A victory for the Celts, however, was a matter to be quickly glossed over for it did not suit the Roman propaganda picture. Rome presents this loss of a consular army as a mere skirmish during the war with Carthage.

However, in spite of the attempts to quickly dismiss the Celtic victory, we learn that when news of this disaster reached Rome, so great was the alarm that all the shops were closed and the streets deserted and silent 'as if it were midnight'. A spontaneous public mourning was the order of the day. The Senate had to instruct the magistrates, the aediles, to order the removal of the mourning symbols. It was bad for Roman morale. Importantly, for the Celts of the Po Valley, the Roman Senate now abandoned the idea of sending any further army across the Apennines, at least for the time being.

In the south of Italy the war with Hannibal went on with skirmishes rather than battles until 214 BC. Syracuse, which had been taken from Carthage as a part of the settlement of the First Punic War, rose in revolt against Rome. Marcellus was sent to retake the city. He laid seige to it with 25,000 men and after two years the Romans forced their way in during a religious festival. Marcellus allowed his frustrated troops to massacre most of the inhabitants. One of the most famous people to be killed in this slaughter was Archimedes (c.287–212 BC), perhaps the greatest mathematician of the age, an astronomer, physicist and inventor, who lived at the court of Hieron II of Syracuse.

In 212BC a Roman army laid siege to Hannibal's capital at Capua. Hannibal tried to relieve the pressure on it by marching south and seizing the town of Tarentum (Taranto). He made a deal with the Greek inhabitants who opened the gates of the city at night. Hannibal sent three divisions of Celtic troops into the town, numbering 2000 men, with two Tarentine guides to each division. His orders were that they should occupy all the main streets and when daylight broke, if the Romans began any trouble, the Celts were to kill them. All Tarentines were to be spared. The seizure was made but it did not have the effect of drawing the besieging Roman army from Capua after him. Capua was forced to surrender in 211 BC. Fifty-three of the city senators were executed and all other officials were sold into slavery as punishment. Rome treated anyone who had co-operated with Hannibal harshly.

Roman morale was looking for a boost from reports of the Scipio brothers in Iberia. But for two years there had been little success. Disaster struck in 212 BC. First Publius Cornelius Scipio was killed and his army defeated and then, a mere twenty-nine days later, Gnaeus Cornelius Scipio was killed when his army was defeated. The Celts of Iberia played a prominent part in this Carthaginian success. In 210 BC, the son of Publius Cornelius Scipio, still only twenty-five and with the same name as his father, was gaining such a reputation in the field that his exceptional military ability brought about his appointment as pro-consul in Iberia. He took over the command that had been his father's. Young Scipio succeeded in playing on local politics and persuading some of the Celtiberian tribes to defect to Rome against the Carthaginians. Setback followed setback for the Carthaginians. Within a few years they had been driven out of their Iberian empire and Rome had taken over. Rome then had to set about her own conquest of the Celtic tribes. It was not until 93 BC that the Celts of Iberia finally submitted to the *pax Romana*. It was over a century of the fiercest warfare Rome had ever engaged in.

With the Roman successes, there was a growing new confidence in the Senate. In 210 BC, the Senate also decided to send another army into Cisalpine Gaul. This consisted of two legions under the command of one of the consuls for that year, Publius Sculpicius Galba. There are no reports of major battles but the Roman colonies, the garrison towns at Placentia and Cremona, were reinforced.

In 208 BC came another setback for Rome. Both consuls, Marcus Claudius Marcellus and Titius Quinctius Crispinus, were killed. They had united both consular armies at Venusia. The consuls, astonishingly, were scouting together with only a few personal guards, when they were attacked by cavalry. Marcellus was killed instantly but Crispinus was wounded, dying from his wounds shortly afterwards. Marcellus' son, also a Marcus Claudius Marcellus, who had been with the scouting group, was also badly wounded. He recovered to become consul in 196 BC.

During 207 BC envoys from the Greek city of Massilia arrived in Rome to report that Hannibal's brother Hasdrubal had arrived in their territory with a new Carthaginian army and was planning to make a crossing of the Alps into Cisalpine Gaul. The Roman Senate ordered Sextus Antistius and Marcus Raecius to Massilia to scout the country and discover what exactly Hasdrubal's plans were. They subsequently reported that Hasdrubal had gathered an immense army which was planning to cross the Alps during the following spring, 206 BC.

Rome now had twenty-five legions on active service. Fifteen of these were in Italy, of which two were now sent to the Po Valley under the command of a praetor, Marcus Porcius Cato, with orders to protect the Roman colonies there. A second army, commanded by Terentius Varro, kept Etruria pacified. Another army was encamped at Bruttium, in Calabria, commanded by Quintus Fulvius Flaccus, while yet another army lay near Tarentum. That year some 137,000 citizens of Rome were under arms without counting the non-Roman allies and levies.

The Senate decided that the two consular armies should take the field with two objectives. Hasdrubal had to be prevented from raising the Cisalpine Celtic tribes while Hannibal had to be prevented from leaving the south of Italy and marching north to join his brother. The consuls for the year were Gaius Claudius Nero and Marcus Livius Salinator, so nicknamed because of the salt tax he had introduced when serving as censor. Both consuls appeared to take their time getting their armies into the field.

Porcius Cato finally sent a dispatch from the Po Valley to tell the Senate that Hasdrubal was already on his way across the Alps. The Po Valley Celts were stirring and a combined army of 80,000 Celts and Ligurians awaited Hasdrubal's arrival. Hannibal's brother was, in fact, having an easy passage through the Alps for he had been joined by large contingents of the Celtic Arverni and other Transalpine tribes. Before long, Hasdrubal was besieging Placentia. Porcius Cato retreated to Ariminum, to which Livius Salinator was also hurrying. Even with a combined force of four legions and a similar number of auxiliaries, Livius Salinator decided he was in no position to face Hasdrubal alone. The Romans retreated south to Sena.

The second consul, Nero, was marching south to Apulia, where Hannibal was wintering. His aim was to block Hannibal's army of 40,000 men from moving north. The Roman army encamped around Tarentum provided Nero with an additional 20,000 troops. Nero meant to catch Hannibal in a pincer movement but the Carthaginian general had eluded him and was already on the march to join his brother.

Hasdrubal, realising the futility of laying siege to Placentia, strongly fortified and well provisioned, decided to leave the garrison town and march along the east coast down towards Picenum. He had sent four Celtic and two Numidian horsemen to Hannibal requesting his brother to join forces with him at the Metaurus river (Metauro) near Ancona. From here, the combined armies could move directly on Rome. These unarmed horsemen managed to ride through enemy-occupied country almost the entire length of Italy. While trying to find Hannibal, however, they were captured by a Roman foraging party and brought before the pro-praetor Quintus Claudius. Under torture, they revealed they were carrying dispatches to Hannibal. The letter was found and handed to the military tribune Lucius Verginius who took it immediately to the consul Nero.

Nero ordered a legion under Quintus Catius to protect the road to Rome from Picenum while he force marched the rest of his legions directly to join Livius Salinator at Sena. At the same time he sent dispatches to Livius to inform him of the news. The two Roman consuls joined forces with great secrecy at night.

Unaware of this, Hasdrubal had marched to Sena and encamped not far from the Roman lines. In fact, his camp was not more than half a mile away. Scouts brought Hasdrubal the news of the enemy positions but too late. While Livius and Porcius tried to dissuade Nero from giving battle until the troops had rested, Nero issued the orders for an immediate action. On the banks of the Metaurus, Cannae was avenged by the Romans. The Carthaginian dead amounted to 57,000 and the prisoners were 5400, reports Livy. Polybius puts the figures more convincingly at 10,000 killed and 2000 captured. The Roman losses were 8000. Livy cannot let the matter go without another attack on the Celtic character. He says that the Celts had drunk heavily and lay in their quarters, incapable of moving. The Romans were supposed to have slaughtered them as they lay in drunken stupor. Polybius is more fair when he says that the Celts, with Hasdrubal and his Celtiberian infantry and ten elephants, had made a last ditch defensive stand. When Nero attacked, 'finding he could make no headway against the Celtic defence, he wheeled round behind Livius' men, and fell on the right flank of Hasdrubal's army'. According to Polybius, the Celts determinedly held the line against the Romans but to no avail. They were outflanked.

Livius Salinator was told the next morning that contingents of Cisalpine Celts and Ligurians had escaped the carnage and were moving off. An officer suggested that they could be wiped up by the pursuit of cavalry. The consul replied: 'No! Let there be some survivors. They can spread the news of our victory and the defeat of Hasdrubal.'

Hasdrubal had been killed. According to Polybius: 'Hasdrubal had shown himself to be a brave man throughout his life; now in his last hour he died in the thick of the fighting, and I must not take leave of him without paying the tribute that is his due.' This admiration was not shared by the Roman consuls. Whereas Hannibal, after a victory, always had the bodies of the Roman officers sought out and given military funerals, the consul Nero had Hasdrubal's head cut off, not with the reverence for the soul of the man which prompted the Celts to remove the heads of those they admired and take them to religious sanctuaries, but for a more brutal reason.

After the battle Nero took his army back to meet Hannibal's advancing troops. One of Nero's officers carried the head to Hannibal's lines. He tossed it across the lines where it was shown to Hannibal. To reinforce the message, two Numidian captives were sent to Hannibal in chains to tell him of the defeat.

It was a personal as well as a professional blow. Hannibal withdrew his army into the south of Italy. Although he remained in Italy for a further four years, the Carthaginian commander never regained the impetus or had similar successes against the armies of Rome that the early years had given him.

Even Carthage was now under pressure following Publius Cornelius Scipio's dramatic conquest of Iberia. Scipio had been elected consul in 205 BC. The Roman Senate, after some reluctance from those who argued that Hannibal should be fought and beaten in Italy, agreed to let Scipio invade Carthage itself. With an army of 20,000 Scipio, soon to be titled 'Africanus' after his victories, landed in midsummer at Utica, less than 20 miles west of Carthage. He was at once confronted by Hasdrubal, son of Gisgo, with a Carthaginian force, including Syphax, king of Numidia and his Numidians with bands of Celtiberians. Scipio was hemmed in on his beachhead and hard pressed to break out. It took eight months to do so. By then intrigue had also played a part. An ambitious Numidian tribal chieftain had been persuaded to desert Syphax and the old king's young wife, Sophonisba, threw in her lot with him. The chieftain Masinissa organised a coup and captured Cirta, the Numidian capital, and Syphax was taken in chains to Rome.

There was still danger from the Po Valley for Mago, another Carthaginian commander, thought by some chroniclers to have been the same Mago who was Hannibal's brother, had landed at Genua (Genoa) in 205 BC and was attempting to raise a new army of Celts and Ligurians. The Ligurians asked for two months to enable them to raise troops but the Celts responded immediately and joined his standards. Livius Salinator crossed from Etruria to join his praetor Spurius Lucretius to counter this new threat. Mago eluded them and did not bring his army to battle. The following year, 204 BC, the praetor Quintus Mamilius Turrinus was given command of the two legions stationed in Cisalpine Gaul and instructed to conduct raids throughout the Po Valley to dissuade Mago and his allies.

In the spring of 203 BC the Carthaginian Suffete, terrified by the nearness of Scipio's army, called for Hannibal to return to Africa in order to protect the city. Shipping his army in 400 transports, Hannibal landed near modern Tunisia with only 12,000 men.

In 203 BC, in the sixteenth year of the Second Punic War, Marcus Cornelius Cethegus was given the task of holding the Po Valley as proconsul. Publius Quintilius Varus was his praetor. Mago and his predominantly Celtic army finally faced the Romans in Insubrean territory. The praetor's legions were in the front line with Cornelius keeping his own legions in reserve. The Roman troops were reluctant to attack the Celts because of the fierceness of the Celtic resistance and the fact that Mago still had elephant detachments.

Quintilius Varus told the proconsul that he felt that only a cavalry charge would dislodge the Celtic lines. He offered to personally command such a charge. The proconsul agreed, taking command of all four legions, while Quintilius took the cavalry with his son Marcus as second-in-command.

Mago ordered his elephants into action. Livy comments:

They had been kept in readiness for the first sign of movement by the Roman cavalry, whose assistance was now rendered useless, as all the horses were as much terrified by the aspect of the brutes as they were by their trumpeting and unfamiliar smell. At close quarters the Roman cavalry, when they could use their lance or sword, would have had the advantage, but not so in the present circumstances when their horses were bolting with them.

The XII Legion had been badly cut up and would have been forced to retire had not the XIII been brought up to reinforce it. Mago then brought up detachments of Celtic reserves to face the Roman lines. The XI Legion now moved to attack the elephants, which had been causing many casualties, with their *hastati* or heavy spears. Once the Roman spearmen had driven the elephants off, the legions could bear down on the Carthaginian lines. Mago, leading his men from the front of the standards, was wounded in the thigh and carried off the field.

The Carthaginian army kept an orderly and regular withdrawal but none the less, it is claimed that 5000 fell. Some twenty-two standards were captured while only 2300 men of the XII Legion were killed. But these included two military tribunes, Marcus

Cosconius and Marcus Maevius. The tribune Gaius Helvius of the XIII was also killed and among those trampled by the elephants were twenty-two patricians of high rank.

Mago, in spite of his wound, broke camp during the night and reached the coast near Genua. Here he found envoys from Carthage telling him that he must return to Carthage as the city was now in danger from Scipio's army. He also learnt that Hannibal had already left Italy with the remnants of his army. Mago set sail immediately with his men, including Celts and Ligurians. There are conflicting reports of his death. Some accounts say that he died of his wound, others that he was captured by a Roman fleet and killed, still others that he was simply lost at sea. At all events, many of Mago's troops from the Po Valley arrived safely at Carthage but without their commander.

A new consul arrived in Cisalpine Gaul, Gnaeus Servilius Caepio who 'achieved no noteworthy successes in Etruria nor in Cisalpine Gaul', reports Livy, but managed to rescue his father from captivity. This was Gaius Servilius Caepio, who had been seized by the Boii in 218 BC near the village of Tannetum, one of the three officials who had been confiscating Boii land to give to Roman colonists. Also rescued was Gaius Lutatius Catulus. The consul took them back to Rome, entering the city between the two of them. 'Though of no great national importance, this was a personal triumph and brought him distinction accordingly,' Livy comments.

The last act of the Carthaginian war was being played out in Africa. Scipio and his Roman army at Utica gave up the siege and marched to the Bagradas (Medjerda) river in the spring of 202 BC. His aim was to draw Hannibal into combat. At a village near Zama the two armies finally met. Hannibal now had an army of 37,000 with eighty elephants. Scipio had been reinforced to similar numbers. Hannibal placed the elephants in the front line. In the centre lines he placed the Ligurians and the Celts, behind them Numidian and Carthaginian infantry under Hanno and behind them a third line of infantry from his allies from Italy. On the left wing were Numidian cavalry and on the right Carthaginian cavalry.

Scipio's men were able to disperse the elephants and advanced on the Celts and Ligurians. The first lines gave way after a gruelling fight. As Polybius says: 'The contest was for long doubtful, the men falling where they stood out of determination.' As Hannibal was about to lead a charge of his veteran troops, the Roman cavalry, under the command of the Numidian turncoat, Masinissa, and Gaius Laelius, struck behind the infantry. It was the end. Some 20,000 of Hannibal's army lay dead and dying on the field. Some 20,000 more were captured. The Roman casualties were reported at only 1500. With the defeat came the total collapse of Carthaginian power. Hannibal was eventually forced into exile in 195 BC and sought the protection of Antiochus III of Syria. But after the Romans defeated Antiochus at Magnesia, Hannibal, in 183 BC, was forced to take poison to avoid being captured by an unrelenting and unforgiving Rome.

That same merciless attitude made Rome turn her gaze more closely on the Celts of the Po Valley. The Celts had always been Rome's most implacable enemies and the Senate revived the plans which had been interrupted by the arrival of Hannibal in 218 BC – the plan to conquer and colonise the entire Po Valley.

Looked at from the Roman perspective, it was a logical step. Hannibal's armies had always been at least fifty per cent Celtic in their composition and often far more. It is true that the Scipio brothers and Scipio Africanus had managed to persuade some Celtiberians and even Celts to serve in the Roman forces. But, generally, the Celts were always found at the centre of the Carthaginian armies. At Utica the Celtic troops had stopped Scipio's victory over the Carthaginians becoming a total rout. At Zama, Hannibal gave the Celts the central position again which they held while Scipio turned the wings of the army. The Celts were the great thorn in Rome's aspiration to empire. But now Rome's star was in the ascendant. The Carthaginian enemy was defeated. The Celts of the Po Valley had no one else to aid them.

[13]

The Conquest of Cisalpine Gaul

THE second and, finally, successful campaign to conquer Cisalpine Gaul began badly for the Romans. In 201 BC the consul Publius Aelius Paetus was ordered to cross the Apennines to commence operations firstly against the Boii. The excuse for the expedition, as if the Romans needed one, was that the Boii had raided the territory of some tribes in alliance with Rome. Aelius sent four cohorts from his own consular army, some 2000 men, to reinforce two more legions commanded by the general Gaius Ampius who had been ordered to march into the territory of the Boii by way of Umbria along the River Sapis. Aelius then took the rest of his army, with 8000 legionaries and auxiliary forces, and marched towards the Boii territory through the mountains from Etruria.

Entering the territory of the Boii first, Gaius Ampius, with 12,000 legionaries and auxiliaries, began burning villages, looting and plundering farmsteads. It was harvest time and we are told that around the fortified Celtic town of Mutilum, Ampius saw that the corn was ripe and ready for harvesting. He apparently ordered his troops to harvest the corn. Livy is critical of Ampius, claiming that he brought disaster on himself by not putting out pickets or forming a reserve guard to protect his men. It seems highly unlikely that a Roman general would be so foolish as to leave his men unprotected while they cut corn, especially in the middle of enemy territory and within reach of a fortified township. Or could the attitude of Ampius simply have been an example of Roman arrogance towards the Celts? If so, it cost him dearly.

What we do know is that Ampius, his two legions, plus the four consular cohorts and whatever other auxiliary forces he had, were suddenly surrounded by a Celtic army and attacked. We are, as I have said, talking about a Roman army of over 12,000 men. The harvesters fled for their lives. Livy makes a slip when he says that 'the armed men also were seized with panic and took to their heels'. So Ampius *had* placed guards in spite of Livy's earlier remarks. We are told by Livy that some 7000 Romans perished in the battle of Mutilum, including their commander Ampius himself.

The Roman survivors abandoned their equipment to the victorious Celts and fled in the direction of the consul Aelius who was approaching through the passes of the Apennines. It seems that Aelius, hearing the news, decided that discretion was the better part of valour for he did not engage the Celts and he 'returned to Rome, without achieving anything worth recording in his sphere of command'. This is not entirely fair comment as the consul managed to conclude a treaty with the Ligurian Inquani tribe. Reading between the lines, the Boii defence of their territory, the casualties at Mutilum, must have brought the Romans up sharply, since they had been led to believe that victory over the Cisalpine Celts was going to be easy in the wake of Carthage's defeat. According to their prejudiced perception, the Celts should have been downcast by Rome's victories over Hannibal.

Rome was also preparing for war with Philip of Macedonia. The Cisalpine Celts, realising that they must consolidate their position, decided to form a new alliance. The Insubres, the Boii and even the Cenomani, who had long held an ambivalent attitude to Rome and had even allied themselves with her, decided to make an alliance in 200 BC with the Celines, Ilvates (Eleiates) and other Ligurian peoples, under the leadership of a Carthaginian general named Hamilcar. Hamilcar seems to have been one of Mago's army who had remained in the area. The new alliance, fielding an army of 40,000 men, attacked the Roman military colony at Placentia, which had been established in 218 BC.

According to Livy:

> They sacked the city and burned down the greater part of it in their fury; leaving scarcely 2000 survivors among the burning ruins, they proceeded to cross the Po, intending to sack Cremona.

The original number of colonists in Placentia had been 6000. If, as sources indicate, the Cisalpine army slaughtered 2000 leaving a further 2000 prisoners, it means that the eighteen years of war had reduced the colonists by a further 2000, one third of the population.

The praetor Lucius Furius Purpurio is said to have rescued the 2000 Placentian captives after the defeat of the Celts.

Hamilcar laid siege to Cremona. The Romans at Cremona, hearing the news of the destruction of Placentia, were able to prepare for the attack, shutting the gates and arming the city ready for a siege. They sent requests for help to Furius Purpurio, who was the senior Roman military commander in the area at Ariminum. Furius only had an army of 5000 men of Latin status, having been ordered by the Roman Senate to transfer most of this command for embarkation to Greece to fight Philip of Macedonia. He sent dispatches to the Senate and reported the deteriorating situation. His own command was too small to march out to meet Hamilcar's forces.

The Senate responded by asking the consul Gaius Aurelius Cotta, who had been assembling an army at Arretium, to march his army to Ariminum and then march to relieve Cremona. His orders were that he would either lead the attack personally if the situation warranted, or else order Furius to do so. The 5000 men commanded by Furius were to be sent as garrison troops for Etruria while Cotta's legions would take over. The Senate also sent envoys to Carthage to demand that the Suffete issue orders recalling Hamilcar. Hamilcar was to be told that he did not have the support of the Carthaginian parliament and that he was making war on Rome in defiance of the treaty Rome had signed with them. Carthage was then to hand Hamilcar over to Roman justice. At the same time the envoys pointed out that not all the Roman deserters to the Carthaginian side had been handed over and a large number of them were known to be living openly in Carthage. These people were to be rounded up and sent to Rome for punishment under the terms of the treaty.

Meanwhile, Cotta's consular army had succeeded in marching from Arretium to Ariminum while the 5000 troops of Furius were transferred to Etruria. The consul Aurelius Cotta had remained in Rome and instructed Lucius Furius to take command of the army. Furius marched on Cremona, taking up his position about a mile and a half from Hamilcar's army. Livy is critical, observing that Furius, in showing consideration for his exhausted troops after their rapid march to Cremona, missed an opportunity to launch a surprise attack on the enemy encampment. Instead, he marched his army into an encampment and allowed them to rest after the forced march.

This gave Hamilcar with his Celts and Ligurian allies time to regroup and prepare for the Roman attack. The next day Lucius Furius moved his army into battle order, placing two legions in his centre commanded by Marcus Caecilius. Marcus Furius, obviously a relative, was given command of a squadron of cavalry on the right wing while Lucius Valerius Flaccus commanded all other cavalry troops. Lucius Furius took up his position on a hill with two staff officers, Gaius Laetorius and Publius Titinius, to observe the course of the fighting so that he could counter any surprise manoeuvres.

Hamilcar launched a mass attack, planning to overwhelm the cavalry on the right, but Marcus Furius held back their attack. The Celts then attempted an encirclement and this obviously caused problems. Lucius Furius, seeing that the manoeuvre might well succeed, decided to extend his lines, moving his two legions to the right flank and left flank. Then he ordered Valerius Flaccus to split his cavalry to attack on both flanks. This prevented the Celts closing the circle around the Romans and it also opened an opportunity for Furius. In extending their lines to encircle the Roman army, the Celts had weakened the centre of their army. Furius now ordered his reserves to make a close order charge on Hamilcar's centre.

According to Livy, Hamilcar suffered heavy casualties here and his centre gave way. Soon they were in headlong flight. It was presumably at this point that the Carthaginian general fell. Livy says that 'three noble Celtic generals fell in the battle'. Infuriatingly, he does not record their names. He does record that 35,000 of the Celtic allied army were slain and 200 Celtic wagons with seventy standards were captured. Fewer than 6000 Celtic warriors managed to escape. The Roman casualties, predictably, were put as low as 2000. Most of these, Livy says, came from the right squadron which had borne the brunt of the initial attack.

> This was a great victory and a joyful day for Rome; and when dispatches brought the news from the city a thanksgiving of three days was decreed.

Consul Aurelius, having allowed his subordinate to fight the battle while he rested in Rome, now set out to join his victorious legions and take whatever praise for the victory existed. A garrison army was instructed to remain in the Po Valley commanded by the praetor Gaius Helvius.

The following year, 199 BC, a Roman invasion of Insubrean territory led to the virtual annihilation of the invading force. Some 6700 Roman dead are referred to and double the number taken as prisoners. The Roman histories are curiously silent about this unhappy event. Only the bare facts are recorded.

In 198 BC Sextus Aelius Paetus, now serving as consul, raised a new consular army and marched to Cisalpine Gaul to conduct a campaign to complete the subjugation of the Celts of the Po Valley. Livy says of his campaign that 'there was nothing memorable in his performance'. In fact, the consul merely spent the entire campaigning season in rounding up Roman colonists who had fled from the colonies and, according to Polybius, sending them back by force if necessary.

It was not until the following year, 197 BC, that the Roman Senate decided to give special attention to the problem of the Po Valley Celts. Gaius Cornelius Cethegus and Quintus Minucius Rufus were consuls for that year. The Senate made the unusual decision that both consuls should be given the job of 'pacifying' the Po Valley once and for all. They were given the traditional two legions each, plus auxiliaries, and jointly charged with bringing the war to a speedy conclusion. The Celts had to be subdued completely.

Quintus Minucius led his army along the coastal route through Etruria across the Arnus into Liguria to Genua (Genoa). He began operations against the Ligurians at once. The Celeiates and Cerdiciates agreed terms with him and he captured Clastidium (Casteggio) and Litubium (Retorbio). Clastidium was reported as burnt. Some fifteen towns and 20,000 warriors had surrendered to Minucius, according to Livy. But the Ilvates were still holding out, as were the Boii. Indeed, they were now the only people south of the Po who had not succumbed to Roman forces. Minucius therefore moved his army on through the Stradella Pass into the territory of the Boii.

By this time, the other consul, Cornelius Cethegus, had marched his army through the Apennines, crossing the Po, into the country of the Insubres.

The tribal army of the Boii had already crossed the Po to reinforce the Insubres and Cenomani. It would seem, reading between the lines of Livy's account, that the kings and chieftains of the Boii had withdrawn northward from their territory, believing that Cornelius Cethegus would follow them and leave their 'civilian population' alone. Livy also adds: 'They had heard that the consuls were intending to conduct their campaign with their combined legions and accordingly they too proposed to make themselves stronger by consolidating their forces'.

However, the first consul, Minucius, and his legions entered the tribal territory of the Boii, and the Romans began burning settlements and farmsteads and slaughtering the old men, women and children. The Boii chieftains demanded that the united force of the Celts should return to protect the people. The Insubres and the Cenomani chieftains were unwilling to leave their own lands unprotected. And so the united Celtic army split. The Boii warriors returned hastily south to defend their people while the Insubres and the Cenomani encamped on the banks of the river.

The consul Cornelius Cethegus and his legions had taken up positions 2 miles from the Celtic encampment. Livy states that Cornelius sent messengers to Brixia, the capital of the Cenomani. He says that Cornelius learned that the tribal assembly, the elders, as he calls them, had not sanctioned their young warriors to join with the Insubres. Cornelius invited the 'leading men' to a conference and made some efforts to persuade them to renounce any connection with the Insubres and order their warriors to return home or even to join the Romans.

The idea of accepting a Roman invitation to join them in wiping out their fellow Celts must have seemed peculiar to the Cenomani who would have known full well that once the Insubres and Boii were defeated, they would be next on the Roman list. Livy blandly says of Cornelius' proposal: 'He did not in fact succeed in this attempt.' However, the Cenomani did promise that they would remain inactive in the fighting which was, perhaps, a diplomatic thing to promise, seeing that a Roman army was encamped just outside the gates of their tribal capital.

The Insubres had, apparently, some suspicion of the pressure brought on their allies so, Livy says, when it came to the battle line they did not entrust either wing of the Celtic army to them in case they succumbed to Roman pressure and gave ground through treachery. The Cenomani warriors were placed in reserve behind the Celtic standards.

The consul Cornelius began the battle by launching a frontal assault on the Celtic lines. Livy says that the Insubres did not even sustain that first assault. He says that, according to some authorities, the Cenomani had attacked the Insubres in the rear and that the Insubres were thrown into confusion. Could the Cenomani have been so duplicitous and so stupid as to have trusted the Roman 'alliance' against their fellows? It seems doubtful and perhaps Livy is once again showing his deprecation of the Celts.

Livy gives identical numbers of killed and captured, as well as of booty taken, to those he gave for the previous victory of Furius: 35,000 Celts killed, 5200 captured alive and 200 wagons taken. However, Livy contradicts his earlier statement that Hamilcar had been killed in the previous battle, by saying that he was captured alive during this battle. If this is so, then perhaps a false rumour had been spread about Hamilcar's death and maybe Hamilcar himself spread it in order to save the Carthaginian Suffete having to accede to the Roman demands for his recall. Livy adds that many towns of the Insubres surrendered to the Romans in the wake of the battle.

Meanwhile, the consul Minucius had been plundering the territory of the Boii without opposition. The warriors of the Boii then returned across the Po river to protect their homelands. This was what Minucius had wanted for he hoped to engage the Boii in a set battle. However, the Boii chieftains, hearing of the defeat of the Insubres and Cenomani, wisely decided to disperse their men back to their villages and henceforth engage in guerrilla warfare with the occupying army. This seems a clever strategy by the Boii leaders who realised that they could not confront the Romans in a set battle at that time. Minucius, in turn, had to change his tactics and abandoned hope of deciding the conquest of the territory by one battle.

Bands of warriors would make lightning raids and disappear as quickly as they appeared. Minucius, in frustration, continued to devastate the countryside, setting fire to buildings and storming individual towns, each one in turn. There was some bad news for the Celts when the Ilvates of Liguria finally surrendered to Rome as winter approached. The legions did not withdraw from the Po Valley this time but retired into winter quarters.

The dispatches of both consuls, announcing their successes over the Cisalpine Celts, reached the Senate in Rome at the same time and were read in the Senate by the city praetor Marcus Sergius. A public thanksgiving of four days was decreed.

The following year, 197 BC, Marcus Claudius Marcellus and

Lucius Furius Purpurio became consuls and Marcellus was given command in Cisalpine Gaul. Marcellus took over the legions of Minucius. His first action was to move north to the Insubrean town of Comum. Here he found that an army of Insubres was arriving to meet him. Obviously the defeats of the previous year had not entirely dampened their spirits.

Rather than await a siege, the leaders of the Insubres decided to engage Marcellus and his legions straight from the march.

The first assault of the Insubres drove back the Roman front lines. Marcellus knew that once these troops were driven back, the remnants of his army would easily be routed. He had with him cohorts of cavalry, notably a cohort of Marsi, a Latin people who were claimed to be notorious as sorcerers and snake-charmers. Marcellus threw all his Latin cavalry against the Celts.

It took two cavalry charges to blunt the Celtic attack and then the Roman infantry charged, breaking through the Celtic lines. The historian, Valerius Antias, quoted by Livy, gives some 40,000 Celts slain in battle, eighty-seven standards captured together with 732 wagons and many golden torques. Quintus Claudius Quadrigarius said that one of these golden torques was of such great weight that it was placed in the temple on the Capitol as a gift to Jupiter. The Insubres' camp was then stormed and plundered and the town of Comum was captured a few days later. Livy says that, soon after, twenty-eight walled Celtic towns surrendered to Marcellus.

Once more, however, the Celts showed resilience. As Marcellus and his triumphant legions were marching back through the country of the Boii, they were attacked. They were constructing a marching encampment, a camp for the night, when a Boii chieftain, leading a large force of warriors, assaulted them. This time Livy, thankfully, gives us the name of the Boii chieftain – Corolamus. The first element of this is well attested among Celtic names and indicates one who throws or casts, especially a spear. The name could mean 'the one who throws/casts (a spear) accurately'. Livy also excuses the ensuing defeat by saying that the Roman soldiers were exhausted having spent the day making a road.

Marcellus lost about 3000 of his men including several distinguished generals such as Tiberius Sempronius Gracchus and Marcus Junius Silanus as well as two military tribunes of the II Legion, Marcus Ogulnius and Publius Claudius. Marcellus, and the survivors, managed to barricade themselves in their encampment. For several days they were besieged by the attacking Boii. Eventually the Boii withdrew and left the Roman survivors to their own devices.

Livy admits that it is a matter of some debate as to whether Marcellus suffered his defeat before or after his victory over the Insubres at Comum. However, I would argue that it is logical that the defeat was suffered *after* his victory at Comum. Professor Toynbee agrees.

The account that puts Marcellus's victory before his defeat is the more convincing of the two. As early as 223 BC the Romans had found by experience that it was difficult to invade Insubria through the Ager Boiorum [Boii territory] and across the River Po, but that it was relatively easy to invade it from the east. In 197 BC they had won a success by combining an attack on Insubria from the east with an attack on the Ager Boiorum from a different quarter. It looks as if the consuls for 196 BC were repeating, with a variation, the pincers movement that had served their predecessors well. In 196 BC as in 197 BC, one consul advanced against the Ager Boiorum from the south – this time from Arretium and over the Apennines, instead of advancing from Genua and through the Dertona gap. In 196 BC again as in 197 BC – the other consul, in this case Marcellus, will have advanced against Insubria from the east.

At the same time as Marcellus' drive on Comum, the second consul, Lucius Furius Purpurio, had entered the Boii territory by way of the Apennine passes from Arretium. It would seem that Marcellus was marching for Bononia when he was attacked by the Boii and that Furius was also heading there. It was obvious that a rendezvous had been arranged. Furius was nearing the town of Mutilum when he learnt that he was in danger of being cut off from his supply routes by the successful army of Boii, which had now been joined by new Insubrean divisions. Furius realised that he would have no help from Marcellus, who was blockaded in his marching camp. He would have to withdraw and take a roundabout route to extricate Marcellus from his position. Eventually, the remnants of Marcellus' legions and Furius' army united. With growing confidence in their united strength, the combined force began to traverse the territory of the Boii, burning and plundering. The town of Bononia was finally forced to surrender to the Romans.

Most of the Boii, except the warriors under arms, had withdrawn out of the path of the rampaging Roman army into the safety of the forests and mountain fastness. As the Romans marched, the Boii warriors followed them, 'by secret tracks', according to Livy, and attacked them when the legionaries were foraging in small parties or by making strikes on groups of stragglers. The same guerrilla tactics of the previous year were proving an irritant to the Romans.

It was near the banks of the Po that finally a full-scale engagement suddenly erupted. It seems, so Livy says, that neither side had really planned it.

> The battle that followed was more sudden in its beginning and more bitter in its fighting than it would have been if the contestants had faced each other with minds prepared for a fight at a predetermined time and place. In this conflict there could be no doubt of the powerful effect of anger in arousing the courage of the fighters. The Romans fought with more lust for blood than for victory; so much so that they left the enemy scarcely a messenger to bring news of the disaster.

Livy does not give details, which is unusual for him as he is implying that the casualties inflicted by the consular armies were overwhelming. All he says is that dispatches telling of the Roman victory over the Boii were sent to Rome and shortly afterwards the consul Marcellus arrived to give details to the Senate. The Senate voted him a triumph. It was said that a great deal of plunder was transported to Rome in captured wagons with many Celtic military standards. This plunder included 320,000 *asses* of bronze and 234,000 pieces of stamped silver. Each Roman soldier participating in the campaign received eighty *asses*; each cavalryman and centurion, three times that amount.

Nevertheless, the outcome of the campaign was that the Boii and Insubres and other tribes of the Po Valley had still not submitted to Rome.

In 195 BC Lucius Valerius Flaccus and his lifelong friend and ally, Marcus Porcius Cato 'The Elder' or 'The Censor' (234–149 BC), were elected consuls. Valerius Flaccus was given command in the Po Valley and we are told that he was able to defeat a Boii army near the formidable Silva Litana, the Litana forest where a consular army had been annihilated scarcely ten years before. The Roman commander did not seem particularly enthusiastic about bringing the Celts to a decisive battle and spent most of the campaigning season setting his troops to repair war damage at Placentia and Cremona.

At the beginning of 194 BC, however, Livy records that he met and defeated a combined army of Boii and Insubres near Mediolanum. It is now that the name of another Celtic king or chieftain of the Boii emerges into history – Dorulatus, perhaps 'one of strength'. In 194 BC he was able to form a new alliance with the Insubres and lead a combined army against the Romans. All we know about this battle is that Valerius Flaccus won the victory and 'ten thousand of the enemy were slain'.

This is also the last time we have a record of hostilities between Rome and the Insubres. It may well be that the Insubres capitulated to Rome after this defeat, concluding their own individual treaty. One would presume that the smaller Celtic tribes within their hegemony, the Laevi around Ticinum, the Vertocomari around Novaria and the Libici around Vercellae, would have been party to that agreement and this might explain why the Boii actually raided the territories of the Laevi and Libici that year to show their displeasure.

In 194 BC the new consul Tiberius Sempronius Longus arrived in the country of the Boii and found them under a king named Boiorix, which simply means 'king of the Boii' and was not necessarily his personal name – it might well have been Dorulatus, still in office. We are told that 'Boiorix' had two brothers who joined him in organising the Boii to defend their homes against this new Roman invasion. Livy tells us that the consul had to fight his way through Boii territory to Placentia in a series of violent battles in which the casualties were heavy on both sides. On at least one occasion, says Livy, the consular army was in danger of being annihilated.

Livy records:

When the consul realised the size of the enemy forces and the height of their confidence, he sent a message to his colleague [the second consul Publius Cornelius Scipio Africanus] asking him to hasten his arrival, if he saw his way to do so; he, himself, he told him, would take evasive action, to prolong matters until the other's arrival.

In other words, in spite of claiming a defeat over Dorulatus and the Boii and their Insubrean allies earlier in the year, the Romans now found the Boii still confident and determined to defend their homeland. The Senate had just decreed that the Po Valley was to be the field of operations for both consuls during that year. However, in spite of Sempronius Longus' predicament, Scipio Africanus, the victor over Hannibal, was sulking. He had wanted to command the Roman army in Macedonia and was disdainful of being sent to the Po Valley to fight 'mere barbarians'. So disdainful, in fact, that he was residing in his own home in Rome. The Senate were adamant in their decision and Scipio Africanus was forced to go north. Livy implies that Scipio did no more than make a pretence of going on campaign while pointing out that other authorities claimed he did his full share of 'traversing the territories of the Boii, plundering on the way, as far as the forests and marshes allow'. But Livy seems certain that 'after achieving nothing worthy of record, he returned to Rome for the elections'.

Meanwhile Sempronius Longus bore the full force of the Boii's attacks. The Boii threw their warriors against Sempronius' army. Sempronius preferred to fortify himself in his encampment. After two days of Celtic insults being shouted, to which the Celts hoped the Romans would respond by coming out to fight, Boiorix ordered an attack on the fortifications. The Boii warriors launched their attacks from all sides of the Roman defence works. Sempronius, realising that the Celts would eventually break in, finally gave the order for his two legions to march out by the main gate. He was too late. The Celts had blocked the gate and surged into the fortifications behind them. Livy says:

> For a long time the fighting raged in these confined spaces, and it was not sword-arms and swords that were engaged but rather shields and bodies, and the combatants pushed with all their might, the Romans striving to force their way out with their standards, the Celts trying to force their way into the camp, or at least to prevent the Romans from issuing from it.

We are told that a senior centurion of the II Legion, Quintus Victorius, and Gaius Atinius, the military tribune of the IV Legion, took the standards from their bearers and threw them into the enemy ranks, so that, out of shame, the Roman soldiers would surge forward to recover them. The II Legion finally managed to break out through the gates but the IV Legion were stuck fast.

The Celtic attack was being pressed home at the rear of the camp. The Celts had broken through at the *porta quaestoria*, the entrance behind the military quaestor's tent. The quaestor Marcus Postumius Tympanus had been killed in the attack. Two other commanders, Marcus Atinius, probably a relative of the military tribune of the IV Legion, and Publius Sempronius, a relative of the consul himself, had also been killed with 200 of their men.

The rear gate of the Roman encampment was now in Celtic hands. The consul desperately ordered his 'special cohort', a crack troop of 500 men, to retake the gate and drive the Celts out. At the same time two cohorts of the IV Legion had managed to break out of the main gate. It seemed that there were three separate battles developing.

The attack had started at dawn and by midday it was still raging. Livy's anti-Celtic prejudice colours his account of the turning point of the battle:

> But then exhaustion and heat compelled the Celts to break off the fight; for the Celts are physically soft and lacking in stamina, and they have very little tolerance of thirst.

The Romans regrouped and drove the Celts back from the main gate of their camp. Livy claims the withdrawal was turned into a rout but he contradicts himself, and it is more likely that the Celts withdrew to reform. Livy says that the consul ordered the sounding of the retreat at this point. Why, if he had sent the Celts packing in a rout, would he then have signalled a Roman retreat? Some Roman troops apparently did not hear the retreat being sounded and followed the Celtic withdrawal. They now became caught in a Celtic counter-attack.

'The Romans,' Livy confessed, 'in their turn were routed and their panic forced them back to the camp ... Thus the fortunes of both sides were mixed, defeat at one moment, victory at another.' Livy claims the Celts lost 11,000 men while the Romans only 5000. Once more, if the Roman victory was so overwhelming, why did Sempron-ius abandon the fortified encampment and take the remnants of his legions hurrying back to the safety of the fortified city of Placentia?

The following year, 193 BC, the Romans renewed their campaign and one of the new consuls, Quintus Minucius Rufus, arrived at Arretium to march on Pisa in order to conduct a campaign against the Ligurians. The second consul, Lucius Cornelius Merula, marched on from Ligurian territory through the Stradella Pass to attack the Boii yet again. The Boii made no effort to close with the Roman army this time, preferring to raid and harass as they had done in previous campaigns. Frustrated, Cornelius marched his legions towards Mutina (Modena). Livy criticises Cornelius, claiming that he had taken no precautions to protect his march. He had not placed scouts ahead nor ordered out flanking patrols around his marching columns 'on the assumption that the surrounding country was pacified'.

> The Boii . . . followed, keeping silence on their march and looking for a spot for an ambush. They passed the Roman camp by night and occupied a defile through which the Romans would have to pass.

That morning, however, Livy says that Cornelius waited until daylight and, unlike on previous days, sent out a troop of cavalry to scout ahead. They returned with a report that the Boii were ahead of them. The consul ordered the baggage of the army to be piled in the centre with the *triarii*, the third-line companies of the legionary battle order, who were to construct a defensive rampart around it. He then proceeded towards the Boii positions with the rest of his forces drawn in battle formation.

The Boii, seeing their ambush had been discovered, changed tactics and reformed in a regular battle line. Livy says the battle began at the second hour of the day. On the left of the Roman line was the former consul Sempronius Longus and another man of consular rank, Marcus Marcellus, commanding some 'special cohorts'. The presence of these senior officers of consular rank in subordinate commands shows just how seriously the Senate took its campaigns against the Celts. It seemed that the new consul Cornelius Merula was having a tough time making his 'subordinate officers' obey his orders and not attack before he gave the signal. They undoubtedly thought, from their previous experience, that they knew better than the new consul.

Cornelius Merula ordered the military tribunes Quintus and Publius Minucius to form the cavalry up on level ground. As he was preparing, the Celts had already attacked the lines held by Sempronius Longus. Merula received a message from him that the Celts were overwhelming his lines and there had been heavy Roman casualties. Indeed, many of the Roman soldiers were now in panicked flight. A humiliating defeat was about to be inflicted. Merula ordered the II Legion to reinforce the battle line.

The II Legion managed to hold back the Celtic advance and now fresh troops, in the form of another newly arrived legion, moved up to replace the left wing.

It was a day of blazing sunshine, which scorched the bodies of the Celts, who cannot endure excessive heat; in spite of this, they resisted the Roman attacks, drawn up in dense array, propping themselves up sometimes on one another, sometimes on their shields. When Merula observed the situation, he ordered Gaius Livius Salinator, in command of the auxiliary horse, to charge at full gallop, with the legionary cavalry in support. This cavalry charge immediately threw the Celtic line into confusion and disorder, and then scattered it; but it failed to cause a rout.

The Celtic leaders put a stop to the retreat. Livy says they belaboured their men with their spear shafts to drive them back into line. Merula, observing this, called for another charge, telling his men that one more brief effort would bring victory. If the Celts were allowed to reform their battle lines, then the legions would be lost. A second charge was made and this time, they broke through and the Boii army was scattered.

Livy tells us that 14,000 Boii were slain and 1092 captured alive, with 721 horsemen and three Celtic chieftains. Some 212 Celtic standards were taken and sixty-three wagons. He puts Roman losses at only 5000 men but the Roman dead included twenty-three centurions and four generals, together with Marcus Genucius and Quintus and Marcus Minucius, all three military tribunes of the II Legion.

Indeed, we have evidence that the victory claimed by Livy over the Boii at Mutina was not such an overwhelming one, for the dispatches of Cornelius Merula about the battle were the subject of a debate in the Roman Senate. It appears that one of Cornelius Merula's subordinates, Marcus Claudius, had written to many friends of his in the Senate, saying that the consul was responsible for the heavy casualties suffered by the army and that the escape of the main body of the Celtic army was due to his bad generalship. The losses sustained by the Romans had been heavier because reinforcements were ordered up too late and the enemy had been able to withdraw in good order because the cavalry had not been allowed to pursue them. The fact that the Romans could claim a victory was only because of luck.

The Senate postponed listening to the charges against the consul until a later date and he was ordered to return to Rome and give an account of himself. However, Marcus Claudius, his accuser, was still with the army in the Po Valley when Cornelius Merula made his speech to the Senate. Cornelius Merula claimed the victory was important and wondered why no thanksgiving or triumph had been proclaimed. He was told he had to answer charges made in the letters from Marcus Claudius criticising his conduct of the campaign.

Quintus Metellus, a former consul and dictator, rose in the Senate to make a damning speech against Cornelius Merula's conduct. Why, he asked, had Cornelius Merula ordered his lieutenant, Marcus Claudius, to stay in Cisalpine Gaul in command of the troops when it would have been more fitting to entrust the army to Sempronius Longus and allow Marcus Claudius to appear before the Senate? It seemed that he had deliberately kept Claudius away in case he could make his charges public and if Claudius' assertions were wrong then the truth could have been established. In opposing Cornelius Merula, Metellus was joined by the tribunes of the plebeians, Marcus and Gaius Titinius, and a thanksgiving and triumph were denied the consul.

Little is recorded about campaigns in Cisalpine Gaul in 192 BC except that we are told a chieftain or *princeps* of the Boii arrived at the camp of the army of a proconsul, Titus Quinctius Flaminius. The Celtic leader brought his wife and family to the encampment and asked for terms of surrender. Livy says that the proconsul seized the family and had them ritually put to death in order to entertain a sulky boyfriend. Flaminius had been consul in 198 BC and had commanded the Roman forces against Philip V of Macedonia. His arrogance and ruthlessness caused him to be struck off the Senate poll in 182 BC for this and other acts considered unworthy of a Roman senator.

The end for the Boii came in 191 BC. We are told that the consul Publius Cornelius Scipio Nasica, a cousin of Scipio Africanus, fought an army of the Boii in a pitched battle with outstanding success. Unfortunately, there appears to be no record of the details of this encounter. The historian Valerius Antias, quoted by Livy, claimed 28,000 of the Celts were killed and 3400 taken prisoner, with 124 standards captured, 1200 horse and 247 wagons. The number of Roman dead was placed at only 1484. Scarcely credible figures. Even Livy comments:

> Although very little confidence can be given to this author in the matter of numbers since no writer shows less restraint in exaggerating such statistics, it is still evident that this was a great victory, as can be seen from these facts; first, the enemy camp was taken; secondly, the Boii surrendered immediately after the battle; thirdly, a thanksgiving was decreed by the Senate in honour of the victory and the [physically] larger Celtic prisoners were slain in sacrifice.

Publius Cornelius took hostages from the Boii and confiscated half of the territory so that Rome could begin to establish colonies there. He then returned to Rome and presented himself before the Senate to demand a triumph. However, the tribune of the plebeians, Publius Sempronius Blaesus, suggested such a triumph be postponed. He pointed out that the Ligurians had not yet been defeated and, as Ligurians and Boii usually rendered each other mutual service, that is, they were allies, a triumph could not be proclaimed until both had been defeated. Having defeated the Boii, Publius Cornelius could have served Rome better by crossing into Liguria and defeating them, or at least going to the aid of Quintus Minucius, who commanded there. Unless the Ligurians were defeated, then the Boii would continue to be a threat to Rome.

The consul was bitter, pointing out that the Ligurians had not been allotted to his sphere of military command. He had done all that Rome had asked him to do.

What he himself was demanding was a triumph over the Boian Celts; he had defeated them in battle; he had robbed them of their camp; he had received the surrender of their whole people two days after the battle; and he had taken hostages from them as a security for peace in the future. However, what was really of greater importance was the fact that he had killed in battle more thousands of Celts than any number – or at any rate any number of Boii – ever encountered in battle by a previous Roman general. More than half of their 50,000 men had been slain; many thousands had been captured; old men and boys were all that the Boii now had left. Could anyone then wonder why a victorious army, having left behind no enemy in the province, should have come to Rome to celebrate the consul's triumph?

It seemed that the campaign of this year was, indeed, a significant one and it is frustrating that there are no details known apart from the meagre facts given in Publius Cornelius' speech. The Senate agreed, however, to vote him the triumph over the Boii. After all, the most important aspect was that following previous defeats, the Boii had never submitted to Rome. Publius Cornelius had finally brought about their submission. Livy points out that the ceremonial parade in Rome included a line of Celtic wagons in which were conveyed the captured arms and standards and the noble Celtic prisoners, the chieftains and their families, together with a herd of captured horses. Also displayed were 1471 golden torques, as well as 247 pounds' weight of gold, 2340 pounds' weight of silver, both wrought and unwrought, vessels of Celtic craftsmanship and vessels of bronze. In addition there were 234,000 silver *bigati* – Celtic silver coins stamped with a pair of horses. The consul paid to each infantry soldier 125 *asses*, with double that amount to each centurion and three times to each cavalryman.

The following day, having made a speech to his soldiers, the consul disbanded his legions. The last major battles between the Celts of the Po Valley and Rome had been fought. There was now nothing to stand in the way of the colonisation of the conquered territory.

The Colonisation of Cisalpine Gaul

CISALPINE Gaul was the first Celtic homeland to be conquered by Rome. It would not be the last, for the Roman empire would eventually swallow up most of the Celtic world which, at this time, stretched as far west as Ireland, east to the central plain of Turkey, Galatia, north to what are now Scotland and Belgium on the Continent, south to Cadiz in Spain and the Po Valley itself. This vast Celtic territory would be slowly reduced over the years until, today, Celtic communities survive only on the fringes of north-western Europe.

The people of the Po Valley, where Rome had finally achieved dominance, were, of course, not all Celts. To the mountainous south-west of the area dwelt the Ligurians, or Celto-Ligurians, perhaps a mixed group of tribes. To the east dwelt the Veneti, who many scholars argue were heavily Celticised by this time. There also remained areas of the old Etruscan population, many of whom were intermixed with the Celts especially in the Apennine Boii territory in which groups of Umbrians were found. All these people had intermarried to varying extents, judging from the archaeological evidence. But the predominant culture, along the extent of the Po river itself, was Celtic.

Clearly the Roman victory over the Boii in 191 BC had been devastating. With the Boii no longer able to defend themselves the way was opened for complete Roman dominance south of the Po, Cispadana as it would become known. Roman policy took various forms. For the time being, treaties of friendship secured the co-operation of the Veneti and the Celtic tribes of Transpadana, or north of the Po. The Romans continued their military campaigns to bring the Ligurians of the west under their control. The Cispadana area was already open to Roman colonisation.

Polybius claimed that the Celts were driven out of the entire Po

Valley. This is clearly not so. Strabo says there was a mass migration of the Boii to the land which was named after them – Bohemia. But then he speaks of the continued habitation of the Celts on the Cispadane plain, that is within the Boii territory, and archaeology supports this claim. The reality seems to lie in a partial migration of some of the twelve septs that made up the Boii confederation, who made their way north-east to what became Bohemia, leaving isolated communities or small tribal groups behind which no longer functioned as independent peoples but were subject to control by the new Roman colonies.

According to Dr Chilver:

As to the Celts, Polybius tells us that they had been driven out of the plain of the Po by his day, and inhabited only the towns at the foot of the Alps ... But Polybius is contradicted by the persistence of the word Gallia, which presumably had some foundation in fact, and by direct statements in other authors, particularly Strabo, who tells us that Cispadana was inhabited by Ligures in the mountains and Celts in the plain and the Transpadana by Celts and Veneti. Our evidence from personal names has already confirmed the existence of Celts in the towns of the plain; for around Cremona any non-Roman would be a Celt rather than a Ligurian or Venetian. Further, that the citizens of the big Transpadana towns, and not merely their *attributi populi*, were of Gallic origin is proved by their special treatment under the *Lex Pompeia*; and even in the principate of Augustus, the simple-minded people of Mediolanum, who preserved a statue of Brutus without reflecting that Augustus might have taken offence, are called Gauls in the story told to Plutarch.

The Boii had been forced to give up half of their territory and hand over three of their towns. Their capital, which had formerly been the Etruscan city of Felsina, was named after the Boii – Bononia (Bologna), the place of the Boii. This became a Roman military colony in 189 BC and 3000 military of Latin origin were settled there. According to Strabo, the main body of the Boii had retraced their steps over the Alps back to the homelands they had left over five centuries before. The Romans seemed in no doubt that the Boii who named Bohemia were the same Boii that had once dwelt in northern Italy. Of course, it might be argued that they were a separate tribe bearing the same name, for tribes bearing similar names were to be found throughout the Celtic world such as the Tolistoboii. If the Boii of Bohemia were the same Boii of the Po Valley then they were ill-fated in their choice of new homelands for they were forced to move on again when the Germans and Slavs began to press from the north and east. The Boii joined the last great Celtic movement into Gaul proper in 58 BC. This was turned back by Julius Caesar, who used the migration as an excuse for Rome to interfere in the affairs of Transalpine Gaul and as the lever to conquer it. According to documents recovered by Caesar from the Celts, there were 32,000 Boii who had joined with the Helvetii, Tulingi, Latovici and Rauraci and other small tribes in this migration. According to Caesar:

> The Boii were given a home in the country of the Aedui, who asked Caesar to consent to this arrangement because the Boii were known as a people of exceptional bravery. The Aedui assigned them land, and later admitted them to equality of rights and liberties with themselves.

The devastated colonies of Placentia and Cremona were reinforced in 190 BC with 6000 new colonists. According to Tenney Frank, Placentia was not only reinforced but rebuilt on a new site. In 187 BC the consul, Marcus Aemilius Lepidus, ordered the construction of a new road from Ariminum to Placentia which became the Via Aemilia; the area through which it ran was known as the Aemilian Plain. Today it still takes the name Emilia Romagna.

According to Professor Toynbee a new town, called the Forum Gallorum, was established as a half-way staging post on the Via Aemilia between Ariminum and Placentia where the road crosses the River Reno. He says:

> ... the only inhabitants of the country between the territories of the two Latin colonies Bononia and Placentia will have been the original Boian owners of it, who will have been allowed to remain there provisionally on sufferance. Through the act of expropriation in 191 BC, Rome had deprived them of their title to the land, but the Roman Government is likely to have left them in precarious occupation, pending the disposal of the expropriated

land in other ways. Those of them who were now synoecised [united into or under one city] at the halfway-house on the new road may have obtained security of tenure there in return for serving a Roman purpose.

Warming to his argument that the Romans did not evict all the Celts from this area, Professor Toynbee says: 'The present day "Celto-Italian" dialect of the Emilia is evidence that, in spite of its colonis-ation by Peninsular Italian settlers, the Boian Gallic population must have survived in the expropriated territory in considerable strength.' He cites as his sources for this claim H. Nissen's *Italische Landes-kunder*, vol. 1, p. 482, and vol. 2, p. 109, together with R. Chevallier, 'Rome et l'Italie du nord' in *Revue des Études Latines*, vol. xxxvii (1959), p. 140. In fact, the extent of Celtic influence in this linguistic area is a matter of some argument, to the extent that the survival of a 'Celto-Italian dialect' in Emilia seems an unreasonable proposition. However, most scholars are in agreement that there was still a small but noticeable Celtic population in the towns along the Via Aemilia well into imperial times.

Professor Toynbee also points out: 'In contrast to the Roman annexation of half the *Ager Boiorum* [Boii territory], the territories of the Cenomani, the [B]Orombovii and the Insubres were left intact.' We have archaeological evidence to support this: excavations at Ornavasso in the Como area show that the Insubres were still in the area in the age of the Roman emperors and probably merged with the Roman settlers and other colonists. The excavations showing the survival of the Celts in these areas were reported in the *Rivista archaeologica della provincia di Como*, in 1907 and 1908.

C. Livius Salinator was elected consul in 188 BC and sent to continue the Roman colonisation of the Po Valley. Livius Salinator established the Forum Livii as another defensive bastion covering Ariminum and protecting lines of communication. In 187 BC a further road was built from Bononia to Arretium. By that year, the Romans had made treaties with the Celts north of the Po. We find that the Cenomani sent ambassadors to the Roman Senate to make a formal complaint about the breaking of one of these treaties by a Roman official. A Roman praetor had marched an army into their territory and attempted to disarm them without any provocation being given by the Cenomani. The Senate heard the case and referred it to the consul Aemilius Lepidus. Livy records that Aemilius Lepidus ordered the praetor to return the confiscated arms and resign his command. This is interesting because it shows that, at this time, Rome was keen to have these Celtic tribes as allies rather than enemies. If the Roman government had disarmed all the Celtic tribes north of the Po, then they would have had to take on their shoulders the military burden of defending these northern territories against any hostile action from the Transalpine Celts. By allowing the Transpadana Celts to remain armed and able to defend their own territories, Roman territory was also defended.

In fact, in 186 BC a new Celtic tribe appeared, having crossed the Carnic Alps. They apparently moved out of the area of Noricum, modern Austria. Henri Hubert believes that they were the Carni, although other scholars believe that the Carni had long been settled in this area, giving the name to the mountains there, and that the invaders were a new, smaller tribe whose name is not recorded. They consisted of 12,000 men, women and children. They declared that their intentions were peaceful and that they merely wanted to settle down to farm in the area. They set industriously about building a township near the future site of Aquileia, modern Aquiléia near Grado on the Golfo di Trieste. A Roman army commanded by a praetor, Marcus Claudius Marcellus, was sent against them in 183 BC, the year Mutina (Modena) and Parma were transformed into garrison towns. The Celts did not want to fight and so they surrendered and were disarmed, stripped of all their goods and movable property and ordered to move back across the Alps. It was a death sentence, since they were without goods to sustain themselves or the means to protect themselves. They were allowed to send emissaries to the Roman Senate but the Senate refused to revoke its decision. However, commissioners were sent to ensure that the personal property of the Celts was returned to them before they were expelled from the area.

It was because of this incursion that the Roman Senate decided to protect its interests in this north-eastern area, establishing in 181 BC another military colony at Aquileia with 3000 infantrymen, cavalrymen and officers and their dependants. In 169 BC the colony was reinforced with an additional 1500 military families.

Mutina and Parma had, as we have seen, been established in Boii territory as Roman military colonies with 2000 settlers apiece. The

Forum Cornelia was set up two years later; the Forum Lepidi also appeared in Boii territory about 175 BC. Military colonies were constructed around this time in Claterna (modern Maggio), Tannetum and Fidentia. The Romans usually adopted the existing names of the towns they chose as Roman colonies. Where there was no existing name they gave the new settlement a descriptive one, such as Fidentia (courage) or Parma (shield). Sometimes, if the name was too outlandish or inauspicious-sounding, it was changed. Obviously the original name of a Boii tribal capital was not to Roman taste and the town was called Regium, modern Reggio, after the word for 'royal' or 'kingship'. Yet the Romans accepted the Celtic name Bononia instead of reverting to the old Etruscan name Felsina, which probably would have sounded easier to their ears. Eporedia (now Irea/Yvrea) was allowed to keep its existing Celtic name, the name derived from the Celtic horse goddess whose worship became accepted even in Rome. Eporedia was colonised by Rome around 100 BC, much later than other places in the area. And, of course, the Insubrean town of Comum, whose Celtic root *com* suggests a stronghold or fortification, remains today as Como.

One town taken over by the Romans for the establishment of a colony was Druentinorum. It has an obvious Celtic ring to it and means 'the place of oaks'. There was a river in Gaul proper called Druentia, a tributary of the Rhône, which is now called the Durance. The location of Druentinorum is uncertain. It has been suggested that it was a synonym for Caesena but this is admittedly a guess. And Dr Ewins hazards that it is the present-day village of Terenzo on the Parma–Luna road. This would seem logical for it was near the Forum Novum (present-day Fórnovo di Taro) and the disappearance of the garrison town could have been explained by the unification of Novum and Druentinorum into one single *municipium*.

While the Roman colonisation was proceeding, with new garrison towns springing up, in 179 BC yet another small Celtic tribe, only 3000 strong, moved south of the Alps and, like their predecessors in 183 BC, declared their peaceful intent. In fact they petitioned the Senate to be allowed to settle under Roman rule. They, too, were ordered to withdraw. This was the last Celtic 'invasion' of Italy prior to the coming of the Cimbri and Teutones and their Celtic allies. Livy says that the Roman Senate now issued a proclamation which forbade any Celtic tribe from entering the new borders of Italy which they finally set at the Alps.

Meanwhile, the friendly relationship with some Po Valley Celts began to show dividends. Livy was able to report that in 178 BC one of the Celtic tribes of the Po Valley, either Cenomani or Insubres, had provided the Roman army with a division of 3000 warriors, commanded by a chieftain nominated by their prince. They served in the Roman expeditionary force in Istria. In 168 BC Cisalpine Celtic cavalry were serving in the Roman army in Macedonia.

The Romans' initial policy had been to attempt to maintain a peaceful relationship with the Ligurian tribes until they had completed their subjugation of the Celts on the southern side of the Po Valley. They were apparently caught unaware when, in 193 BC, a 20,000 strong Ligurian army attacked Luna and moved on towards Pisae. Livy is not clear whether the army came from a particular Ligurian tribe, the Apuani; he says it was the undertaking of 'the whole nation', but whether he means the 'nation' of the Apuani or all the Ligurian tribes is not certain. Certainly during that same year the Eliates, with an army of 10,000, headed for Placentia.

The consul Quintus Minucius Thermus had been ordered to deal with the Ligurians and he set off into Apuanian territory. Livy explains that only his Numidian cavalry saved him from being annihilated. By 190 BC Minucius returned from his campaign to report that all the Ligurian peoples had capitulated and the war was over. He was then told to join Publius Cornelius Scipio Nasica to assist him in 'mopping up' in the territory of the Boii. But Minucius Thermus' report on the submission of the Ligurians was premature. It was another sixteen years before Rome was able to declare her war with Liguria really over and then it took the combined activities of both consuls and six full legions and auxiliaries.

Among the remarkable feats during this period was that of Marcus Sempronius Tuditanus in 185 BC who fought his way overland from Pisae to the mouth of the River Macra and the port of Luna. He was the first Roman commander ever to do so. The Ligurians had as many successes as setbacks; in 176 BC they made a daring invasion of the Po Valley and were even able to capture Mutina. The proconsul Claudius Pulcher was forced to expend time and energy retaking the garrison town. In the wake of this success he was able to send to the Senate a boastful dispatch which claimed that as a result of his operations there was no enemy of Rome under arms south of the Alps.

However, the Ligurians were still not defeated and later that year the new consul Quintus Petilius Spurinus lost his life in leading an attack on the Ligurian strongholds at Mount Letus and Mount Ballista. But Rome finally began to achieve domination. They commenced the mass deportations of the Ligurians to the plains where they could be more easily controlled by military means. In 166 BC, Claudius Marcellus was celebrating a victory over the Eliates and, significantly, the Celtic Contrubrii. However, as late as 155 BC triumphs were being recorded for battles against the Ligurians, especially the Cisalpine Eliates who were still fighting against the Romans.

Rome was continuing to busy herself with the confiscation of Celtic lands along the Po Valley and their resettlement by colonists. Various Italic groups, such as settlers from Stellatina in Campania, the Mevaniola from Mevania in Umbria and many others, were now encouraged to move in as colonists. The reason for encouraging these non-Romans was, it seems, judging by Livy, a reluctance among Roman citizens to go to the area. The new Roman towns appeared to grow up in an individual unplanned manner. Dr Ursula Ewins asks the question: 'Why did Rome allow these towns to grow up thus, haphazard, instead of dividing the whole area into colonies, each thoroughly organised from the start? The answer lies in past history. Colonies had always been founded for military reasons, and the tradition did not end until the time of the Gracchi.' She therefore believes the system was one of *viritum*, man by man, or individually. However, she contradicts herself by suggesting that the colonies were not made for purposes of military defence but 'it was simply natural Roman procedure for dealing with land left empty after the conquest'. There is evidence that the Romans were, in fact, engaged in some degree of 'ethnic cleansing', forcibly evicting the Celtic occupants and seizing their land to colonise. But I think this haphazard growth was probably due to nothing more than the individual priorities of each succeeding consul.

In 175 BC we hear that the Celts of Cisalpine Gaul and the Ligurians joined forces and rose in revolt against the Romans. Livy gives little detail but says the revolt 'was quickly suppressed, with no great effort'. By 170 BC Cisalpine Gaul was quiet again and it is reported that one of the consuls for that year, Aulus Hostilius Mancinus, went there.

> Having satisfied himself that it would be a peaceful year, he sent home the soldiers of the two Roman legions within sixty days after his arrival in the province. Then, after taking a small force of allies of Latin status into winter quarters at Luna [on the borders of Liguria and Etruria] and Pisa, he went with the cavalry on visits to many of the towns in the province of Cisalpine Gaul.

Livy's description of Cisalpine Gaul as a 'province' is a little early for the reality. It was not a province at this time and didn't become one until about 81 BC. In fact, by 173 BC the region was, for administrative purposes, still divided into two – Cispadana and Transpadana. There were no colonies north of the Po at this time because the Cenomani and Veneti especially were considered allies; even the Insubres had agreed treaties with Rome. It has been argued that the Romans actually resettled a tribe of Ligurians at Acelum among the Veneti in 172 BC. The argument rests solely on a remark by Livy (XLII, 22) but it is unlikely that the Romans would suddenly place a Ligurian tribal settlement in the middle of friendly Venetian territory. From inscriptions and references, the Roman colonisation north of the Po does not appear to have begun until after 143 BC.

When the historian Polybius visited Cisalpine Gaul around 150 BC he was able to report:

> Words fail to describe the fertility of the country. Corn is so abundant that in our own time a Sicilian *medimnus* of wheat has more than once been seen to fetch only four *obols*, a *medimnus* of barley two *obols*, and a *metretes* of wine no more than a measure of barley. Millet and panic produce enormous crops. A single fact may give an idea of the quality of the acorns furnished by the oaks which grow at intervals on the plains; many pigs are slaughtered in Italy both for daily life and for the supply of camps, and it is from this district that most of them come. Lastly, here is conclusive proof of the cheapness and plenty prevailing there. Travellers stopping at the inns do not make terms over each item separately but ask what the rate is per head; as a rule the innkeeper undertakes to give them all they want for a quarter of an *obol*

[less than half a penny] and this price is seldom exceeded. Need I speak of the enormous population of the country, of the stature and good looks of the people and of their warlike spirit?

Clearly, Polybius is contradicting himself and talking about Celts with his stereotypical references to stature, his Greek concern with Celtic good looks and Celtic warlike spirit. This also is another confirmation of the argument that the Celts remained south of the Po and eventually merged into the new Italian identity. As for Polybius' special attention to the taverns of the area, there is a distinct echo of Irish taverns (*bruden* or *brughean*) in this passage. In early medieval times these Irish taverns obtained universal admiration among the many nationalities travelling in Ireland. Ireland was then a centre of European education. At the great monastic college of Durrow in the seventh century AD students from eighteen different nationalities were listed. Each clan territory had to have its public hostel in which lodging, food and entertainment were provided. These hostels or inns were regulated under the ancient Irish law system, the laws of the Fénechus, more commonly called the Brehon laws, after the word for a judge, *breitheamh*, cognate with *breto* (judgement) in Continental Celtic. Caesar claimed that someone called Vergobret was elected chief magistrate and judge of the Aedui in 52 BC: in fact, Vergobret is a title, a job description, rather than a name, deriving from *vergo* (effective) and *breto*. Under ancient Irish law a public innkeeper had to keep his wayside inn in order. Beds had to be provided, a kitchen fire had to be perpetually alight, and he should always have plenty of food and drink for guests. In Ireland it was also the duty of the hostel-keeper to maintain the roads leading to his inn and to keep a light burning at night outside the inn to announce its presence.

A stranger in Celtic territory often did not need the services of an inn, for hospitality was a matter of honour among the Celts. Strangers would be invited to share whatever a Celtic family had to offer. Diodorus Siculous observed: 'They invite strangers to their feasts, and do not inquire until after the meal who they are and of what things they stand in need.'

The years of warfare, with Roman armies constantly marching through the countryside and devastating it, had interrupted the maintenance of the drained swampland along the Po, its tributaries and

affluences. The problem the Roman colonisers had to turn to was the
task of repairing the dykes and canals and securing land reclamation.
Marcus Aemilius Scaurus in 109 BC had to drain lands around Parma
and build a navigable canal from Parma to the Po. The road between
Bononia and Mutina had to be reinforced and still ran along an
embankment through the swamps in Cicero's time. Strabo's journey
from Ravenna to the Po took two days and two nights by canal.
Ravenna was designated as a naval station by Augustus. Strabo noted
it was a healthy place.

> In the swamps, the biggest city is Ravenna. It is built entirely on
> piles, and it has water flowing all through it. Its internal communi-
> cations are maintained by bridges and ferries. At high tide it has
> a large intake of sea-water. What with this and with the action
> of the rivers, all the mud is scoured away, and this gets rid of the
> foul air.

Ravenna was, in these early days, what Venice subsequently became.

In 143 BC the Celtic Salassi in the north-west of the Cisalpine
region (modern Savoy) rebelled against Rome and were defeated.
Half of their territory was seized for colonisation. Even so the tribe
continued to be in a state of insurrection and it was not until 25 BC
that they were finally suppressed and reduced to slavery. Roman civil
servants estimated that the tribe comprised 44,000 people, including
8000 warriors, who were resettled in the colony of Augusta Praetoria.

By the first century BC, Latin had become the official language
and schools were established for the children of the wealthy colonists
and natives. The richer Celts began to change their names to Latin
forms. Briona became Quintus. It became a fashion to adopt the
names of Roman families who settled in the various areas of Cisalpine
Gaul, such as the Caecilii, the Livii and the Valerii. But this did not
mean all aspects of local culture disappeared. Celtic deities persisted
and were worshipped, such as Belenus, Epona, the Matronae, the
Fatae Dervones and others.

At the time of the defeat of Carthage, Rome's land frontiers had
been clearly placed at the south-western foot of the Apennines. With
the conquest and colonisation of Cisalpine Gaul, she had moved her
frontier to the southern foot of the Alps. This mountain barrier
frontier was, of course, a greater obstacle to a potential invader than

the Apennines. While the mountains provided a barrier to the west and north, to the east there was an easy passage on to the Italian peninsula between the Carnic Alps and the head of the Adriatic, from the basin of the River Save into the basin of the River Isonzo. Invasions had come from this direction before and would do so in the future. So Rome felt it had to provide, in human form, what nature had failed to do.

The Romans formed an alliance with the Veneti but beyond them were the Carni, a Celtic people, and beyond them were the Histri and other Illyrian tribes. The movement of the Celtic tribes in 186 BC and 179 BC made this a particularly sensitive area and therefore Marcus Claudius Marcellus was given the task of invading Istria. The invasion of 178 BC nearly ended in disaster for the Romans and produced panic in Rome. Both consular armies were tied down in Istria during the winter of 178–177 BC. Campaigning continued and the Romans built a military link road between Genua and Aquileia around 148 BC with its fortifications running along it. When Augustus started his reign as emperor in 27 BC, Rome's north-eastern frontier still remained at Aquileia. Cisalpine Gaul had become Gallia Togata, the land of the Celts who wear the toga. A land of Romanised Celts.

[15]

The Last Kicks at Rome

IT took Rome a further hundred years after the conquest to begin to feel secure on her new northern borders. In 154 BC the consul Lucius Opimius, in answer to a complaint from the Greek colony of Massilia about Ligurian raiders, marched an army into the area to deal with them. In 125 BC Massilia repeated the request for further aid against the Ligurians and the new consul Marcus Gulvius Flaccus was given command of an army which then crossed the western Alps, by Mont Genèvre, in order to surprise the Ligurians from an unexpected quarter. Gulvius Flaccus spent two years campaigning against the Ligurians without a really successful conclusion before being relieved by Caius Sextius Calvinus who managed to establish a Roman colony (*castellum*), consisting of army veterans, at Aquae Sextiae, modern Aix, to protect the hinterland. Calvinus finally reduced the Ligurians to the *pax Romana*. In doing so, however, he found himself at odds with the main Celtic tribe in the area, the Allobroges, who had been so helpful to Hannibal in his crossing of the Alps.

The 'flashpoint' occurred when the Allobroges refused to surrender to the Romans a fugitive Ligurian chieftain who had sought asylum with them.

In 121 BC the proconsul Gnaeus Domitius Ahenobarbus fought the first battle between Rome and the Celts of Transalpine Gaul within their own territory. The battle took place near modern Avignon. With the aid of an elephant corps, Ahenobarbus was able to rout the Allobroges' army. This victory gave the Romans control of the whole left bank of the Rhône as far north as Geneva. Worried by this fact, the Arverni, in the Auvergne, decided to raise an army against the Romans commanded by their king, Bituitus son of Lovernius. The Arverni marched to the confluence of the Rhône and the Isere. Here a Roman army commanded by Quintus Fabius

Maximus managed to repulse them. The greater disaster for the Arverni occurred when the Celts, withdrawing from the battlefield and crossing the Rhône bridge, were precipitated into the turbulent waters when the bridge broke. Fabius Maximus claimed that he had slaughtered 120,000 Celts with a loss of fifteen Romans, figures that certainly need to be treated with a great deal of scepticism.

However exaggerated his report, both the Arverni and the Allobroges had clearly been defeated and Rome now controlled the southern lands of Gaul along the Mediterranean shore. In the defeat of the Arverni, the perfidy of the Romans was demonstrated when the consul Ahenobarbus persuaded the king of the Arverni, Bituitus, to journey to Rome to conduct the peace negotiations between the two peoples in person. Once in Rome, Bituitus was seized and made a prisoner. The Senate took full advantage of the violation of the safe-conduct promise of Ahenobarbus, by keeping Bituitus confined as a prisoner in Alba Longa on Mons Albanus. Here, Bituitus was joined by his son Comm or Congentiatus. Domitius Ahenobarbus set up a victory monument, the Tour Magne at Nîmes.

Domitius Ahenobarbus had managed to acquire for Rome large tracts of lands comprising modern Languedoc and the Upper Garonne Valley, including the towns of Nemausud (Nîmes) and Tolosa (Toulouse), the capital of the Tectosages, who were given the euphemistic title of 'allies of Rome'. Thus Rome had managed to carve out a new imperial province from the Alps to the Pyrenees and Domitius constructed a highway to which he gave his name. On this route a military colony was also established called Narbo, modern Narbonne. The area was for a time called Narbonensis Gaul but, as Romans called it the 'provincia', it simply became known as 'The Province' and today remains Provence.

Rome's hold over Italy was finally complete and unquestioned. It had exerted its dominions through the entire peninsula and even beyond, east to Greece and Anatolia and west to Iberia through southern Gaul. Rome was now confident that she was invincible. Then the unexpected happened, and the Romans were uncomfortably reminded of their mortality and of the Celtic capture of Rome nearly 300 years before. Like so many nasty shocks that the Romans experienced, this one seemed to come from a movement of the Celts.

Two great tribal armies, those of the Cimbri and the Teutones, spilled towards the Italian border. In 113 BC they reached Noreia

(Neumarkt, near Ljubljana) and were met by the consul Gnaeus Papirius Carbo. The area had been settled by the Taurini, perhaps driven from their lands around Turin. The town had become a rich trading centre and naturally Rome's envious gaze had been drawn there.

The chieftains of the Cimbri and Teutones, realising a Roman consular army was in the vicinity, at first sent word to the consul that they would not approach the border of Rome's possessions. But Carbo, not trusting their promises, decided to launch an attack on them anyway. He apparently thought it would be an easy triumph for his legions. The tribes were on the march with their women, children and elderly as well as large baggage trains. The Romans were defeated.

Who were these Cimbri and Teutones?

Several historians of the Roman empire speak of these peoples as Germans. Cicero, Sallust and Appian, however, regarded them as Celts. Who was right? Certainly the names are Celtic. Teutones means 'tribe' or 'people', cognate to the Irish *tuath* and the Welsh *tud*. Festus says that Cimbri meant 'brigands'. There is a Celtic root *cimb*, meaning 'tribute, ransom' (hence *cimbid*, a prisoner). Festus says, '*Cimbri lingua Gallica latrones dicuntur.*' And the names of these Teutones and Cimbri leaders, given by the historians, are all Celtic. One Teutones chieftain was called Teutoboduus, and one Cimbrian chieftain Claodicus. Significantly, there also appears a Boiorix, king of the Boii, among them, a Gaesorix, king of the Gaesatae, and a Lugius, whose name seems to incorporate the Celtic deity Lugh.

Plutarch also mentions that the Ambrones were a crack corps of the Teutones' army. The name seems to be akin to the names of the many rivers in the Celtic lands called Ambra which means 'water' and is cognate to the Sanskrit *ambhas*. Festus calls these 'dwellers by the water' a *gens Gallica*. When the Roman consul, Gaius Marius, asked Sertorius to set up an intelligence service to find out more about these peoples, it is significant that they had to learn Celtic and found that language sufficient for their needs, according to Theodor Mommsen. Apart from the fact that their personal and tribal names were Celtic, the Teutones and Cimbri were armed in the Celtic manner. Isidor of Seville, Plutarch and Martial are among many who describe the weapons, helmets, body armour and shields in Celtic terms. And if we have doubt about the Cimbri and Teutones then we can have no doubt about the peoples that subsequently flocked to their support – the Helvetii, the Tigurini, the Tugeni and other Celtic tribes – so that eventually Rome was facing a grand Celtic coalition.

Not elated by their sudden and overwhelming victory over the consular army of Carbo, the Teutones and Cimbri disappeared for a period of four years. Then, in 109 BC, they suddenly reappeared west of the Rhône in the Roman province of Narbonensis Gaul, where the consul Marcus Iunius Silanus hurried with his legions. The tribes sent an embassy to the consul and said they were looking for land to settle and did not want any conflict with Rome. In fact, they offered to become mercenaries in the Roman army in order to pay for the land. Silanus, with some arrogance, misread the signs as weakness and broke off negotiations. He attacked the tribes. The Teutones and Cimbri routed and destroyed the Roman army again. Two Roman consular armies had been annihilated.

Once more, the Teutones and Cimbri had the opportunity to turn into northern Italy but they did not do so. A Celtic tribe called the Tigurini detached themselves from the main body of the coalition and moved through Narbonensis Gaul from the west bank of the Rhône into the land of the Volcae Tectosages, in modern Languedoc. The Volcae Tectosages had unwillingly accepted the *pax Romana*. Now they enthusiastically joined forces with the Tigurini and besieged the Roman military garrison occupying their capital of Tolosa.

In 107 BC the new consul, Lucius Cassius Longinus, arrived with another army and hurried to do battle with the Celts. The Tectosages and Tigurini pretended to retreat, withdrawing into the country of the Nitiobriges near Agen, modern Gascony. It was a well-executed ambush with the Celts commanded by a Tigurini chieftain named Divico, whom Caesar eventually met when Divico was an elderly man. The consul Longinus was killed in the action and his army had to surrender; the survivors, including his second-in-command, Caius Popillus Laenas, were yoked like oxen by the Celts, and paraded through the country as a reparation for the ill-treatment of Celtic captives. It was the third Roman consular army to be destroyed.

However, yet another consular army, commanded by Quintus Servilius Caepio, managed to capture Tolosa and loot the sanctuary of the Tectosages. The treasure Rome captured was said to include 100,000 pounds of gold and 110,000 pounds of silver which then disappeared mysteriously on its way to Rome. The treasure was supposed to have been part of that taken by the Tectosages from the temple of Delphi in 279 BC, as recounted in *Celt and Greek*. Servilius Caepio was accused of making off with it. In 1892 a treasure of coins, ingots and Celtic torques was found at Taillac Libourne. The coins belonged to the Celtic tribes of the Bellovaci, Ambarri, Arverni and others and were from this period. It has been speculated that this is part of the 'lost treasure'.

In 105 BC the Cimbri, Teutones, Ambrones and Helvetii were reunited and moving down the Rhône. At Orange, the proconsul Caepio and consul Gnaeus Mallius Maximus managed to secure a victory by dispersing them. The Cimbri headed for Iberia while the Teutones moved off to central Gaul. In 103 BC the Cimbri moved back and were reunited with the Teutones. Now they formed a plan to invade Italy. The Teutones were to cross the western Alps, following the River Durance, the Cimbri were to move north around the Alps and through the Brenner Pass, the Tigurini were to cross from the east, through Noricum, and bring reinforcements through the Julian Alps.

Rome waited fearfully for the onslaught.

Gaius Marius (157–86 BC), a member of an equestrian family, who had served as an officer at the siege of the Celtic fortress of Numantia in Spain, one of the worst disasters for the Celts in a weary history of defeat and disaster, and who married an aunt of Julius Caesar, had been elected consul in 109 BC. He had been sent to Numidia to conduct a war against the Numidian king, Jugurtha. In 107 BC he was elected again and ended the war in Numidia by capturing Jugurtha and bringing him to Rome in 104 BC. The Senate asked him to undertake the defence of Italy against the Cimbri and Teutones.

He set up an intelligence service to find out more about his enemy and then moved rapidly so that he was able to meet up with the Teutones before they had even begun to cross the Alps. In fact, he found them at Aquae Sextiae, modern Aix, in 102 BC. He manoeuvred them into a narrow valley with no room for retreat. In a brutal battle, showing no quarter, Marius defeated and destroyed them.

The Cimbri had already crossed the Alps and arrived at the banks of the Adige where Quintus Lutatius Catulus, commanding the only other consular army, had been placed to defend the Po Valley. The Cimbri mauled the Roman army and dispersed it. The victorious Cimbri encamped in the Lombardy area to await the arrival of the Teutones and Tigurini. There is no reference to any Celts within the Po Valley joining with the Cimbri. It would be surprising if none of them did so: if not tribal groups then individual young men who had learnt the stories of their heroic struggle against Rome from their grandfathers and grandmothers around the fire at night. Instead of the Teutones arriving to join them, the Roman general Marius, and his legions, came through the passes and met up with the remnants of Catulus' army at Vercellae. It was the spring of 101 BC.

The battle proved a day-long slaughter and the Cimbri were utterly defeated. We hear of 300,000 dead at Aquae Sextiae among the Teutones and an equal number of Cimbri at Vercellae. Even allowing for the Roman exaggeration of enemy casualty figures, it was cataclysmic.

At the same time Cornelius Sulla had been sent to confront the Tigurini in Noricum. Hearing the news of the fate of their allies, the Tigurini departed swiftly to take shelter among the Helvetii in modern Switzerland. The terror of the Teutones and Cimbri had vanished.

Strangely enough, it was the Celtic world of Gaul proper that had been turned upside down rather than the lands south of the Apennines. For 400 years Transalpine Gaul had been a country where the Celts lived as agriculturists, in farms and open villages with only a few fortified towns surviving from the early Halstatt period. Now fortresses were erected again, and towns were refortified throughout Gaul. Within fifty years Rome was to start moving into Transalpine Gaul and the Celtic world began to diminish rapidly.

Marius' greatest triumph was his reorganisation of the Roman army from a conscript militia into a standing army of professional soldiers. The old militia divisions of *hastati*, *principes* and *triarii* were abolished. All soldiers were armed with standard weapons, the *pilum* and the *gladius*. The maniple was superseded by the cohort, ten cohorts to a legion, with a total legionary strength of 6000 men. Sixty regular centuries comprised the legion. The soldiers, each man highly trained, developed a new *esprit de corps*. It was centred around regimental loyalty, symbolised by the legion's new standard of a silver eagle. Legionaries now had to carry their own entrenching tools and other equipment – they became known as *muli Mariani*, Marius' mules – but with these tools, they were less dependant on the baggage train and could construct well-defended marching camps at speed. The new Roman army would continue to create an empire that would last for a further 500 years. There is irony in the fact that the Roman army, the legionary fighting force which has seized popular imagination over the centuries, was created as a direct result of a war with the Celts which had previously resulted in the annihilation of several consular Roman armies.

For a decade or so, there was quiet among the people of the Po Valley.

Between 90 and 88 BC a war broke out in Italy as the result of a proposal by M. Livius Drusus, tribune of the plebs, to extend the Roman franchise to all Italians. The proposal had failed through bitter conservative opposition and Livius was assassinated. This led to a revolt among Rome's Italian allies. The war became known as the Social War (from *socii*, allies) and later as the Marsian War because the Marsi had begun the rebellion. It was a curious war in which some fought to gain Roman citizenship while others, like the Samnites, still hoped to destroy Rome's predominance in Italy. While the fighting was inconclusive, the Romans did concede the main issue. Full citizenship was granted to all Italians south of the Po.

The Celts of the Po Valley, surprisingly, did not join the Italians in the uprising against Rome. Rome, in fact, was able to raise auxiliary troops among them. Dr Tizzoni in 'The Late Iron Age in Lombardy' comments:

The silence of the Latin historians on this subject can be explained as follows: on the one hand the Romans had no interest in reminding the Cisalpines of their past as Celtic warriors, now that they were accustomed to send their children to Rome for education and in this way they helped the spread of Roman culture in their land (as did the Gaulish mercenaries coming back to their country). On the other hand the Cisalpines (new Roman citizens) who had a bureaucracy formed by their own people and enjoyed the new Roman way of life, did not want their 'barbarian' past and their wars against the Romans to be remembered. The interpretation of the Romanisation as a cultural phenomenon alone, can explain the apparently contrasting data we have on this period.

Between 90 and 89 BC all the rich inhabitants of the Latin settlements in Cisalpine Gaul were given Roman citizenship and the wealthy of the communities which had been classed as 'non-Latin allies of Rome' were given the status of Latin colonies by Gnaeus Pompeius Strabo. Professor Toynbee believes that these 'non-Latins' who now received citizenship were the remnants of the Celts of the area. He points out that the Libici were united into the administration of the town of Vercellae, the Vertacomori were incorporated into Novaria, the Laevi into Ticinum, the Insubres into Mediolanum, the remaining Boii into Laus Pompeia, the (B)Orombovii into Bergamum and the Cenomani into Brixia. The *Lex Pompeia*, however, did not enfranchise the masses as some assume. Dr A. Ferrura argued from a reading of Cicero that all the inhabitants of Cisalpine Gaul received a vote. As Dr Brunt points out: 'the [argument] on the importance of the Gallic vote misses the fact that in a timocratic assembly it was the votes of the rich that counted; ex-Latins who had obtained citizenship "*per magistratum*" would be rich; hence even Transpadane votes mattered'. According to some sources, it was in 82 BC, under the constitutional reforms of Lucius Cornelius Sulla (*c*.138–78 BC), that Cisalpine Gaul was created a province with the River Rubicon recognised as its southern boundary. Dr Brunt argues that we cannot really be sure whether it was due to Sulla or to the earlier *Lex Pompeia* of 89 BC. Cisalpine Gaul was certainly not a province before 90 BC. It had been simply a conquered territory. In 49 BC Julius Caesar extended Roman citizenship to all dwellers beyond the River Po (Transpadana). Another change was also made. It had been the policy of the Senate to place all settlers in Cisalpine Gaul, for voting purposes, in the Roman tribe of the Pollia, with the notable exception of the settlers in the Forum Livii. The new citizens now became distributed among twenty out of the thirty-one Rome tribes for the purposes of the franchise.

Finally, in 42 BC, the province of Gallia Cisalpina was incorporated into Italy and eventually vanished as a separate political unit. During the reign of the Emperor Augustus, Gallia Cisalpina constituted four administrative *regiones* of Italy, that is Aemilia (VIII), Liguria (IX),

Venetia (X) and Transpadana (XI). During this time, Augustus embarked on a 'pacification' of the Celtic tribes of the Alpine foothills.

The population of the Po Valley even then was not totally submerged. Even during the reign of Claudius the deeds of the Celts of Gallia Cisalpina were still fresh in the minds of the Romans. In his *Annals*, Tacitus recounts that in the year when Aulus Vitellius and Lucius Vipsanius were consuls, that is AD48, some of the leading families of Gallia Comata, 'hairy Gaul' or Tansalpine Gaul, were lobbying for the right to sit as magistrates and have full civil honours. Tacitus says, 'The demand became the topic of public discussion, and, in the emperor's cabinet, met with a strong opposition.' Interestingly, Tacitus has members of Claudius' government arguing: 'Is it not enough that the Veneti and Insubreans have forced their way into the Senate? Are we to see a deluge of foreigners poured in upon us, as if the city were taken by storm?'

While it is arguable among current scholarship whether the Veneti were Celts, the Insubreans certainly were and the fact that Tacitus is saying that it was well known that Insubres had made it to the Roman Senate in these times, shows that the Celts of Cisalpine Gaul, or at least a proportion of them, had not completely lost their cultural identity, otherwise the fact would not be remarked upon and they would not be called 'foreigners'.

The argument among Claudius' cabinet throws up some interesting points.

'All posts of honour will be the property of wealthy foreigners; a race of men, whose ancestors waged war against the very being of the republic; with fire and sword destroyed her armies; and finally laid siege to Julius Caesar in the city of Alesia.'

Here, of course, Tacitus, or his source, has his history wrong for it was Julius Caesar who laid siege to Alesia, a stronghold of the Mandubi on the plateau of Mont Auxois, about 30 miles north-west of Dijon – modern Alise Ste Reine. Caesar besieged Vercingetorix, commander-in-chief of the Celtic forces, fighting against the Roman conquest in 52 BC.

But the senator whom Tacitus is quoting goes on:

'But these are modern instances; what shall be said of the bar-barians who laid the walls of Rome in ashes and dared to besiege the Capitol and the temple of Jupiter? Let the present claimants, if it must be so, enjoy titular dignity of Roman citizens, but let the senatorial rank, and the honour of the magistrates, be preserved unmixed, untainted and inviolate.'

We are told that the Emperor Claudius was more liberal, pointing out that his ancestral pedigree derived from a Sabine family, from Attus Clausus. The Julii clan had come from Alba, the Coruncani came from Camerium and the Portii from Tusculum. Peoples from Etruria, Lucania, indeed all of Italy, had become Roman citizens 'and blended with the Roman name'. Claudius continued:

'In a period of profound peace, the people beyond the Po were admitted to their freedom. Under colour of planting colonies, we spread our legions over the face of the globe; and, by drawing into our civil union the flower of the several provinces, we recruited the strength of the mother-country. The Balbi came from Spain, and others of equal eminence from the Narbonensis Celts; of that accession to our numbers have we reason to repent? The descend-ants of these illustrious families are still in being; and can Rome boast of better citizens? Where do we see more generous ardour to promote her interests?'

Claudius warmed to his defence of the Celts:

'The Spartans and the Athenians, without all question, acquired great renown in arms; to what shall we attribute their decline and total ruin? To what, but the injudicious policy of considering the vanquished as aliens to their country? The conduct of Romulus, the founder of Rome, was the very reverse; with wisdom equal to his valour, he made those fellow-citizens at night, who, in the morning, had been his enemies in the field. Even foreign kings have reigned at Rome. To raise the descendants of freedmen to the honours of the state, is not, as some imagine, a modern innovation.

'But, we are told, the Senones waged war against us; however, were the Volscians and Aequi always our friends? The Celts, we are told, well nigh overturned the Capitol; but did not the Tuscans oblige us to deliver hostages? Did not the Samnites compel a Roman army to pass under the yoke? Review the wars that Rome had upon her hands, and that with the Celts will be found the shortest. [This is a reference only to the conquest of Gaul proper.] From that time a lasting and an honourable peace prevailed. Let them now, intermixed with the Roman people, united by ties of affinity, by arts, and congenial manners, be one people with us. Let them bring their wealth to Rome, rather than hoard it up for their own separate use. The institutions of our ancestors, which we so much and so justly revere at present, were, at one time a novelty in the constitution. The magistrates were at first, patricians only, the plebeians opened their way to honours; and the Latins, in a short time, followed their example. In good time we embraced all Italy. The measure which I now defend by examples will, at a future date, be another precedent. It is now a new regulation; in time it will be history.'

Tacitus says that the first Celtic peoples from Gallia Comata to send a representative to a seat in the Roman Senate were the Aeduans. 'Of all the Celts, they alone were styled the brethren of the Roman people, and by their strict fidelity deserved the honour conferred on them.'

A few years later, of course, the liberal-minded emperor was poisoned by his ambitious wife, Agrippina; her son, Lucius Domitius Ahenobarbus, whom Claudius had adopted, taking the name Nero, became emperor (AD 54–68). There was much unrest throughout the Celtic world during his despotic rule, notably the insurrection of Boudicca in Britain caused by Nero's policies.

Tacitus gives us invaluable information on the Druids as historians and in his *Histories* he cites a prophecy of the Gaulish Druids made at the fall of Nero which shows not only that they had not been entirely suppressed at that time but that the historiography of the Celts remembered the deeds of their fellow Celts in Italy. Following Nero's death, during 'the year of the four emperors', Romans were fighting Romans and Aulus Vitellius' troops had captured the Capitol and set fire to it. This action, more than anything, had put new hope into the Celts in Gaul that they could shake off Roman rule. Tacitus says:

The Celts began to breathe new life and vigour, and were persuaded that the Roman armies, wherever stationed, were broken and dispirited. A rumour was current among them, and universally believed, that the Racians and Sarmatians had laid siege to the encampments in Maesia and Pannonia. Affairs in Britain were supposed to be in no better situation. Above all, the destruction of the Capitol [by Vitellius] announced the approaching fate of the Roman Empire.

The Druids, in their wild enthusiasm, sang their oracular songs, in which they taught that, when Rome was formerly sacked by the Celts, the temple of Jupiter being left entire, the commonwealth survived that dreadful shock; but the calamity of fire, which had lately happened, was a denunciation from heaven, in consequence of which, power and dominion were to circulate round the world, and the nations on their side of the Alps were in their turn to become masters of the world.

So, over four centuries later, the Druids of Gaul still retained by oral tradition the details of how their fellow Celts, the Senones, had captured Rome.

It has not been fashionable to accept that Geoffrey of Monmouth (*c*.AD 1100–*c*.1155) was speaking the truth when he claimed to have merely translated his Latin *Historia regum Britanniae* (History of the Kings of Britain) from 'a certain very ancient book written in the British language', given to him by Walter, Archdeacon of Oxford. I have shown in *The Druids* that there is some evidence for believing that he did speak the truth and the original text in an early British Celtic form might well have existed. If it is true, then the book represented a setting forth of British Celtic oral traditions in Christian times. The story of the Celtic sack of Rome appears there. In Geoffrey's text, however, the sons of Dunwallo Molmutius are called Belinus and Brennius. They argue about the succession to the kingship of Britain. Belinus becomes king and the brothers are reconciled but Rome is seen as a threat to this peace and Brennius marches an army to Rome, besieges it and plunders the city. Geoffrey says that Brennius' army is made up mostly of Senones, the actual tribe which did attack Rome, and not of British Celts. We are told that after Rome's fall Brennius settled among the Celts of Italy and no further mention is made of him. Perhaps, as with most mythologies, the accounts given in *Historia regum Britanniae* have more than a little truth and could well be the result of centuries of Celtic oral historical tradition.

That year of AD 69, 'the year of the four emperors' (these were Servius Sulpicius Galba, commanding in Spain; M. Salvius Otho, commanding in Germany; Aulus Vitellius, commander of the Lower Rhine army; and finally Titus Flavius Vespasian who founded the Flavian dynasty) is also interesting for the fact that Nero's downfall was set in motion by an uprising led by Celts. In March AD 68 Caius Julius Vindex was governor of Gallia Lugdunensis, the area centred on modern Lyon. Vindex was a Romanised chieftain of the Aquitani, one of those Gaulish Celts who, under Claudius' liberal laws, managed to obtain magisterial rank and military command.

Vindex, having been affected by the suffering under Nero, sent messages to Galba in Spain and asked him to 'champion the human race', promising him that if he made a bid to overthrow Nero then he would lend his support. Galba dithered, although he indicated to the Senate that he would place himself 'at the disposal of the Senate and the Roman people'. Vindex made the mistake of not waiting for assurances from Galba and he raised insurrection among his own Celtic province. According to Cary and Scullard: 'Vindex may have wanted nothing more than a better emperor; he probably did not envisage restoring republican authority, and it is not clear how far he may have championed a Gallic [Celtic] nationalist movement, seeking either autonomy or greater freedom for Gaul.' In fact, some historians accuse him of trying to create a Celtic empire. But Vindex had coins issued which, significantly, do not bear his name but have words like 'freedom' stamped on them.

Whatever Vindex's aims were, he was viewed by some Roman legions as simply fomenting a new Celtic uprising. L. Verginius Rufus, commander of the army in Upper Germany, marched his legions across the Rhine and met Vindex at Vesontio, modern Besançon. Although Vindex managed to convince Verginius Rufus of his case, Verginius' subordinates took matters into their own hands and incited the legions to fall on Vindex's Celtic troops. They were slaughtered and Vindex, reviving an old Celtic tradition, took his own life. However, Vindex, the Aquitani Celt, had set in motion the train of events which were to lead to the Senate taking courage, turning on Nero and deposing him, sentencing the former emperor to death by cudgelling. In the summer of AD 69 Nero, after long hesitation, persuaded a freedman to thrust his sword home and thus took his life. Among his recorded last words were the famous: '*Qualis artifex pereo*', What a loss I shall be to the arts. His death led the way to the conflict between the four claimants, and most of the major battles of the civil war that followed were to be fought in the territory of the Po Valley.

Before all this, of course, the Romans had had one final shock in Italy. Some Celts made their dying kick at the *pax Romana* by joining Spartacus' insurrection in 73 BC. Initially a band of gladiators, led by Spartacus, said to be of Thracian origin, broke out of a school of gladiators at Capua. It is said that Spartacus had gained military experience in the auxiliary forces of the Roman army. He called on runaway slaves to join him and fight for their liberty, establishing himself as a guerrilla leader on the slopes of Mount Vesuvius. It has been suggested that Spartacus himself may have been a Celt as Thrace had only ceased to have kings with overtly Celtic names one hundred years before this time. Whether he was a Thracian Celt or not, one thing is certain, that the majority of his army was made up of Celts. He was joined by thousands of Cisalpine Celts, Celtiberian and other Celts, taken as prisoners in the various Roman campaigns and made slaves or second- or third-generation slaves born in captivity.

Spartacus' two able lieutenants were Crixos and Cenomaros. Crixos' name is well attested among Celtic personal names and means 'curly, crumpled or wrinkled', surviving the Welsh *crych* and the Breton *crech*. Cenomaros means 'he who is sprung from the race of the strong', specifically that he was of the Cisalpine Cenomani. When Crixos was killed in 72 BC, Spartacus slew 300 Roman prisoners in retaliation. Initially, however, he had great success, defeating with comparative ease two Roman armies, including the army of the governor of Cisalpine Gaul. Spartacus' army traversed Italy. As it moved towards the Po Valley it expanded, recruiting other nationalities who were part of the Roman slave economy. Its strength was said to be 100,000 men under arms. It seemed that Spartacus' plan was to march his army out of the orbit of Rome across the Alps but there was dissension among his men and, while the debate was going on, Marcus Licinius Crassus, with 40,000 veteran legionaries, trapped them in Apulia. Spartacus was killed with most of his men in a hard-fought battle in 71 BC.

Gnaeus Pompeius Magnus, returning with his army from Spain, was just in time to mop up the remnants of Spartacus' army and take the credit for ending the insurrection. Crassus celebrated the victory by crucifying 6000 prisoners along the entire Via Appia.

Perhaps the only good result of Spartacus' uprising was to educate the more thoughtful Romans into treating slaves more leniently; some began to substitute free for servile labour, and the concept that servitude makes a sad waste of human talent started to take root. Spartacus soon became a legend not only for his daring successes but for his reputation for personal bravery and his qualities of strength and humanity.

Once again, Rome managed to recover from this shock and a hundred years later had, more or less, reached the greatest extent of the borders of her vast empire. But in the process of the creation of the Roman empire, the Celts of the Po Valley vanished. They did not vanish as quickly as Polybius would have us believe when he claimed that in his day the Celts had already been driven out. Aulus Gellius (c.AD 130–c.180) talks about the Celtic language surviving in the Po Valley in his time. And in early imperial times certainly we find evidence of pure Celtic names surviving on various inscriptions.

[16]

The Cisalpine Celtic Legacy to Rome

FOLLOWING the military conquests and the colonisation of the Po Valley, when did Celtic civilisation disappear from Cisalpine Gaul? In a sense, it is still there in the surviving place-names for those who can decipher them. It is also there in the various archaeological finds, and in inscriptions, mostly preserved in museums and other repositories. Perhaps the question should be, When did a living Celtic culture disappear?, in which case we would have to answer that it had been submerged probably by the second century AD and certainly by the fourth century AD.

One of the most striking examples of Celtic cultural survival is in Celtic religious worship. The direct evidence for the Celtic religious cults in Cisalpine Gaul lies in epigraphic, sculptured monuments, votive dedications in local languages as well as in Latin but to deities other than ones bearing Latin names.

From the early decades of this century much work has been done in trying to decipher the Celtic inscriptions in the area. There is evidence that pure Celtic names survived well into the period of the Roman emperors. 'Boduac Tritiac' is cited from a stone found in the late nineteenth century which, sadly, no longer exists. The first name is related to the Boudicca of Iceni fame and means 'victorious'. Cognates of this name appear among the five names on an inscription found at Brescia: '*Boduisso Coipilloni et Bena Criponiet, Ponto Boduissonis et Ersea Vorvodisius. Crera Boduissonis s.e.*' However, some scholars are of the opinion that pure Celtic names ceased to be used in the Po Valley sometime after 42 BC.

Sir John Rhŷs, who spent much of his time between 1906 and 1914 studying the Celtic epigraphy in the Po Valley, would disagree. In several papers to the British Academy he produced readings of many gravestones and monuments inscribed in Celtic. Other scholars have argued with his readings. Professor Thomas O'Rahilly was not happy with the accuracy of some of his interpretations. Of course, John Rhŷs was a pioneer in the field and not all of his readings have been challenged. For example, in February 1913, at Verigate, an inscribed stone was found of which Professor Francesco Novati of the Historical Society of Lombardy sent a photograph to Rhŷs plus pencil sketches of the inscription. Rhŷs was excited by it for he observed it was a verse in a hexameter. Rhŷs gave the reading as:

> To Belgos son of Bruiamitos:
> Kinsmen, call a banquet at his grave . . .

The following year Rhŷs went to the Gallarate Museum, where the inscribed stone had been sent. 'It turns out that I had been so well provided with reliable rubbings, sketches (by Dr Nicodemi), and a photograph – all supplied me by the Commendatore Lattes and the Lombard Institute – that I have very little that is new or important to say about the inscription.'

Dr Chilver argues for a swift assimilation of the Celtic population by intermarriage. Of course there is ample evidence that the Roman settlers intermarried with the native Celts, especially at Cremona. But Latin names often conceal native origins. Of the funereal inscriptions which might seem to feature pure Latin names, Dr Chilver comments that sometimes it is only the names of the wives in the ancestry which indicate that the subject is a Celt and lately raised to citizenship. Sometimes it is necessary to go back two or more generations to find the native origins. The parents of C. Aebtius, who appear on a stone at Turin, have Roman names but their patronymics are cognomens and typically Celtic.

Funereal memorials to soldiers often show Celts disguised in Roman form. The XXI Rapax Legion was raised in Cisalpine Gaul after 27 BC. Two soldiers of that legion are called Sugasis and Staius on their tomb and another soldier is called M. Curusius Sabonus: all good Roman names. Only when one examines the names of their wives, parents and grandparents does one see that Celtic names emerge.

Dr Chilver quotes several examples of Celtic names disguised in military memorials. A. P. Tutilius of Mediolanum became the standard bearer of the V Legion. He was born in 43 BC and died in AD 29, in retirement. On his tomb are marked the names of four people, all relatives and all with Celtic names. Two Celtic veterans of the VIII Legion are remembered on funereal stones: C. Alebo Castici, buried at Mediolanum, and Albucius Vindilli, whose gravestone was found on the shores of Lake Como. A Celtic veteran of the XV Legion was M. Aebutius Verus. The tombstone of C. Valerius Rugus and Q. Valerius Rufus, apparently Romans, is inscribed with the names of four generations, showing their Celtic origins. They had become citizens of the Valeria *gens*, the most common Roman clan in Cisalpine Gaul, but their father, grandfather and great-grandfather were not citizens at all but had native Celtic names – Bivei, Messava, Triumo and Deivarus.

It is fascinating that during Strabo's time, the later half of the first century B C, the Po Valley contributed more manpower to the Roman legions and the Praetorian guard than all the rest of the Italian provinces. We seem to be seeing a similar situation to the recruitment of Irish, Scots and Welsh regiments to the nineteenth-century British army. A. Passerini, in *Le Coorti Pretoriane*, 1939, says that for every four legionaries from the rest of Italy, Cisalpine Gaul contributed ten. When Julius Caesar became governor of Cisalpine Gaul he was able to raise most of the manpower for his eight legions and auxiliary troops in the area.

We have already discussed the influence that the Celts had on the Romans in terms of the development of their weapons and armour, and also of transport technology, as evidenced by the significant Celtic vocabulary in these fields which was adopted into Latin. What is more fascinating is that, following the Roman conquest, the Celts of Cisalpine Gaul began to give their considerable talents to Latin literature as, indeed, their descendants have done in subsequent centuries to the literature of later conquerors – English and French.

Earliest Latin inscriptional remains are almost contemporary with the earliest Celtic inscriptional remains. The oldest Roman stone inscription, the Lapis Niger from the Forum, dates from about 600 B C. Another of the early inscriptions is from a fibula reading 'Manios med fhefhaked Numasioi', which, in more recognisable Latin, would be 'Manius me fecit Numasio' (Manus made me for Numasius). However, it is difficult to find many Latin inscriptions prior to the third century B C.

A Latin literature did not really start to develop until the end of the third century B C. Greek was the customary language of learning.

We have references to the existence of 'The Code of the Twelve Tables' having been collected around 450 BC but there is no sign of any original text. The quotations from the Twelve Tables which survive from the age of Cicero (106–43 BC) are couched in a contemporary idiom from the time of their quotation. Certainly from about 200 BC we can safely say that a Latin literature was taking shape with the work of poets such as Gnaeus Naevius (c.270–190 BC) and Quintus Ennius (239–169 BC), both of whom actually came from the Greek areas of southern Italy. Two of the earliest Roman historians are the senator Quintus Fabius Pictor, whose work survives in quotations in later writers, and his contemporary Cincius Alimentus, who served in the army and was captured by Hannibal.

It was Marcus Porcius Cato ('The Elder' or 'The Censor', 234–149 BC) who achieved the reputation of being the 'Father of Latin' prose. A plebeian from Tusculum (Frascati), he had risen under the patronage of L. Valerius Flaccus to high office. His contribution to Latin literature was immense. Cicero knew of 150 of Cato's speeches, as well as works on rhetoric, medicine, military matters and his surviving *De Agricultura*, sometimes known as *De re rustica*. His seven books of *Origines*, unfortunately now lost, dealt with the foundation legends of Rome and the rise of the Italian cities. It was the first work of its kind in the Latin language because, as previously mentioned, the early annalists wrote in Greek. It was Cato who used the phrase *Carthago delenda est* (Carthage must be destroyed), which takes its place in the languages of the world as an ironic reminder, says Dr Eugene Ehrlich in his study *Nil Desperandum* (1985), that a ruling clique in a powerful nation can have its way in crushing a helpless rival if it masters the rhetoric to stir irrational passions.

As Rome rose as an imperial power through the second and first centuries BC, so too did Latin begin to rise as a literary medium. Because it ceased to be a *lingua materna* and became a *lingua franca*, with many diverse peoples and cultures contributing to it, it became a vibrant language producing a richer and more varied output of writings than any Mediterranean people except the Greeks and the Israelites. The story of Latin's rise to prominence as a language is very similar to the rise of English. And to this Latin literature, the Celts, throughout the Celtic world, made an extraordinary contribution, worthy of a separate study in itself, especially if we consider the input of every Celtic area over many centuries. It began with the first Celtic peoples to fall within the early Roman orbit – the Celts of Cisalpine Gaul.

We have already seen how Caecilius Statius, the young Insubrean warrior taken prisoner at Telamon, was brought to Rome as a slave and then rose to become a freedman and the leading comedy playwright in Rome. It could be argued that Caecilius Statius was the pioneer of Celtic writing in other languages. After the conquest of Cisalpine Gaul, during the first century BC, a 'Celtic school' of writers emerged. H. W. Garrod, in his introduction to the *Oxford Book of Latin Verse*, was one of the first to point out that Cisalpine Gaul became the home of a vigorous school of poets with a common quality which could be identified as Celtic. Dr Chilver, however, is not entirely convinced. 'There remains much that is vague and unsatisfying about this "Celtic spirit",' he says. Dr Chilver believes more in the dynamic of economics than that of culture. Although it has to be admitted that sometimes, because of the tendency to adopt Latin forms of names, it is difficult to identify who is and who is not a Celt, there are many writers whose background we can be sure of.

Cornelius Nepos (*c.*100–*c.*25 BC) was from Cisalpine Gaul but, alas, his exact birthplace is not known. His annalistic history *Chronica*, a universal history in three books, has not survived, but we do have his *De Viris Illustribus*, 'Life of Famous Men', in sixteen books. His fellow Cisalpine, Catullus, dedicated a poem to him and Nepos was also a friend of Cicero and Titus Pomponius Atticus (110–32 BC) of whom he wrote a life.

Gaius Valerius Catullus (*c.*84–*c.*54 BC) was born in Verona, and was, arguably, of Cenomani origin. He went to Rome as a young man and became part of a fashionable literary circle called '*neoterics*' or 'the moderns'. Cicero sarcastically called them in Greek *hoi neoteroi* or 'the young ones'. Professor Rankin has argued:

Catullus is the most important of the poets from Celtic territory of northern Italy and he deserves to be taken as our main representative of the school of 'new poets' in the second half of the first century BC who took the poetry of Hellenistic Alexandria as their literary model ... Catullus may have characteristics which are capable of being argued as distinctively Celtic within the confines of the cultural tradition in which he lived and worked, which was that of the dominant Roman society. His work could also be considered to have elements in common with the poetry of a much later date in Celtic.

Catullus was the supreme satirist. His name, it is argued, derived from *catus*, battle. Many names in modern Irish, Cathal (strong in battle), Cathassach (vigilant in war), Cathbarr (protector), Cathchern (battle lord), still include this element.

Certainly his satire was sharp and cutting. He once ridiculed the work of a man named Volusius who had written some *Annales*. This history was 'no better than lavatory paper', says Catullus. Professor Rankin identifies Volusius as a Celt from the north of Italy who was residing in Padua. Catullus suggested the pages of the *Annales* be used for wrapping marinaded mackerel in. Professor Rankin submits that this Volusius might be the same person as Tanusius Geminus whom Suetonius used as a source for his life of Julius Caesar.

Another member of this school of 'young ones' was Gaius Helvius Cinna, of Cenomani origin from the town of Brixia, who incorporated several Celtic words in his work. The fragments of his poetry that survive contain many examples, often connected with equestrian interests. Catullus refers to his friend Cinna as having written a long and complex poem called *Zmyrna* about the mother of Adonis which he greatly admired. Cinna accompanied Catullus on a journey to Bithynia in 57 BC. He was lynched by an angry Roman mob in 44 BC in mistake for Lucius Cornelius Cinna who had spoken out against Julius Caesar.

Horace and Cicero criticised the 'Celtic accents' of the new poets of Rome. Horace – Quintus Horatius Flaccus (65–8 BC) – openly ridiculed it. He regarded the accent as absurd. Professor Rankin says of their poetry: 'Another characteristic of the northern poets was their fascination with onomatopoeia and word-play, which need not be attributed to outright bilingualism, but could easily be stimulated by the linguistic and cultural influence of a Celtic substrate.'

Among other Celtic poets of the 'new school' were Valerius Cato and Furius Bibaculus. Bibaculus (*c.*103–25 BC) was said to have been born of an Insubrean Celtic family in Cremona. He wrote epigrams about Valerius Cato, who is reported to have satirised Julius Caesar and others. Bibaculus, or Vivaculus, had a reputation as a sharp satirist and in later years the historian Publius Cornelius Tacitus was to write:

> The verses of Bibaculus and Catullus, though keen lampoons on the family of the Caesars, are in everyone's hands. Neither Julius Caesar nor Augustus showed any resentment against these envenomed productions; on the contrary they left them to make their way in the world. Was this their moderation, or superior wisdom? Perhaps it was the latter. Neglected calumny soon expires; show that you are hurt, and you give it the appearance of truth.

One of the most influential poets and philosophers of this period was Titus Lucretius Carus (98BC–*c.*55 BC). From Eusebius Hieronymus, St Jerome, (*c.* AD 347–420) we learn that he took his own life at the age of forty-four. Only his *De rerum natura* (On the nature of things) has survived, in which he demonstrates himself to be a theoretician of the Epicurean school. He won the admiration of many poets including Virgil. Friedrich Marx in 'Der Dichter Lucretius', in *Neue Jahrbücher für das Klassische Alterum* (1899), argued the case for Lucretius Carus being of Celtic origin and points out that the name 'Carus' is to be found not only in Romanised Cisalpine Gaul but in the earlier Celtic inscriptions, for example in the name 'Boduacus Carus'. It also occurs in the La Graufesnque graffiti in the form 'Caros'. Professor Rankin says: 'I incline to the view he was from Celtic territory . . . his style has arguably northern characteristics.'

Another Insubrean Celt interested in Epicurean philosophy was T. Catius who wrote on the subject and whose work was admired by Marcus Fabius Quintilianus – Quintilian (*c.* AD 35–*c.*AD 95). It is interesting that many of these Celtic writers found themselves supportive of the ideas of the Greek philosopher Epicurus (341–271 BC), who stated that there was no providential God and no survival after death (contrary to Celtic belief), that the universe was created by accident and that therefore the aim of life was pleasure, by which he meant the harmony of body and mind, to be achieved only by virtue and plain living.

Lucius Pomponius of Bononia, who flourished in the early part of the first century BC, is one of the first we know of who wrote satires about his fellow Celts. Among the many farces attributed to him was one called *Galli Transalpini* (Transalpine Gauls). It does not survive but Pomponius appears to have been presenting his fellow Celts to his Roman audiences in the same way as certain Irish playwrights of the nineteenth century, such as Dion Boucicault, developed the 'stage Irishman' for the consumption of English audiences.

Many other writers of the same period came from Cisalpine Gaul. While we may not definitely claim them all as Celtic in origin, Professor Rankin has argued that a Celtic influence may be seen in most of their work. Publius Vergilius Maro – Virgil (70–19 BC) – was born at Andes near Mantua (Mantova) in Boii territory. He has succeeded in leaving the mark of his literary individuality on world history. Professor M. C. Howatson of Oxford, editor of the *Oxford Companion to Classical Literature*, has no doubts that he was of Celtic origin and educated at Cremona and Mediolanum. However, some have argued for an Etruscan origin. Professor Rankin sums up by saying: 'We need not deny Celtic influences in the background of Virgil's life. Etruscan and Ligurian elements can be suggested with no greater assurance than Celtic can be excluded. The region of Mantua was mixed in population. There is no reason to deny that there was a Celtic component in the local culture . . .' It was a Miss Gordon (*Journal of the Royal Society*, xxiv, 1934) who first argued an Etruscan origin for Virgil on the basis that Maro bore a resemblance to an Etruscan priestly title, *maru*. Dr G. E. F. Chilver devoted an entire chapter to 'Virgil and Cisalpine Culture' in his study *Cisalpine Gaul*, but ends his essay: 'It is safest, therefore, to avoid attributing anything to Virgil's Celtic blood, if we are not sure that he was a Celtic at all.' However, those who argue his Celtic origin are not ascribing anything to Virgil's 'blood' but to his cultural origins and influences. Of his work, Professor Rankin is clear: 'A Celtic flavour has been perceived in it . . .'

Dr Chilver, in analysing works such as the *Aeneid*, the *Georgics* and the *Eclogues*, points out that Virgil was one of the innovators of a wider 'Italian' patriotism as opposed to a narrow Roman one. While Virgil was undoubtedly a propagandist for Augustus and the empire, he presents a picture of Augustus triumphing due only to Italian, as distinct from Roman, patriotism. In the *Georgics*, Virgil treats the entire Italian peninsula as the home of a nation. His literary propaganda endorsed the political facts. Prior to the mid-fifth century

BC, the term 'Italy', which seemed to derive from *Vitelia*, land of calves, had applied only to the southern half of the toe of Italy. By 400 BC the name applied to all of the south-west peninsula, now Calabria, and also Lucania; by the following century to all the peninsula south of the Apennines; and by Virgil's day to all the country south of the Alps. The conquest of all the inhabitants of the peninsula by Rome and their merger into a Latin political nationality was not completed until Virgil's time.

Dr Chilver argues that this 'greater Italian nationalism' of Virgil is explained by the fact of his own nationality. 'It is tempting to reply that his Cisalpine birth made him exceptionally proud of Italy at this time, when Italy had just been extended to the Alps. We have seen how Cisalpines later in the first century were proud of their "Italian birth", though they show us little of the nationalist feeling which Virgil gives us. For Virgil there were the two factors, his birth, and his relations with the government.'

The idea of a Celt rejecting his own nationality to enthusiastically espouse another, a 'composite' nationality which embraces the conquered peoples, is not unusual. In March 1997 a Welshman, Christie Davies, a professor of sociology, could enthusiastically argue, in a booklet called *Loyalty Misplaced*, for the death of the Welsh language. In a televised discussion on the subject, launching his arguments, on 28 February that year, he could assure the audience that the Welsh language was 'alien'. When Lord Elis Thomas, chairman of the Welsh Language Board, asked in bemusement what Welsh was alien to, Professor Davies triumphantly shouted across the studio, 'To *Britain*!' He had put his finger on his confusion of Britain as a *nation*, which he saw as English in culture, with Britain as a multinational *state* encompassing several languages and cultures. Virgil, too, had been arguing for a similar concept – Italy, originally a land of several different nationalities and cultures, emerging as a single Latin-speaking nation.

It was H. W. Garrod, in the *Oxford Book of Latin Verse*, who first clearly identified Virgil as a Celt and argued that his Celticness permeates his poetry. While Dr Chilver is again not entirely convinced, he adds:

Nevertheless, few people would care to deny that there is something in Virgil's poetry, and not only in the *Eclogues*, which

Mackail could call, and call happily, 'the note of brooding pity', and which Mr Garrod thinks was akin to the poignant expressions of Catullus' romantic temperament. In arguing that Celtic birth gave Virgil this power, Mr Garrod uses mainly a process of elimination. Greece and Rome could never have produced this effect by themselves; there must be a third element, the Italian or in this case the Celtic.

Of all the writers from Cisalpine Gaul, Titus Livius, Livy (57 BC–AD 17), is – as we have seen – certainly no admirer of the Celts. He was from Patavium (Padua) and the origins of his family are unknown. It has been argued that he was of an early Roman colonising family; of settler origin rather than native. It has also been suggested that he was a Veneti. Gaius Asinius Pollio (76 BC–AD 4) accused him of 'Patavinitas'. Pollio was not only an historian but a literary patron and a friend of Catullus. He served as a legate in Transpadana and came to the assistance of Virgil when the latter's farm was confiscated in 42 BC after the Civil War. It seems that Asinius Pollio was a Cisalpine too. Professor Rankin makes this pertinent point:

> He [Livy] has little good to say of the Celts. He describes them as being of highly emotional temper, this makes them prone to engaging in tumultuary raids; they are bold at first in battle and almost inhumanly ferocious but they soon fall off into a weakness that he describes as being more than feminine. They cannot endure hardship and are essentially unpredictable. He brings them out as a foil to Roman fortitude and virtue. He speaks of them either as one who is proud not to be a Celtic or as a Celt who is ashamed of being one and is at pains to conceal the fact – an all too familiar figure in the history of the Celtic peoples.

Indeed, whether he was from a Celtic family or from a settler family among the Celts, Livy was almost certainly influenced by his cultural environment. His style has a richness and a sinuosity which distinguish it from that of any other prose author in Latin. His books are reminiscent of epic poetry and many events seem straight out of Celtic mythology rather than Roman history. We have already talked about the single combat of Valerius Corvus. Dr Chilver comments that Livy 'had, or affected to have, an enormous admiration for the ancient Roman virtues, and was willing to believe a story or not according as it offered something for the generation of his own day to emulate.'

Livy was, in today's parlance, a right-wing reactionary. He was accused of puritanism and conservative republicanism during the civil wars.

Dr Joshua Whatmough examined Livy's work from the point of view of a linguist and philologist and came to the conclusion that the charge of 'Patavinism' did not simply mean peculiarities of syntax, grammar or choice of words, or even solecisms in spelling and pronunciation. Quintilian certainly mentions Livy's peculiarities in spelling. Dr Chilver comments: 'It is true no odd spellings are found in Livy's *extant* works, but such curiosities would have disappeared at the hands of shocked scribes and editors very early in the history of the text . . .' Whatmough believes that 'Patavinism' meant an attitude of mind governed by cultural environment.

A fellow citizen of Patavium was Publius Clodius Thrasea Paetus, a Stoic philosopher who, like Livy, was something of a conservative republican. He became a senator and was condemned to death by Nero for his political views but decided instead to take his own life in AD 66. He wrote a life of Cato of Utica. He was married to Arria and their daughter married Helvidius Priscus who shared his father-in-law's views. Exiled, Priscus returned after the death of Nero but his republican views brought him into conflict with Vespasian and he was put to death about AD 75. His son, of the same name, was a friend of Tacitus and Pliny the Younger. Thrasea Paetus' wife, Arria, was the daughter of parents who had also been forced to commit suicide by the Emperor Claudius. Her mother, also Arria, and her father, Caecina Paetus of Patavium, were condemned to be executed. They took their own lives and Arria is said to have stabbed herself, handing her reluctant husband the weapon with the words '*Paete, non dolet*' – It doesn't hurt, Paetus!

Yet another distinguished native of Cisalpine Gaul was Gaius Plinius Secundus (AD 23–79), Pliny the Elder, who was born at Comum. He was a man of extraordinary industry and thirst for knowledge although he spent many years as a soldier and became a procurator in Gaul proper for a while. His book *Naturalis Historia* contains information on the Celts and the intellectual Druid caste. He was killed in the eruption of Vesuvius.

His nephew, Gaius Plinius Caecilius Secundus, or Pliny the Younger, was seventeen years old at this time. He had also been born in Comum and he inherited his uncle's estates. He became as well known as his uncle, the author of a copious correspondence with his Cisalpine compatriots and a panegyric to the Emperor Trajan under whom he had been consul in AD 100. Pliny the Younger died in AD 113.

A man named Publius Alfrenus Varus from Cremona, mentioned by Catullus and also by Horace, was a jurist and patron of literature and helped Virgil save his farm from confiscation during the Civil War. This may be the same person as, or related to, Quintilius Varus from Cremona who is mentioned as a friend of Horace and who is said to have been the son of poor Celtic parents living in the town. His father had been a barber and Quintilius Varus had to work as a barber also. But he went to Rome and studied law under Publius Sulpicius Rufus. Alfrenus wrote some tracts on philosophy, though none have survived, but in 39 BC he went on to become consul, one of the earliest Cisalpine Celts to reach such high office. The first appears to have been Lucius Calpurnius Piso Caesonus who became consul in 58 BC. Cicero criticised Piso on the grounds that his grandfather had been nothing better than an Insubrean Celt. Piso's daughter, Calpurnia, had ironically married Julius Caesar who had conquered more Celtic peoples in his career than any other Roman general. Piso himself had a magnificent villa at Herculaneum where he indulged his interests in Epicurean philosophy. He was a friend of the Greek Epicurean Philodemus and when the villa was excavated in the nineteenth century, having been buried during the Vesuvian eruption in AD 79, charred rolls of Philodemus' writings were found. These were probably Piso's own copies. Piso refused to side with Cicero against Clodius and did his best to prevent the outbreak of the Civil War in 44 BC. Cicero attacked him in two speeches, *De proviniciis consularibus* and *In Pisonem*. Piso shows how far the Romanised grandson of an Insubrean Celt could make it in the Roman world.

There are some Celts from Narbonensis Gaul whom we should mention while we are talking about Cisalpine literary contributions. They mixed with the Cisalpine Celtic writers of the 'young ones'. One was Gaius Cornelius Gallus (c.69–26 BC), a friend of the Emperor Augustus who had been born at the Forum Julii (Fréjus) in Gallia Narbonensis of a Celtic family. He had been sent to Rome for his education and served in the Roman army under Octavian. Octavian had appointed him as a commissioner to oversee the confiscated lands in the former Cisalpine Gaul in 41 BC. After Octavian became the Emperor Augustus, Gallus fell out of favour and committed suicide.

Another Narbonensis Gaul was Pompeius Trogus (c.27 BC–AD 14) who was a Vocontii. Trogus' father had served Julius Caesar in Egypt and is identified as Pompeius Rufus, mentioned in Caesar's work on the Civil War. But it was Trogus' grandfather who had first managed to get the patronage of Gnaeus Pompeius Magnus, Pompey the Great (106–48 BC) and obtained Roman citizenship, adopting the name of his patron. Trogus' uncle became a cavalry commander in Pompey's army. Young Trogus also became Romanised. He went on to write a universal history in forty-four books entitled *Historiae Philippicae* (Philippic histories), based on Greek sources. We have only an epitome of it from Justin in the third century AD, which is still a very valuable history. The name Trogus is Celtic and many Gaulish names begin with the root *trog*, equating with the Irish *trog* and Welsh *tru* meaning 'miserable'. Trogus was at least proud enough of his Celtic origins to point out he was a Vocontii.

Yet another Narbonensis Celt who achieved fame at this time was M. Terentius Varro (b.82 BC) who wrote satires, love elegies and a war epic *Bellum Sequanicum* which is thought to have been an account of the conquest of his own people, the Sequani, by Julius Caesar. Sadly, only a few lines of this survive.

Another Vocontii Celt was Sextus Afranius Burrus who died in AD 62. Burrus reached the highest rank any Roman citizen of equestrian rank could obtain to – he became prefect of the Praetorian Guard. He was a friend of Lucius Annaeus Seneca, 'The Younger' (c.4 BC–AD 65) and, with Seneca, was the Emperor Nero's adviser from AD 54 until his death. This was the time of Nero's reign when Rome actually enjoyed a period of good government. There is an irony in a Celt governing the Roman empire under Nero.

Narbonensis Gaul produced many easily identifiable but Romanised Celts who rose to high office. Others, as in Cisalpine Gaul, are difficult to identify because of their Roman names. However, Valerius Asiasticus, senator and consul in AD 35, was claimed as an Allobroges Celt. Domitius Afer, consul in AD 39, was said to be of Helvetii Celtic origin. Even the famous Gnaeus Julius Agricola, senator and one time governor of Britain, came from the Forum Julii but whether he was a Vocontii or from a family of Roman settlers is uncertain. What is certain is that there was a Celtic family in nearby Glanum who took Roman citizenship and adopted the name Julius in the 40s BC. Their family tomb can still be seen at Glanum.

As Rome extended her conquests through the Celtic world, from Cisalpine Gaul to Narbonensis Gaul and then to Iberia, to Galatia, on to Gaul proper, and eventually to Britain, many Celts achieved literary fame by turning to write in Latin, the language of the empire. Speaking specifically of the Cisalpine Celts, Professor Rankin states: 'Beyond doubt, the region was fertile in literary talent. This distinguished crop of poets and literary men in many instances have arguably Celtic origins and backgrounds. There is no doubt also that there was a sense of community amongst the writers who came from this region to succeed or otherwise in Rome.'

Dr Chilver tends to regard this concentration of literary talent as due more to economic and social conditions than to cultural ones.

Those who disregard the Celtic theory must still admit that the number of north Italians among the poets of the first century BC is very striking. This fact may be explained, not by the poetic temper of their race, but by their vigour in most directions at this time. The poets are the product of this vigour; and at times they seem near giving verbal expression to the rising importance of their country. They had little race-consciousness, but there are signs of a consciousness of a common origin in a geographical sense.

One could argue with Dr Chilver that 'race consciousness', by which one presumes he means a consciousness of community origins and a common history, was certainly part of the Celtic psyche. If the Druids of Transalpine Gaul could in AD 69 remember the details of the Senones' capture of Rome in 390 BC and identified their common history with the Senones, then how much more would their Cisalpine cousins have remembered?

After the start of the Christian epoch Cisalpine literature appears to have suffered a lessening of production and diversity. Dr Chilver says:

> Cisalpine literature then suffers a decline. Isolated names are not worth recording because it is hard to find anyone who really represented the region by his thought, except in so far as they illustrate how little individuality it was beginning to have.

While not of the same magnitude and influence as in the first century BC, the contribution by the Cisalpines to literature continued into the first century AD and one noteworthy poet was Tiberius Catius Asconius Silius Italicus (c.AD 26–101) who appears to have been a Cenomani born at Patavium. He was a consul in AD 68, the last year of Nero's reign, and survived the politics of the time to win praise for his work as proconsul in Anatolia in c.AD 77. He is the author of the longest surviving Latin poem, an epic in seventeen books on the Second Punic War, *Punica*.

There has, so far, been no detailed study of the origins of the later Latin writers. However, according to Professor Toynbee:

> The present-day linguistic map of Italy testifies to the survival of a once Celtic-speaking population, not only in Lombardy, but also in the Emilia and down the Adriatic coast as far as the south-eastern end of the former *Ager Gallicus*. The Italian dialects now spoken in these districts still display this Celtic imprint.

Dr Chilver again believes that the decline in literature was due to economic rather than cultural factors, arguing that during the early empire Cisalpine Gaul did produce visual art and architecture.

> Reasons why sculpture and architecture flourished more than literature under the Empire are not hard to find in the general circumstances of the imperial régime. That they did not do so before was due largely to economic conditions. For in the first century BC a poet from the north might find his way to Rome and write there, perhaps displaying in his poems the special north Italian temperament. But if a sculptor did the same it is most unlikely that we should know about it, and in any case he would

normally belong to a poorer order of society than the poet. Equally, however, he could not practise his art at home, because the essential patronage was not to be found until the country grew richer. So Cisalpine monuments in stone belong naturally to the period when the country was prosperous; and it happened that then Roman influence was dominant.

Certainly, many Celts became more Roman than the Romans as, in later years, certain Welsh, Cornish, Scots, Manx and Irish were to assimilate into the composite English – or British, as many prefer to describe it – nationality. Some Bretons became more French than the French. Jules Verne (1828–1905), France's 'founding father' of science fiction, was a Breton born in Nantes with a typical Celtic name derived from *varna*, alder tree. That absorption was certainly happening in Rome to the disgust of many Romans like Gaius Suetonius Tranquillus (b.*c*.AD 70) who, in his 'Life of Caesar', condemns Caesar for 'admitting to the Senate men of foreign birth, including semi-civilised Celts, who had been granted the Roman citizenship.' Suetonius actually records a popular song of the day:

> Caesar led the Celts in triumph,
> led them to the Senate house,
> then the Celts took off their breeches
> and put on the *laticlave*.

A *laticlave* was the senator's toga with the broad purple stripe of office.

As Cisalpine Gaul, now firmly part of the Italy which Virgil had envisaged, moved into the second century AD, the mixture of the cultures and the acceptance of Latin as the *lingua franca* caused the Cisalpines to become so fused that there is little immediately Celtic to be identified in the late empire period. The conflict of cultures between Celt and Roman had been the dynamic for producing the fine poetry and literature of the first century BC, which declined into merely provincial Latin writings once the Celtic language and culture had been absorbed. In this 'disappearance' of the Celtic identity one might see a parallel for the disappearance of the Cornish language, although the awareness and knowledge of Cornish still hang on by a thread in the modern world. In it also we can possibly foresee the eventual end of the dominance of Irish writers in English literature. T. S. Eliot once warned that if the 'peripheral languages' of the British Isles were forced to die then English, too, would become the poorer. In his *Notes Towards the Definition of a Culture* (Faber and Faber, 1948) Eliot expressed his theory of 'a harmony of diversities'. Ireland, for example, would become a provincial 'West Britain' lacking the cultural conflict between English and her own language and culture with which to create the dynamic for the more vibrant literary form. Dr Chilver, on the other hand, is more concerned with economic influences than cultural. He comments on the economic effects in Cisalpine Gaul in the first century:

They enjoyed a full century of real prosperity, and became perhaps the richest people in the Empire. But if anything the land proved too easy for them. There is no invention and no initiative: the advances in science here as elsewhere in the Roman Empire in the first century are astonishingly trivial. There is no assurance that if things begin to break down some resistance to the march of events will be offered. The rich environment might have produced a brilliant nation, not as a political unit, but as a self-conscious and robust part of the Empire. But just as the art of the region is forced and without permanence, so the attempts to create a common consciousness are with very few exceptions superficial. The Romanisation had been too strong, and the difficulties of the people, economic and social, had to be solved from the centre.

I would have argued the reverse: that the solution lay not in more centralisation but in devolution; in the reassertion of the people's identity and culture. The conditions Dr Chilver saw in ancient Italy can be seen throughout Europe today and in the inherent problems of what are called 'ethnic minorities'. But such concepts as the linguistic and cultural rights of minorities and the right of national self-determination have come too late for the native peoples of Cisalpine Gaul. The Celts of Italy have vanished. Perhaps, when we consider the centuries of bloody conflict between the north Italian Celts and their southern Roman neighbours, we might dwell on the fact that the Celts gave the Latin language not only words for weapons of war, for transport, chariots, wagons and horses – even for a measure of distance for a long journey – but also the words for beer (*cervisia*), trousers (*bracae*), lark (*alauda*) and soap (*sapo*)!

Acknowledgements and Bibliography

The material relating to the Celts in northern Italy, their history, literary remains and archaeology, in the English language for the general reader, is notable for its paucity. In fact, this is the first such account of the Cisalpine Celts to be available. The lack of material in English is reflected in this bibliography. As usual, the intention of my work is to present a history for general readership and thus copious footnote references have been dispensed with although necessary references, and a discussion of their validity, is often made clear within my text. The primary historical sources are, obviously, those Classical authors quoted in the text and their works are, of course, generally available in various English translations.

A special word of appreciation is in order for the late Professor Enrico Campanile (died 14 October 1994) of the University of Pisa. His work, especially in the field of linguistics, cannot be too highly valued in the field of Celto-Italian studies.

I would like to express my gratitude to Professor H. David Rankin (formerly Professor of Philosophy at Southampton University); to Professor Gearóid Mac Eoin (formerly Professor of Old and Middle Irish and Comparative Philology at University College Galway); to Professor Kenneth McKinnon, Hon. Research Fellow in Celtic Studies at the University of Edinburgh; to my indefatigable researcher, Elizabeth Murray; to Harry Bourne for numerous discussions and advice on archaeological matters; and finally to my wife Dorothy who, many years ago, introduced me to the real Italy.

Books

Anati, Emmanuel. *The Camonica Valley*, Jonathan Cape, London, 1964.
Bertrand, Alexandre L. J. and Reinach, Salomon. *Les celtes dans les vallées du Pô et du Danube*, Paris, 1894.

Brunt, Peter Astbury. *Italian Manpower 225 BC–AD 14*, Clarendon Press, Oxford, 1971.

Cary, M. and Scullard, H. H. *A History of Rome*, Macmillan, London, 1935 (1994 ed.).

Chadwick, Nora. *The Celts* (Introductory chapter – 'The Origins of the Celts; The Archaeological Evidence' by J. X. W. P. Corcoran), Pelican, London, 1970.

Chilver, G. E. F. *Cisalpine Gaul; a social and economic history from 49 BC to the death of Trajan*, Clarendon Press, Oxford, 1941.

Conway, Robert Seymour, Johnson, S. E., & Whatmough, Joshua. *The Prae-Italic Dialects of Italy*, privately published, London, 3 vols, 1933.

Cottrell, Leonard. *Enemy of Rome*, Evans Brothers, London, 1960.

Cunliffe, Barry. *The Celtic World*, Constable, London, 1992.

De Beer, Gavin. *Alps and Elephants*, Geoffrey Bles, London, 1955.

Déchelette, Joseph. *Manuel d'archéologie préhistorique celtique et gallo romaine*, Paris, 1924.

De Marinis, R. *Il periodo Golasecca IIIA in Lomarbadia*, Bergamo, 1981.

Dillon, Myles. *Celt and Hindu*, University College, Dublin, 1973.

Dillon, Myles. *Celts and Aryans*, Indian Institute of Advanced Studies, Simla, India, 1975.

Ducati, P. *Storia di Bologna*, Bologna, 1928.

Ellis, Peter Berresford. *The Celtic Empire*, Constable, London, 1991.

Ellis, Peter Berresford. *The Druids*, Constable, London, 1994.

Ellis, Peter Berresford. *Celtic Women: Women in Celtic Society and Literature*, Constable, London, 1995.

Ellis, Peter Berresford. *Celt and Greek: Celts in the Hellenic World*, Constable, London, 1997.

Evans, David Ellis. *Gaulish Personal Names*, Oxford University Press, Oxford, 1967.

Fell, R. A. L. *Etruria and Rome*, Cambridge University Press, Cambridge, 1924.

Filip, Jan. *Celtic Civilization and its Heritage*, Publishing House of Czechoslovakia, Prague, 1962.

Garrod, H. W. *Oxford Book of Latin Verse*, Oxford University Press, Oxford, 1912.

Grant, Michael. *History of Rome*, Faber & Faber, London, 1979.

Grassi, M. T. *I Celti in Italia*, Biblioteca di Archeologia 16, Longanesi, Milano, 1991.

Green, Miranda J. (ed.) *The Celtic World*, Routledge, London, 1995.

Hatt, Jean-Jacques. *Celts and Gallo-Romans*. The Ancient Civilizations series, trans. J. Hogarth, Barrie & Jenkins, London, 1970.

Holder, A. *Alt-Celtische Sprachschatz*, Stuttgart, 3 vols, 1896.

Homo, L. *L'Italie primitive et les débuts de l'impérialisme romain*, Renaissance du Livre, Paris, 1925.

Hubert, Henri. *The Rise of the Celts*, Routledge, London, 1934 (new ed. intro. Professor Gearóid Mac Eoin), Constable, London, 1987.

Hubert, Henri. *The Greatness and Decline of the Celts*, Routledge, London, 1934 (new ed. intro. Profesor Gearóid Mac Eoin), Constable, London, 1987.

I Gallia e L'Italia. Catalogo della Mostra, Soprintendenza Archaeologica di Roma, Rome, 1978.

James, Simon. *Exploring the World of the Celts*, Thames & Hudson, London, 1993.

Jullian, Camille. *Histoire de la Gaule*, 8 vols, Paris, 1908–26.

Kruta, V. *I Celti in Italia, Italia omnium terrarum alumna. La civiltà dei Veneti, Reti, Liguri, Celti, Piceni, Umbri, Latini, Campani e Iapigi*, Milano, 1988.

Lejeune, Michel. *Lepontica*. Monographies Linguistiques 1, Société d'édition, Paris, 1971.

Les Celtes en Italie, Dossiers Histoire et Archéologie, No. 112, Dijon, 1987.

MacNamara, Ellen. *Everyday Life of the Etruscans*, B. T. Batsford, London, 1973.

MacNeill, Eoin. *Phases of Irish History*, M. H. Gill, Dublin, 1968 edition. First published in Dublin in 1919.

Mommsen, Theodor. *Histoire romaine*, English trs. London & New York, 1911.

Moscati, Sabatino & etc. *I Celti*, Bompiano, Milano, 1991. English trs. *The Celts*, Thames & Hudson, London, 1991.

Murley, Joseph Clyde. *The Cults of Cisalpine Gaul as Seen in the Inscriptions*, Menasha, Wisconsin, 1922.

Nash, Daphne. *Coinage in the Celtic World*, Seaby, London, 1987.

Negroni Catacchio, N. *Indigeni, Etruschi e Celti nella Lombardia orientale, Cremona romana*, Cremona, 1985.

Nissen, H. *Italische Landeskunder*, Weidemann, Berlin, vol. 1, 1883 & vol. 2, 1902.

O'Rahilly, Thomas F. *Early Irish History and Mythology*, Dublin Institute for Advanced Studies, Dublin, 1946.

Pallottino, Massimo. *The Etruscans*, Penguin Books, London, 1955 ed. First published 1942.

Pascal, Cecil Bennett. *The Cults of Cisalpine Gaul*, Collection Latomus Vol. LXXV, Latomus: *Revue d'Études Latines*, Brussels, 1964.

Piggott, Stuart. *The Earliest Wheeled Transport: From the Atlantic Coast to the Caspian Sea*, Thames & Hudson, London, 1983.

Pleiner, Radomir. *The Celtic Sword* (with contributions by B. G. Scott), Clarendon Press, Oxford, 1993.

Poggi, V. *Sullo svolgimento della forme onomatische durante il period della romanizzazione presso i Cisalpini*, Milano, 1886.

Powell, T. G. E. *The Celts* (preface by Professor Stuart Piggott new ed.), Thames & Hudson, London, 1980. First published 1958.

Rankin, H. D. *Celts and the Classical World*, Croom Helm, London, 1987.

Robinson, Cyril E. *A History of the Roman Republic*, Methuen, London, 1932.

Sherwin White, A. N. *Racial Prejudice in Imperial Rome*, Cambridge University Press, Cambridge, Mass. USA, 1967.

Strong, Donald. *The Early Etruscans*, Evans Brothers, London, 1968.

Toynbee, Arnold J. *Hannibal's Legacy: The Hannibalic War's Effects on Roman Life*, Vols I and II, Oxford University Press, London, 1965.

Whatmough, Joshua. *The Prae-Italic Dialects & etc.* See under Conway.

Whatmough, Joshua. *Dialects of Ancient Gaul*, University Microfilms, Ann Arbor, USA, 1949–51, also 1963.

Articles, papers and pamphlets

Arslan, Ermanno. 'Celti e Romani in Transpadana', *Études celtiques*, XV, 1978.

Baserga, G. 'Memorie falliche e gallo-romaine', *Rivista Archeologica della'Antica Provincia e Diocesi di Como*, 1916.

Bocchio, G. 'Tomba gallica Polpenazze, località Capra (1970)', *Annali del Museo di Gavardo*, 1971.

Bonfante, G. 'Indo-Hittite and Areal linguistics', *American Journal of Philology*, 268, 1946.

Brizio, E. 'Tombe e necropoli galliche della provinciadi Bologna', *Atti e Memoire Deputazione di Storia Patria per le Province di Romagna*, series III, 1887.

Brizio, E. 'Il sepolcreto gallico di Montefortino presso Arcevia', *Monumenti Antischi* No 9, 1899–1901.

Calzavara Capuis, L. and Chieco Bianchi, A. M. 'Osservazioni sul celtismo nel Veneto euganeo', *Archeologia Veneta* III, 1979.

Chevallier, R. 'Rome et l'Italie du Nord: Problèmes d'Histoire et d'Archéologie', *Revue des Études Latines*, 37th Year 1959. *Journal of the Société des Études Latines*, Paris, 1960.

Cisalpina, publication of papers on Cisalpine archaeology, Vol. 1 only extant, Istituto Lombardo, Milan, 1959.

De Marinis, R. 'The La Tène culture of the Cisalpine Gauls', *Keltske Studje*, Brezice, Posavki muzej, 1977.

De Marinis, R. 'L'età gallica in Lombardia (IV-I sec. a.C.): risultati delle utimericerche a problemi aperti', La Lombardia tra protostoria e romanità, *Atti del II Conv. Arch. Regionale*, Como, 1984.

Dobesch, G. 'Die Kimbren in den Ostalpen und die Schlacht bei Noreia', *Mitteilungen Osterreichischen Arbeitsgemeinschaft Ur- und Frühgeschichte* No. 35 (1982).

Dobesch, G. 'Zur Einwanderung der Kelten in Oberitalien. Aus der Geschichte der keltischen Wanderungen im 6, und 5. Jh.v.Chr.', *Beitäge zur Alten Geschichte, Papyrologie und Epigrahie* No. 4, 1989.

Ellis, Peter Berresford. 'Etruria-Celtica: A rebuttal of the Etruscan-Celtic Theory', *The Incorporated Linguist*, Vol. 23, No. 1, Winter, 1984.

Evans, David Ellis. 'The Labyrinth of Continental Celtic', Rhŷs Memorial Lecture, 1977, in *Proceedings of the British Academy*, London, 1981.

Ewins, Ursula. 'The Early Colonization of Cisalpine Gaul', *Papers of the British School at Rome*, London, 1952. Vol. XX (New Series, Vol. VII).

Fogolari, G. 'I Galli nell'alto Adriatico', *Antichità Altoadriatich* XIX, 1981.

Frey, Otto-Herman. 'The Celts in Italy', in *The Celtic World*, ed. Miranda Green, Routledge, London, 1995.

Frova, A. 'Una tomba gallo-ligure nel territorio della Spezia', *Rivista di Studi Liguri*, 1968.

Gabba, E. 'I Romani nell'Insubria: trasformazione, adeguamento e sopravienza delle strutture socio-economiche galliche', La Lombardia tra protostoria e romanità, *Atti del III Conv. Arch. Regionale*, Como, 1984.

Homo, L. 'The Gallic Wars of Rome', Chapter XVII in Vol. VII of the *Cambridge Ancient History*, Cambridge University Press, Cambridge, 1928.

Kruta Poppi, L. 'Les Celtes à Marxabotto (province de Bologne)', *Études celtiques* XIV, 1975.

Kruta Poppi, L. 'Les vestiges laténiens de la région de Modène', *Études celtiques* XV, 1978.

Kruta Poppi, L. 'La sépulture de Ceretolo (prov. de Bologne) et le faciès boien du IIIe siècle avant n.é.', *Études celtiques* XVI, 1979.

Kruta Poppi, L. 'La sépulture de Casa Selvatica à Berceto (prov. de Parme) et la limite occidentale du faciès boien au IIIe siècle av n.é.', *Études celtiques*, XVIII, 1981.

Kruta Poppi, L. 'Contacts transalpins des Celtes cispadans au IIIe siècle avant J.C.: le fourreau de Saliceta San Giulano, province de Modène', *Études celtiques*, XXI, 1984.

Kruta, V. 'Celtes de Cispadana et transalpins au IVe et au IIe siècle avant n.é.', *Studi etruschi* XLVI, 1978.

Kruta, V. 'Les Boiens de Cispadane, essai de paléoethnographie celtique', *Études celtiques* XVII, 1980.

Kruta, V. 'Les Sénons de l'Adriatique d'après l'archéologie (prolégomènes)', *Études celtiques* XVIII, 1981.

Kruta, V. 'L'Italie et l'Europe intérieure du Ve siècle au début du IIe siècle av n.é.', *Savaria* 16, 1982.

Kruta, V. 'Quali Celti? La Lombardia tra protostoria e Romanità', *Atti de II Convegno Archeologico Regionale*, Como, 1984.

Kruta, V. 'I Celti e la Lombardia', *La Lombardia dalla Preistoria al Medioevo*, Milano, 1985.

Landolfi, M. 'Presenza galliche nel Picenoa sud del fiume Esino' in *Celti e Etrusschi*, ed. D. Vitali, 1987.

Mazzini, U. 'Monumenti celtici in Valdi Magra' in *Giornale storico e Letterio della Liguia*, 1908.

Negroni Catacchio, N. 'I ritrovamenti di Castate nel quadro di celtismo padano', *Atti del Conv. celebrativo del Centenario*, Como, 1974.

Negroni Catacchio, N. 'Per una definizione della facies culturale insubres: i rinvenimenti tardo celtici di Biassono (MI)', *Sibrium* No. XVI, 1981.

Patroni, G. 'S. Crustina. Tombe gallo-romane trovate nella frazione di Bissone', *Notizie Scavi*, 1906.

Peyre, C. 'La Cisalpine gauloise du IIIème au Ie siècle avant J.C.', *Études d'Histoire Archaéologie*, Presses de l'Ecole Normale Supérieure, Paris, 1979.

Piani Agostinetti, P. 'Per una definixone deiconfini della Civitates celtiche della Transpadana xentrale', *Scienze dell-Antichità*, 2, 1988.

Rhŷs, John. *Transactions of the Philological Society*, 1891.

Rhŷs, John. 'Celtae and Galli', *Proceedings of the British Academy*, 1905–1906, Oxford University Press.

Rhŷs, John. 'The Celtic Inscriptions of France and Italy', *Proceedings of the British Academy*, Vol. 2, 1906.

Rhŷs, John. 'The Celtic Inscriptions of Gaul', *Proceedings of the British Academy*, Vol. 5, 1911/12.

Rhŷs, John. 'The Celtic Inscriptions of Cisalpine Gaul', *Proceedings of the British Academy*, Vol. 6, 1913–14.

Rhŷs, John. 'Gleanings from the Italian field of epigraphy', *Proceedings of the British Academy*, Vol. 6, 1913–14.

Saronio Masolo, P. 'Una tomba gallica di Pavia', *Studi in onore di F. Rittatore Vonwiller*, Como, 1981 (Vol. 1, Part 1).

Schmidt, Karl Horst. 'Keltisches Worgut im Lateinischen', *Glotta*: Zeitschrift für griechische und lateinische Sprace, Vol. XLIV/XLV, 1967/1968, pp. 151–174.

Schmidt, Karl Horst. 'On the Celtic Languages of Continental Europe',

The Bulletin of the Board of Celtic Studies, XXVIII, Cardiff, 1979.

Stary, P. F. 'Foreign Elements in Etruscan Arms and Armour: 8th to 3rd Centuries BC', *Proceedings of the Prehistory Society*, Vol. 45, December 1979.

Stead, I. M. and Meeks, N. D. 'The Celtic Warrior Fubula', *The Antiquaries Journal*, Vol. 76, 1996.

Szabo, Miklós. 'I Rapportsentre le Picenum et l'Europe extra-méditerranéenne à l'âge du Fer', *Savaria* 16, 1982.

Tizzoni, Marco. 'La Gallia Transpadana nel IIe nel I secolo a.C.', *Atti del Colloquio Internationale Popoli e facies culturali celtiche a nord e a sud della Alpi dal V al I secolo a.C.*, Milano, 1983.

Tizzoni, M. 'La cultura tardo La Tène in Lombardia', *Studi Archeologici* No. 1, Bergamo, 1981.

Tizzoni, M. 'La Tarda Età del ferro nel Lodigano', *Archivo Storico Lodigano*, No. 101, 1982.

Tizzoni, M. 'The Late Iron Age in Lombardy', *Papers in Italian Archeology IV*; The Cambridge Conference (Part iii – *Patterns In Protohistory*, ed. Caroline Malone and Simon Stoddart), BAR International Series 245, Cambridge, 1985.

Tizzoni, M. 'I materiali della tarda Età Ferro nelle Civiche Raccolte Archeologiche di Milano.' *Rassegna di Studi Civico Mus. Arch. e Civico Gabinetto Numismatico, Milano Suppl. 3*, Milan, 1984.

Vitali, Daniele. 'Una tomba di guerriero da castel del Rio (Bologna). I problemi dei corredi con armu nell-area cispadana tra IVe II sec. a. C.', *Atti memorie della Deputazione di Storia Patria di Romagna*, 1986.

Vitali, D. 'L'elmo della tomba 14 di Monte Bibele e Monterenzio (prov. di Bologna)', *Études celtiques* XIX, 1988.

Vitali, D. 'Monterenzio e la valle dell'Indice', *Archaeologia e storia di un territorio, catalogomostra*, Monterenzio, 1983.

Vitali, D. 'Un fodero celtico con decorazione a lira zoomorfa da Monte Bibele (Monterenzio, Bologna)', *Études celtiques* XXI, 1984.

Vitali, D. 'Monte Bibele (Monterenzio) und andere Fundstellen der keltischen Epoche im Gebiet von Bologna', *Kleine Schriften Vorgeschichtliches Seminar*, Marburg 16, 1985.

Vitali, D. 'Monte Bibele, criteri disributivi nell'abitato ed asetti del territorio bolognese dal IV al II sec. a.C., La formazione della città preromana in Emilia-Romagna', *Atti del colloquio di Studi Bologna-Marzabotto*, 1985, Bologna, 1988.

Vitali, Daniele. (ed.) 'Celti ed Etruschi nell'Italia centro settenrionale dal V secolog a.C. allia Romanizzazione'. *Proceedings of the International Colloquium at Bologna*, Imola, 1985.

Whatmough, Joshua. 'Continental Celtic', *Proceedings of the Second International Congress of Celtic Studies*, Cardiff, 1966.

Zuffa, M. *I Celti nell'Italia adriatica, Introduzione alle antichità adriatiche*, Pisa, 1975.

Index

Abruzzi, 132
Acelum, 227
Acerrae, 163, 165
Acta Triumphalia, 164
Adria, 24
Adriatic Sea, 28, 29, 37, 81, 135
Aedui, 22, 26, 37, 221, 228, 241
Aegates (Egadi), 48
Aelius, 201, 202
Aelius Paetus, Publius, 201, 205
Aemilia, 238
Aemilius Lepidus, Marcus, 150, 221, 223
Aemilius Mamercinus, Lucius, 127
Aemilius Paullus, L., 58, 153, 155–9, 186–8
Aemilius Scaurus, Marcus, 229
Aequi, 2, 46, 67, 81, 84, 240
Africa, 58, 149, 199
Agathokles, 119
Agendicum, 151
Ager Boiorum, 209
Agrigentum, 145, 147
Agrippina, 241
Ajax, 156
Alaudae, 109
Alba, 105, 111, 132, 240; Longa, 121, 232
Alesia, 93, 239
Alexander the Great, 142, 143
Alimentus, Lucius Cincius, 176, 249

Allia, 21, 36, 38–9, 46, 85, 112–13, 128, 131, 135, 189
Allobroges, 175–6, 179, 231, 232
Alpi Carniche, 38
Alps, 22–8, 32, 41–2, 60, 153, 163, 168, 176–7, 179, 194–5, 220, 229, 231–2, 235–6, 242, 244, 254; Carnic, 223, 230; Cotian, 28; Julian, 235; Pennine, 29
Alt-celtische Sprachschatz, 36
Ambarri, 22, 37, 235
Ambicatus, King, 22, 23
Ambrones, 51, 233, 235
Ampius, Gaius, 201–2
Anamari, 37
Ananes, 37
Anares, 29, 37, 160
Anatolia, 232, 260
Ancona, 81, 82, 117, 118, 119, 195
Andes, 253
Andria, 159
Aneroestes, 153, 154–6, 159
Animals in Celtic Myth and Life, 74
Annales, 77, 108, 239
Annius, Titus, 171
Antalcidas, Peace of, 21
Antias, Valerius, 208, 217
Antigonus (Gonatus), 142–3
Antiochus III of Syria, 200

Antistius, Sextus, 194
Antium (Anzio), 70, 118
Apennine mountains, 2, 4, 21–2, 28–9, 35, 39, 42, 43, 60, 79, 83, 119, 132–3, 135, 140–2, 144, 146, 153, 155–6, 166, 181, 201–2, 205, 209, 219, 229–30, 254
Apollinaris, Sidonius, 33
Apollo, 54–5, 67, 80
Appian of Alexandria, 23, 49, 70, 78, 188, 233
Apuani, 225
Apuleius, Lucius, 67, 100
Apulia (Puglia), 79, 81, 105, 117, 125, 144, 186, 195, 245
Apulians, 132
Aquae Sextiae (Aix), 231, 235, 236
Aquileia, 54, 55, 223, 230
Aquitania, 101, 243
Archéologie celtique et gauloise, 19
Archimedes, 193
Ardea, 66, 67, 69, 72
Argentocoxus, 51
Aricia, 45, 124
Ariminum (Rimini), 81, 119, 141, 150, 153, 155, 166, 175, 178–9, 181–2, 195, 203, 221–2
Aristotle, 58, 80
Arpinum (Anzio), 131
Arretium (Arezzo), 138, 139, 182, 203, 209, 214, 222
Arrianus, Flavius, 99
Arruns of Clusium, 23
Arverni, 22, 37, 50, 195, 231, 232, 235
Asculum (Ascoli Satriano), 144
Asinius Pollio, Gaius, 255
Ategnatos, 41
Athenaeus, 50, 108, 118
Athenians, 143, 240

Atilius, Gaius, 153, 156–7, 172, 174–5, 178, 181
Atilius, Lucius, 188
Atilius Regulus, Marcus, 147–8
Atinius, Gaius, 213
Atinius, Marcus, 213
Atis, 150
Attus, Clausus, 240
Augusta Praetoria, 229
Augustus, 8, 64, 220, 229–30, 238, 239, 252, 253, 258
Augustus, Julia, 51
Aulerci, 22, 37
Aurelius Cotta, Gaius, 203
Aurelius, Marcus, 57, 204
Aurelius Propertius, Sextus, 52, 95, 163
Auriga, 44
Aventine hill, 67
Avignon, 175, 231

Baal-Hammon, 145
Balbi, 240
Balzac, Honoré de, 130
Banff, 93
Banostar, 37
Barbarians, 89
Barca, Hamilcar, 148–9, 167
Battaglia, Raffaello, 41
Beissirissa, 27
Belenus (Bile), 54–5, 229
Belgium, 219
Beligna, 55
Bellovaci, 235
Bellovesus, 22–8
Belvedere, 55
Beneventum (Benevento), 146
Bergramum, 238
Berlin, 106
Bertrand, Alexandre, 19, 20–21
Bíle, 56
Bithynia, 251

Bituitus, King, 50, 95, 231–2
Bituriges, 22, 37
Bocconi, 41–2
Bohemia, 220, 221
Boii, 18–9, 31, 37, 42, 49, 104,
    133, 140, 144, 150–51, 153,
    156–60, 165, 171, 174–6,
    179–80, 191–2, 199, 201–2,
    205–12, 214–21, 223–5, 238
Boiroix, 49, 211–12, 233
Bologna, 39
Bomilcar, 187
Bonfante, Dr, 96
Bononia (Bologna), 37, 180,
    209–10, 220–22, 224, 229, 252
Borthwick, the Rt. Hon. The Lord,
    152
Boucicault, Dion, 253
Boudicca, 51, 52, 241, 246
Boulogne, 37
Brancus, 175–6
Brennus, 2–6, 10–11, 16, 61–2,
    65–6, 69, 72–3, 77–9, 85, 104,
    180
Bres, 44
Brigit, 54
Britain, 103, 242, 254, 259
Brixia (Brescia), 26, 28, 36, 172,
    206, 238, 246
Brixianus, 36, 172
Broghill, Lord, 58–9
Brunt, Dr P.A., 34, 39, 238
Bruttians, 146
Bruttium, 194
Brutus, Marcus and Decimus, 56,
    220
Busta Gallica, 76

Cabillonum (Châlons-sur-Saune),
    96
Cabum, 123
Caecilius, Lucius, 139, 159

Caecilius, Marcus, 204
Caecilius Metallus, Lucius, 148,
    189
Caecilius Statius, Caius, 59,
    159–60, 250
Caedicius, Marcus, 68, 70, 71, 72
Caere, 14, 79
Caesar, Julius, 11, 40, 48–9,
    54–8, 74, 93, 96–7, 100, 109,
    129, 151, 221, 228, 234–5,
    238–9, 248, 251–2, 257–8, 261
Caesonus, Calpurnia, 257
Caesonus, Lucius Calpurnius Piso,
    257
Calabria, 77, 254
Cambridge Modern History, 130
Cameria, 135, 240
Camillus, Marcus, 80–81, 83–4,
    89–90, 101, 104, 106–7, 162,
    185
Camonica Valley, 26–7
Campania, 45, 110, 131
Camunians, 27
Cannae (Cannosa), 186, 188–9,
    196
Canosa di Puglio, 105
Canossa, 41
Cantilius, Lucius, 189
Canusium, 190
Capena, 66; Gate, 121
Capitol, 64–6, 69–77, 84, 153,
    159–60, 208, 240–42
Capitoline hill, 12, 21, 56, 62, 65,
    72
Capua, 189, 191, 193, 244
Carbantorate, 95
Carbantoritum, 95
Carisioli, 132
Carmenta, 72
Carni, 38, 223, 230
Carnutes, 22, 37
Carpentorate, 95

Carthage, 46, 116, 145–9, 156, 160, 167–8, 172, 189, 191–2, 197, 199, 202–3, 229
Carthaginians, 86, 98, 145–6, 147–9, 153, 156, 168–70, 172, 175–6, 178–9, 183–6, 190, 193–4, 200
Carthago Nova (New Carthage, Cartagena), 167, 170
Carthalo, 189
Cartimandua, 51–2
Cary, M., 10, 243
Cassius, Dio, 51–2, 126, 153
Cassius, Hemina, 70
Cassius Longinus, Lucius, 234
Castelletto Ticino, 42
Castelli Romani, 121
Castiglioncella, 89
Catius, Quintus, 195
Catius, T., 252
Catumandus, 80
Cavari, 175
Cavereno, 36
Celeiates, 205
Celines, 202
Celt and Greek, 118, 146, 235
Celt and Hindu, 53
Celtiberians, 90, 97–8, 118, 145, 168, 170, 184, 186–8, 193, 196–7, 200, 244
Celtic Empire, The, 39, 190
Celtic Women: Women in Celtic Society and Literature, 51
Celtica, 49–50
Celts and Aryans, 53
Cenomani, 28–9, 34, 36–7, 104, 153, 161, 165, 202, 205–7, 222, 225, 227, 238
Cenomaros, 244
Centenius, Gaius, 184
Cerdiciates, 205
Cernunnos, 27, 54

Cerveteri, 88
Chadwick, Dr Nora, 19
Château Queyras, 177
Chevallier, R., 222
Chieti, 81
Chilver, Dr, 38, 220, 247–8, 250, 253, 254–6, 259–62
Chiomara, 52
Chouans, The, 130
Chronica, 250
Chulainn, C, 126
Cicero, 44, 56, 102, 109, 129, 229, 233, 238, 249–51, 257
Cimbri, 224, 232–6
Cineas 143–4
Cirta, 197
Cispadana, 28, 219–20, 227
Citadel, 84
Clan Bascna, 152
Clan Morna, 152
Claodicus, 233
Clastidium (Casteggio), 163–5, 190, 205
Claterna (Maggio), 224
Claudius, Appius, 94
Claudius Crassus, Appius, 123
Claudius, Emperor (Tiberius Claudius Nero Germanicus 10BC-AD54), 239–41, 243, 256
Claudius Marcellus, Marcus, 162–4, 190, 193–4, 207–10, 214, 216, 223, 226, 230
Claudius Nero, Gaius, 195–7
Claudius, Publius, 208,
Claudius Pulcher, Publius, 148, 190, 225
Claudius Quadrigarius, Quintus, 71, 104, 108–10, 208
Cleisthenes, 47
Clodius Paetus, Publius Thrasea, 256

Clusium (Chiusi), 4–8, 39, 67, 104, 134–6, 138–9, 154–5, 171
Clymene, 44
Col de Grimone, 175
Col de la Traversette, 177
Collina, 48
Colline Gate, 62, 81, 111, 189
Cominius, Pontius, 71–2
Comm (Congeniatus), 232
Comum, 208–9, 224, 257
Concolitanus, 153–6, 159
Conn of the Hundred Battles, 92
Coorti Pretoriane, Le, 248
Corcoran, Dr John X.W.P., 17
Corinth, 116
Coriolanus, 208
Cornelius Cethegus, Gaius, 205–6
Cornelius Cethegus, Marcus, 198
Cornelius Cinna, Lucius, 251
Cornelius Dolabella, Publius, 140
Cornelius Gallus, Gaius, 258
Cornelius Maluginensis, Publius, 2, 107
Cornelius Merula, Lucius, 214–16
Cornelius, Sulla, 236, 238
Corsica, 145, 149
Cortona, 183
Coruncani, 240
Cosconius, Marcus, 199
Cottrell, Leonard, 179, 189
Cremona, 166, 171, 194, 202–3, 211, 220–21, 247, 251, 253, 257
Crixos, 244
Cromwell, Henry, 59
Croton, 46, 116–17
Crustumeria, 1
Culloden, 86, 92
Cumae, 45
Cumberland, Duke of, 86

Curius Dentatus, Manlius, 139–40, 146
Cycnus, 44

Dagda, The, 27
Dalberg, John Emerich Edward (first Baron Acton), 129–30
Danu, 17–18, 44, 53–4
Davies, Christie, 254
De Agricultura, 249
De aquis urbis Romae, 32
De architectura, 33
De Viris Illustribus, 250
De Virtute Mulierum, 52
Decius Mus, Publius, 127, 135, 136–8
Degad, 152
Delphi, 67, 79–80, 83, 190, 235
Desmond (south Munster), 152
Dialects of Ancient Gaul, 40
Diana, 54
Dillon, Professor Myles, 18, 53
Dinéault, 74
Diocletian, Emperor, 57
Dionysius I of Syracuse, 116–19
Dionysius II of Syracuse, 118, 124
Dionysius of Halicarnassus, 21, 23, 91, 101–2, 143
Divico, 234
Dobesch, Dr G., 19
Domitian, Emperor, 52
Domitius, Afer, 259
Domitius Ahenobarbus, Gnaeus, 231, 232
Domitius Ahenobarbus, Lucius, 241
Domitius, Gnaeus, 49–50
Dorulatus, 211–12
Dream of Rhonabwy, 126
Drepanum (Trepani), 148
Druentinorum, 224

Druids, 48–9, 55, 242–3
Druids, The, 242
Druteos, 41
Ducarius, 184
Dulpicius Lagus, Quintus, 75
Durrow, 228

Earliest Wheeled Transport, The, 94
Economus, 147
Egnatius, Gellius, 134, 136, 138
Egypt, 33, 90
Ehrlich, Dr Eugene, 249
Elea (velia), 116
Eléments de Grammaire Celtique, 164
Eliates, 225–6
Eliot, T.S., 262
Elitovius, 28
Emilia Romagna, 19, 221
England, 129
Ennius, Quintus, 77, 160, 249
Epaminondas, 118
Epicurus, 252
Epiros, 142
Epona, 54, 99–100, 126, 229
Eporedia (Ivrea), 37, 224
Eri, 44
Eshmoun, 145
Esquilina, 48
Etruria, 4–6, 14, 24, 44, 47, 60, 67, 118, 133–4, 138, 153–6, 166, 174, 181–3, 194, 197, 201, 203, 205, 240
Etruscan, culture, 31, 35, 39–40; empire, 2, 178
Etruscans, 2, 26, 28–9, 39, 42, 45–6, 70, 79–82, 87–8, 90, 92, 118–19, 132–8, 140, 143, 145, 178, 190
Eutropius, 78
Evander, 6

Everyday Life of the Pagan Celts, 94
Ewins, Dr Ursula, 151, 166, 224, 226
Expurgatio Hibernica, 100

Fabii clan, 6–9, 12, 70–71, 85, 104, 116, 121, 139–40
Fabius Ambustus, Marcus, 1, 5
Fabius Dorsuo, Gaius, 70
Fabius, Gaius, 116
Fabius, Marcus, 121
Fabius, Maximus, 190–91
Fabius Maximus, Quintus, 135–6, 138, 185–6, 188–9, 231–2
Fabius Pictor, Quintus, 71, 90, 184, 190, 249
Fabius Quintilianus, Marcus, 252
Fabius, Quintus, 1, 5, 7–8, 167–8
Fabricius, Gaius, 144
Faesulae (Fiesoli), 155, 182
Falerri, 67
Fasti, 64
Fatae Dervones, 229
Fazies Cenegrate group, 42
Felsina, 37, 220, 224
Ferentium (Feremto), 124
Feretrius, Jupiter, 62
Ferrura, Dr A., 238
Festus, 233
Fiachadh, High King, 152
Fianna, 151–2
Fidenae, 1
Fidentia, 224
Filottrano, 81–2
Finne, The, 29
Flaminius, Gaius, 151, 160, 162, 166, 180–84
Flavius Justinianus, Petrius Sabbatius, 23
Flavius Vespasian, Titus, 243, 256
Floronia, 189

Florus, 64, 95, 102
Folius, Marcus, 15
Formorri, 126
Forum, 13, 62–3, 65, 84, 248;
    Boarium, 14, 56, 189; Cornelia,
    224; Gallorum, 221; Julii,
    258–9; Lepidi, 224; Livii, 222,
    238; Novum, 224
Fossa della Bettina, 1
France, 129, 152
Frank, Tenney, 166, 221
Frey, Professor Otto-Herman, 19,
    42
Fucens, 132
Fulvius, Gnaeus, 135, 138, 181
Fulvius Flaccus, Quintus, 194
Fulvius, Quintus, 160
Furius Bibaculus, Lucius, 188,
    251–2
Furius Camillus, Lucius, 123–6
Furius Camillus, Marcus, 4, 42,
    66–9, 71–2, 76–80
Furius, Publius, 160
Furius Purpurio, Lucius, 203–4,
    207, 208, 209–10

Gabii, 79
Gades (Cadiz), 145
Gaesatae, 101, 103, 151, 153,
    156–8, 163–5, 233
Gaesorix, 233
Galatia, 169, 259
Galatus, 150, 219
Gallarate Museum, 247
Gallia, Cisalpina, 238–9; Comata,
    239, 241; Lugdunensis, 243;
    Togata, 165–6, 230
Gamhanrhide, 152
Ganges, 55–6
Ganna, 52
Garrod, H.W., 250, 254–5
Gaul, 22, 24, 151, 168, 170, 221,

224, 232, 235–6, 259;
Cisalpine, 21, 30–5, 50, 54, 73,
    78, 94–5, 118–19, 126, 165,
    169, 172, 190, 194, 197,
    201–30, 238–9, 244, 246–63;
Transalpine, 35, 37, 54, 82, 98,
    151, 163, 169, 221, 236
Gellius, Aulus, 23, 71, 108, 110,
    245
Geneva, 231
Genua (Genoa), 166, 197, 199,
    205, 209, 230
Genucius, Marcus, 215
Geoffrey of Monmouth, 242
Geographica, 33
Georgics, 32
Gerald of Wales (Giraldus
    Cambrensis), 100
Germans, 221, 233
Germany, 243
Gisgo, 187, 197
Glotta, 41
Golasecca, 42
Gordon, Miss, 253
Gorge des Gas, 176
Gourney Moenneville, 36
Gracchi, 226
Great St Bernard Pass, 27, 28, 29,
    54
Greece, 232
Green, Dr Miranda, 27, 74, 100
Gulvius Flaccus, Marcus, 231

Hallstatt, culture, 17–18, 31;
    period, 26, 41–2, 236
Hamilcar, 202, 203–4, 207
Hannibal of Carthage, 28, 98, 143,
    148, 166–200, 202, 212, 231,
    249
Hanno (brother of Hannibal), 170,
    173
Hanno (nephew of Hannibal), 187

Hanno, 148, 186
Hasdrubal (brother of Hannibal), 170, 186, 188, 194–6
Hasdrubal (son of Gisgo), 197
Hasdrubal, 148, 167
Hawkes, Drs Jacquetta and Christopher, 17
Helios, 44
Heloris, 117
Helvetii, 221, 234–6
Helvidius Priscus, , 256
Helvius Cinna, Gaius, 251
Helvius, Gaius, 199, 204
Heracleia, 143
Heracles, 54
Herculaneum, 257
Hercules, 6, 25
Hermes, 6
Hernici, 116
Herodotus, 44
Hieron II, 193
Hieronymus of Cardia, 143–4
Hieronymus, Eusebius, 252
Hiketas, 119
Histoire de la Gaule, 126
Historia regum Britanniae, 242–3
Histories, 241
History of Rome, 10
Histri, 250
Holder, Dr A., 36
Homo, Dr L., 31
Horace, 95, 251, 257
Hostilius Mancinus, Aulus, 227
Hostilius Mancinus, Lucius, 185
Howarton, Professor M.C., 253
Hubert, Dr Henri, 19, 20, 38, 41–2, 90, 126, 223

Iberia, 168, 170, 172, 174, 180, 182, 193, 197, 232, 235, 259
Iberians, 168, 170, 183
Idige, 35

Iliberris (Elvira), 170
Ilvates, 202, 205, 207
Inquani, 202
Insubreans, 33, 162, 212, 239
Insubres, 26, 29, 34, 36–7, 42, 54, 104, 119, 144, 151, 153, 157–8, 160–5, 171, 175, 178, 180, 202, 205–11, 222, 225, 227, 238
Ireland, 24, 59, 60, 74, 103, 219, 228
Isidor, 233
Istria, 225, 230
Italische Landeskunder, 222

James, Dr Simon, 36, 50, 103
Janiculum hill, 13–14
Journal of the Royal Society, 166
Joyce, Dr P.W., 60
Jubainville D'Arbois de, 25, 36, 164
Jugurtha, 56, 235
Julii clan, 240
Julius Agricola, Gnaeus, 259
Julius Frontinus, Sextus, 32, 82–3
Julius Vindex, Caius, 243
Jullian, Camille, 126
Junianus Justinus, Marcus, 83
Junius Silanus, Marcus, 208, 234
Juno, 62, 67, 72–3
Jupiter, 14, 27, 36, 54, 62, 73, 83, 208, 242
Juvenal, 95, 100

Katzeldorf, 36
Kretschmer, Paul, 41
Kruta, Dr Venecelas, 82

La Tène, 18–19, 36, 82; period, 26, 27, 98
Labici, 110
Ladicus, 27

Laelius, Gaius, 200
Laetorius, Gaius, 204
Laevi Ligures, 28
Laevi, 29, 37, 211, 238
Laevius, Laverius, 143
Lake, Como, 40, 54; d'Iseo, 26;
    Garda, 36, 43; Lugano, 40;
    Maggiore, 40, 42; Neuch,tel, 18;
    Orta, 40; Trasimene, 183
Lampsacos, 169
Languedoc, 232, 234
Late Iron Age in Lombardy, The,
    237–8
Latina, 124
Latins, 81, 122, 208
Latium, 46, 80, 118, 121, 131
Latovici, 221
Lattes, Commendatore, 247
Laus Pompeia, 238
Lebeccii, 29
Lejeune, Professor Michel, 40
Lentulus, Gnaeus, 188
Lentulus, Lucius, 77
Leontini, 145
Leoponti, 37
Lepontic area, 40
Libici, 37, 211, 238
Libui, 28, 37
Licinius Crassus, Marcus, 83,
    244–5
Liguria, 42, 159, 166, 169, 205,
    238
Ligurians, 25, 40, 45, 179, 181,
    195–9, 214, 217, 219, 220,
    225–7, 231
Lilybaeum (Marsala), 148
Lingones, 28–9, 37
*L'Italie primitive et les débuts de
    l'impérialisme romain*, 31
Litana, 191, 211
Litubium (Retorbio), 205
Livius, Drusus, 82, 237

Livius, Marcus, 137
Livius Salinator, Gaius, 215, 222
Livius Salvinator, Marcus, 195–6,
    197
Livy (Titus Livius), 1, 3, 4–16, 19,
    21–9, 34, 36–9, 51, 62–85, 87,
    93–4, 96, 98, 102, 104–18,
    122–7, 132–8, 166, 169,
    171–9, 182–4, 186–92, 196,
    198–9, 201–18, 223–7,
    255–6
Lombard Institute, 247
Lombardy, 19, 41
Lovernius, 50, 231
Loyalty Misplaced, 254
Luca (Lucca), 181
Lucan, 32
Lucania, 139, 143–4, 146, 240,
    254
Lucretius Carus, Titus, 252
Lucretius, Lucius, 181
Lucretius, Spurius, 197
Lucumo, 4, 23
Lugdunum (Lyon), 126
Lugh, 54, 56, 126, 233
Lugius, 233
Luna (Spexia), 166, 225, 227
Lutatis, Gaius, 171
Lutatius Catalus, Gaius, 148
Lutatius Catulus, Quintus, 236

MacCarthy MUr, The, 152
MacDonalds of the Isles, 92
Macedonia, 143,145, 212, 225
MacNEill, Professor Eoin, 164
Maecius, Geminus, 127
Maesia, 242
Maevius, Marcus, 199
Magalus, 171, 173–4, 177
Magna Graecia (Megale Hellas),
    46, 116, 141–2, 146
Magnesia, 200

Mago, 170, 180, 186, 190, 197, 198, 199, 202
Maharbal, 186, 188–9
Mallius Maximus, Gnaeus, 235
Mamilius Turrinus, Quintus, 197
Mandubi, 239
Manlius Capitolinus, Marcus, 108, 133
Manlius Imperiosus, Lucius, 108
Manlius, Lucius, 171–2, 178
Manlius, Marcus, 12, 74–6
Manlius Torquatus, Lucius, 135
Manlius Torquatus, Titus, 127, 137
Manlius, Titus, 104–5, 108–11, 133, 135, 160
Mantua (Mantova), 54, 253
Marburg, 41
Marcellinus, Ammianus, 50–51
Marcius, Gaius, 138
Marius, Gaius, 51, 56, 87, 233, 235–7
Mars (Ares), 14, 54, 73
Marsi, 46, 208, 237
Martial, 95, 233
Martius, Ancus, 13
Marx, Friedrich, 252
Masinissa, 197, 200
Massilia (Marseilles), 21, 24, 34, 47, 80, 169, 172–3, 194, 231
Massiliots, 25, 172–3
Matronae, 54, 229
Matzjausen, 74
Mechel, 37
Mediolanum (Milan), 26, 36, 159, 161, 165, 211, 220, 238, 247, 253
Mediunemusus, 41
Meeks, Dr, 82
Melkart, 145
Melpum, 42
Mercury, 54

Messana (Messina), 147
Metamorphoses, 100
Metellus, Quintus, 216
Metrodorus of Scepsis, 43
Mevaniola, 226
Milan, 54
Minerva, 54, 62, 161
Minucius Felix, Marcus, 100
Minucius, Marcus, 188, 205–8, 215
Minucius, Publius, 215
Minucius, Quintus, 215, 217
Minucius Rufus, Marcus, 184, 185
Minucius Rufus, Quintus, 205, 214
Minucius Thermus, Quintus, 225
Molmutius, Dunwallo, 242; Belinus (son), 242; Brennius (son), 242
Mommesen, Theodor, 233
Mons Albanus (Monte Cavo), 121–3
Mont, Auxois, 239; Geneve, 177, 231; Lassois, 52
Monte Bibele, 35, 39; Viso, 28
Montefortino, 82
Monterenzio, 35
Montillet, Gabriel de, 82
Morbihan, 38
Moscano di Fabiano, 82
Mount, Ballista, 226; Eryx, 148; Letus, 226; Soracte, 66; Vesuvius, 137, 244
München-Obermenzing, 36
Munster, 152
Mutilum, 201–2, 209
Mutina (Modena), 166, 171, 214, 216, 223, 225, 229
Mylae (Milazzo), 147

Naevius, Gnaeus, 249
Nantosuelta, 126

Naquane, 26–7
Narbo (Narbonne), 232
Narnia, 132
Nasc Niadh, 152
Nash, Dr Daphne, 119–20, 144,
    146–7
Natural History, 23–4
Naturalis Historia, 256–7
Neapolis (Naples), 131, 190
Negau, 41
Nemausud (NOmes), 232
Nepos, Cornelius, 21, 42, 250
Nero, 57, 241, 243–4, 256, 260
Nervii, 24
Nicodemi, Dr, 247
Nicomedia, 99
Nil Desperandum, 249
Nissen, H., 222
Nitiobriges, 234
Noctes Atticae, 108
Nola, 191
Noreia, 232–3
Noricum (Austria), 26, 223, 236
*Notes Towards the Definition of a
    Culture*, 262
Novaria, 37, 211, 238
Novati, Professor Francesco, 247
Numantia, 235
Numidia, 170, 235
Numidians, 149, 173, 178–9,
    183–4, 186–8, 199, 225

Octavian, 258
Octavianus, 100
Ogimos, 54
Ogulinius, Marcus, 208
Olympiad, 98th, 21
Onomaris, 52
Opimia, 189
Opimius, Lucius, 231
O'Rahilly, Professor Thomas,
    246–7

Orange, 93, 235
Origines, 37, 249
Ornavasso, 222
Orombovii, 222, 238
Osci, 46
Osequens, 32
Osimo, 81
Otho, M. Salvius, 243
Ovid (Publius Ovidius Naso), 64,
    95
Ovidius Naso, Publius *see* Ovid
Ovingdean, 36

Paetus, Arria, 256
Paetus, Caecina, 256
Palatina, 48
Palatine hill, 46
Pandosia, 143
Pannonia, 242
Panormus (Palermo), 148
Papirius Atratinus, Marcus, 63
Papirius Carbo, Gnaeus, 233–4
Papirius Crassus, Marcus, 127
Papirius, Marcus, 63
Papirius Mugilanus, Lucius, 63
Parma, 223–4, 229
Parmenides, 116
Parthinus, 27
Pasparido, 27
Passerini, A., 248
Patavium (Padua), 21, 31, 38, 255,
    260
Pausanias, 97–8
Pennines, 29
Periplus, 81
Perseus of Macedonia, 58
Perugia, 39, 88, 138
Petilius Spurnius, Quintus, 226
Phaethon, 44
Philip of Macedonia, 202–3, 217
Philodemus, 257
Phocaea, 25

Picardy, 119, 144
Picenum, 79, 104, 118, 120, 132,
    140–41, 150, 184–5, 195
Piggott, Professor Stuart, 18–19,
    94–5
Pisae (Pisa), 156, 166, 175, 214,
    225, 227
Placentia (Piacenza), 160, 166,
    171, 178–81, 194–5, 202–3,
    211, 214, 221, 225
Plato, 118
Pliny the Elder, 23, 25, 31–3, 37,
    42, 83, 92, 98, 256–7
Pliny the Younger, 257
Plutarch (Ploutarchos of
    Chaeronea), 4–6, 8–10, 15, 20,
    23–4, 39, 51–2, 63, 66–9,
    71–3, 78–81, 89–90, 105–7,
    142–7, 162, 187–8, 220, 233
Po Valley, 3–4, 19–20, 22–4, 29,
    30, 32, 37–9, 42–4, 48, 54, 60,
    79, 83, 140–44, 159–67,
    170–78, 180, 182, 194, 198,
    204–7, 210–12, 216, 219,
    221–2, 225–6, 236–9, 244–8
Poenine Pass *see* Great St Bernard
    Pass
Poeninus, 27, 29, 54
Poetelius Balbus, Gaius, 110, 111
Pollia, 48, 238
Polyaenus, 83, 90
Polybius, 21, 23, 29–34, 37–9,
    54, 66, 71, 79, 81, 83, 86–7,
    90–91, 101, 103, 111, 124,
    127, 131, 133, 139–40, 148–9,
    150–62, 165–6, 170, 173–6,
    180, 183, 186, 188, 196,
    199–200, 205, 219–20, 227–8,
    245
Pompeius Magnus, Gnaeus, 245,
    258
Pompeius, Trogus, 21, 23, 80, 258

Pompey, 83
Pompilius, Numa, 8
Pomponius Atticus, Titus, 250
Pomponius, Lusius, 252–3
Pomponius, Mela, 55, 58
Pomponius Matho, Marcus, 175
Pontine, 124
Pontius, Heracleides, 80
Popilius Laenas, Marcus, 121–3
Popillus Laenas, Caius, 234
Porcius Cato, Marcus, 23, 33, 37,
    194–6, 210, 249
Porsenna (King of Clusium), 134
Porta Collina, 16
Portii, 240
Poseidonius, 11, 50, 56, 98, 108
Postumius, 192
Postumius Albinus, Lucius, 14–15,
    191
Postumius Megallus, Lucius, 135,
    179
Postumius Tympanus, Marcus, 213
Praeneste (Palestrina), 112, 118,
    121
Privernum (Piperno), 116
Ptolemy Cerraunnos, King of
    Macedonia, 142, 145
Publicius Bibulus, Lucius, 190
Punic War: First, 147–9, 150;
    Second, 23, 35, 71, 198, 260
Punica, 78, 260
Pydna, 58
Pyrenees, 168–70, 172–3, 232
Pyrgion, 21
Pyrrhos, 142–7, 150, 176
Pythagoras, 116

Quinctius Crispinus, Titus, 194
Quinctius Flaminius, Titus,
    216–17
Quinctius Poenus, Titus, 107
Quinctus, Titus, 111

Quintilian, 95, 188, 256
Quintus, Victorius, 213
Quirimus, 14, 16, 70
Quirinal hill, 70

Racians, 242
Raecius, Marcus, 194
Rankin, Professor, 81, 141,
    250–53, 255, 259
Rauraci, 221
Ravenna, 229
Regium (Reggio), 224
Rhegion, siege of, 21
Rhegium, 21
Rhine, 17
Rhône, 17, 25, 53
Rhŷs, Sir John, 19–20, 40, 43,
    246–7
Rigomagus (Trino), 37
Rome, 1–2, 5, 7–16, 20–23,
    33–4, 38, 44–9, 62–85, 92,
    94–5, 98–9, 104, 107, 109–13,
    116–24, 127–9, 131–5, 139,
    140–50, 152–4, 159–62,
    164–9, 172, 174, 178–9,
    181–2, 185–6, 188–95, 197,
    199–204, 207, 210–12,
    216–19, 221, 223–4, 226–7,
    229–45, 249–51, 254, 259
Romulus, 14, 62, 240
Roquepertise, 74
Ross, Dr Anne, 94
Ruscino (Tour de Rousillon), 170

Sabelli, 132
Sabines, 2, 20–21, 46, 122, 132,
    153
Saguntum (Sagunto), 167–8
Salassi, 25, 28, 37, 229
Sallust, 233
Salui (Saluvii), 25
Samnites, 118–19, 132, 134–6,

    138–9, 143–4, 146, 237, 241
Samnium, 136, 138–9
Samos, 116
Sardinia, 145, 149, 153, 156
Sarmatians, 242
Sarsinati, 153
Sartre, Jean-Paul, 129
Satires, 100
Schedlt, 24
Schmidt, Professor, 40
Scipio Africanus, Publius Scipio,
    178, 190, 193, 197, 199–200
Scipio Calvus, Gnaeus Cornelius,
    174–5, 180
Scipio, Cornelius, 193
Scipio, Gnaeus Cornelius, 162,
    165, 193
Scipio, Lucius Cornelius, 121, 135,
    137–8
Scipio Nasica, Publius Cornelius,
    217–18, 225
Scipio, Publius Cornelius, 172–4,
    178–80, 193, 211–12
Scotland, 219
Scott, Sir Walter, 92
Scullard, H.H., 10, 243
Sculpicius Galba, Publius, 194, 243
Sellos, Phoulouios, 100
Sempronius Blaesus, Publius, 217
Sempronius Gracchus, Teberius,
    208
Sempronius Longus, Tiberius, 175,
    178–9, 180–81, 211–12,
    214–16
Sempronius Tuditanus, Marcus,
    225
Sempronius Tuditanus, Publius,
    190
Sempronius, Publius, 213–14
Sena, 81, 195–6
Seneca, 95, 258
Senigallia, 140

Senones, 2–10, 16, 22, 29–30,
36–7, 42, 60–61, 79, 81–3,
104, 117–20, 127, 131–3,
139–40, 144, 146, 150–51,
163, 240, 242
Sentium (Sassoferrato), 96, 102,
135, 136
Seogovesus, 22–3
Sequana, 55, 258
Sergius, Marcus, 207
Servilius Ahala, Quintus, 111
Servilius Caepio, Gnaeus, 199
Servilius Caepio, Quintus, 234–5
Servilius Fidenas, Quintus, 1
Servilius, Gaius, 171, 181
Servilius Geminus, Gnaeus, 180,
182, 184–5, 188
Servilius, Quintus, 121
Servius Honoratus, Marcus, 29
Seutonius, 251
Sextis Burrus, Afranius, 258
Sextius Calvinus, Caius, 231
Sibyl, 45
Sicily, 46, 116, 147–8, 175, 178
Siculus, Diodorus, 11, 21, 23, 49,
51, 55–6, 58, 79, 88–9, 93–4,
96, 98, 100–103, 108, 118, 228
Silius Italicus, Tiberius Catius
Asconius, 78, 260
Silvanus, 54
Simylos, 20–21
Slavs, 221
Social War (Marsian War), 237
Somma Ticinese, 42
Sophonisba, 197
Sora, 132
Sosilos, 173
Spain, 149, 153, 167, 219, 235,
240, 243, 245
Sparta, 24, 143
Spartacus, 83, 244–5
Spartans, 98, 118, 240

Spina, 24
Stary, Dr P.F., 86, 87–92
Stead, Dr, 82
Stellatina, 226
Stokes, Dr Whitley, 43
Strabo, 31, 33–4, 38–9, 49, 52–3,
56, 79, 98–9, 220, 229, 238,
248
Stradella Pass, 205, 214
Strategemata, 90
Studi estuschi, 7, 41
Styria, 41
Sucusana, 48
Suetonius Tranquillus, Gaius, 82,
109, 261
Suetonius, 95, 140
Suleviae, 161
Sulis, 161
Sulpicius, Gaius, 112–15, 121,
124
Sulpicius Lagus, Quintus, 1–2, 9,
12, 65–7
Sulpicius Rufus, Publius, 257
Sulpicius, Saverrio, 144
Sutrium (Sutri), 81
Sybaris, 46
Syphax, King of Numidia, 197
Syracuse (Siracusa), 45–6, 116,
119, 145–7, 192–3

Tacitus, 33, 51, 166, 239, 241–2,
252
Taillac Libourne, 235
Táin Bó Chuailgne, 126
Tannetum, 172, 199, 224
Tanusius, Geminus, 251
Taranis, 94
Tarentum (Taranto), 46, 117–19,
142–3, 146, 193–5
Tarpeia, 20–21
Tarpeian Rock, 21, 75, 109
Tarquinii, 116

Tarquinius, Priscus, 22–3
Tarquinius, Superbus, 62, 121
Tarquinius the Elder, 23
Taurini, 26, 32, 37, 153, 156, 158, 165, 177–8, 233
Taurinorum (Turin), 26, 177, 178
Telamon, 59, 89, 96, 101, 103, 156–7, 160–61, 163, 182, 250
Terentius Varro, Gaius, 76, 95, 186–8, 190, 194
Terentius Varro, Marcus, 14, 72, 258
Terentius, Publius, 159
Terracina, 131
Teutoboduus, 233
Teutones, 224, 232–6
Thames, 55–6
Thebans, 98
Theodotus, 21
Theopompus of Chios, 116
Thessalians, 143
Thomas, Lord Elis, 254
Thrace, 244
Tiberius, Emperor, 33, 82
Tibur (Tivoli), 110–11, 118
Ticino, 19, 40, 211
Ticinum, 238
Tigurini, 234–6
Timagenes, 21
Timolean of Corinth, 119
Titinius, Gaius, 216
Titinius, Marcus, 216
Titinius, Publius, 204
Tizzoni, Dr Marco, 19, 237
Todi, 41
Tolistoboii, 169, 221
Tolosa (Toulouse), 232, 234
Toynbee, Professor Arnold, 30, 129, 209, 221–2, 238, 260
Trajan, 57
Transpadana, 28, 38, 219–20, 223, 227, 239

Trasimeno, 185
Trebia, 166
Trent (Trento), 32, 36
Tricastini, 23, 175
Triconi, 177
Tridentum, 32, 36
Tugeni, 234
Tulingi, 221
Tullianum, 56
Tullius, Servius, 48
Tullius, Sextus, 112–15
Tungri, 52
Tunisia, 198
Tuscans, 240–41
Tusculum, 67, 111, 127, 240, 249
Tyre, 145
Tyrrhenians, 22

Udine, 38
Umbrians, 28, 39, 46, 132, 134–6, 153, 201, 219
Umbro-Sabellians, 46
Urnfield culture, 17, 42
Utica, 197, 199–200
Uxellinus, 27

Vaison, 74
Val, d'Aosta, 22; d'Ossola, 37; Leventina, 37; Policella, 55
Valerius, Asiasticus, 259
Valerius, Cato, 251
Valerius Catullus, Gaius, 36, 95, 199, 250–252, 255
Valerius, Corvus, 255
Valerius Flaccus, Lucius, 204, 210–11, 249
Valerius, Lucius, 72
Valerius, Manlius, 147
Valerius, Marcus, 112, 115, 125–6, 133
Valerius Martialis, Marcus, 57
Valerius Maximus, , 14

Valerius Publicola, Publius, 121–2
Valli de Commachio, 37
Vara valley, 41
Varus, Publius Afrenus, 257
Varus, Publius Quintilius, 198, 257
Vegetius Renatus, F., 91
Veii (Veio), 2, 6, 11, 14, 21, 42,
    66–7, 70–72, 75, 83–4,113,
    127
Velitae (Veletri), 116
Vendryes, Joseph, 90
Veneti, 29, 38, 79, 153, 166,
    219–20, 227
Venetia (Venice), 38, 239
Venetian Hadra, 117
Venetii, 38, 230
Venusia (Venosa), 188, 190, 194
Vercellae (Vercelli), 37, 211, 236,
    238
Vercingetorix, 56, 151, 239
Vergilius Maro, Publius see Virgil
Verginius Rufus, L., 243
Verginius, Lucius, 195
Verigate, 247
Verne, Jules, 261
Verona, 28, 36, 250
Verrucosis, Quintus Fabius
    Maximus, 184
Vertacomori, 37, 211, 238
Vesontio (Besançon), 243
Vesta, 13
Vestal Virgins, 13–14, 189
Via, Aemilia, 221–2; Appia, 245;
    Aurelia, 166; Flaminia, 166;
    Salasa, 111

Virgil (Publius Vergilius Maro), 3,
    32, 95, 252–5, 257, 261
Viridomarus, 163
Vispanius, Lucius, 239
Vitellius, Aulus, 239, 241, 243
Vitruvius Pollio, M., 33
Vix, 24, 52
Vocontii, 21, 37, 175
Volcae Tectosages, 173, 179,
    234–5
Volcae, 37
Volsci, 46, 81, 84, 125, 131,
    240
Volumnius, Lucius, 136
Volusius, 251
Vopsicus, Flavius, 52
Vulcan, 44

Waldalgesheim, 52
Walter, Archdeacon of Oxford,
    242
Watkins, Dr Calvert, 53
Watson, Dr W.J., 43
West Indies, 59
Wetwang Slack, 52
Whatmough, Dr Joshua, 40, 256
Wolkersdorf, 36

Xanthippus, 147–8
Xenophon, 118

Zama, 200
Zeus, 44
Zignano, 41